ABOUT THE AUTHOR

EwenChia

A GRADUATE OF THE Singapore Institute of Management, Ewen Chia holds a BS in management, with honors. His first full-time job was in sales and marketing, and he struggled to make ends meet just like any other working person. In 1997, he started learning and experimenting with an Internet business. For five full years, motivated by the desire to build a better future for his family and to clear mounting credit-card debt, Ewen worked tirelessly on his business from 11:00 PM to 3:00 AM every single day, while holding a full-time day job. Years of painstaking effort and sleep deprivation finally paid off when an online fortune began to roll in in 2002.

Drawing on his expertise as an Internet entrepreneur, Ewen set up Autopilot Internet Income in 2007. By providing proven training and advice on Internet marketing, Autopilot Internet Income aims to promote

Internet entrepreneurship worldwide, encouraging the use of the Internet medium to generate extra income and profits.

Today a world-famous and highly respected marketer, Ewen is often consulted for his ingenious marketing advice, especially in the areas of affiliate marketing, affiliate management, list building, e-mail marketing, product creation, and online branding. He is also widely known as the World #1 Super Affiliate; his name is synonymous with affiliate marketing. Ewen is considered the secret weapon of many Internet marketers for his uncanny ability to trounce the competition and bag the coveted number-one reseller spot in almost every major marketing rollout!

An award-winning international speaker, Ewen has toured the world sharing his Internet business knowledge and experience. He has worked extensively with Success Resources, the World Internet Summit, and many other organizations.

Ewen truly believes that anyone who's willing to put in the effort will be able to achieve complete financial freedom using the Internet. The success stories and testimonials of his many students speak for themselves. Many have been able to quit their day jobs, live the Internet lifestyle, and achieve real financial freedom, thanks to his proven techniques and money-making secrets! You can find out more about Ewen and his life-changing solutions by visiting the following Web sites:

http://www.EwenChia.com

http://www.eEntrepreneur.com

http://www.Featuring.com

http://www.WorkingFromHome.com

CONTENTS

ACKNOWLEDGMENTS

To my beloved wife, Irene Pua, and my children, Clayden and Coen—thank you for all your help and understanding throughout the years when I was starting my own Internet business and learning to become a successful entrepreneur. Today's success would not be mine if you hadn't been my strong pillars of support. I love you all.

To my Mum, Lily, and sister Hsin-Ee—thank you for being there for me through thick and thin. No words can express my gratitude and love for both of you.

Special thanks to all my students around the world, particularly in Singapore, for allowing me to share my knowledge and experience with you. I hope I've helped you make a change in your own life. To my staff at AutopilotInternetIncome.com, thank you for your friendship, dedication, and support. You guys are instrumental in helping the business grow.

To Lorna Tan of the *Sunday Times*, thank you for your amazing interview. It was one of the most exciting times of my life! To Karen Kwek, thank you for your help in editing my manuscript—you've done an excellent job.

I would also like to express my deep gratitude to all my business partners, including Jo Han Mok, Tom Hua, and Brett McFall of World Internet Summit; Richard Tan and Veronica Chew of Success Resources; and Adam Khoo and Stuart Tan of Adam Khoo Learning Technologies Group—thank you for the opportunity of working together. I've learned so much from all of you.

To everyone whom I've had the pleasure of knowing online and offline during this wonderful Internet marketing journey—Joel Comm, Mark Joyner, Chris Reynolds, Derek Gehl, Stephen Pierce, John Delavera, JP Schoeffel, Jeremy Gislason, Simon Hodgkinson, Russell Brunson, Stone Evans, Gary Ambrose, Ben Settle, Ben Shaffer, and many, many more—thank you all for being my friends. You guys rock!

INTRODUCTION

LET ME BEGIN BY EXTENDING my sincerest gratitude to you for choosing to invest in *How I Made My First Million on the Internet ... And How You Can Too!* In so doing, you have shown good faith in my ability to help you build a successful and highly profitable online business.

You've also demonstrated a commitment to yourself. I take this commitment, and your trust, very seriously. It is my intention that this book will deliver on everything promised, and more. In fact, I believe that the information in this book will provide you with the clearest, most comprehensive blueprint on Internet marketing and business available.

> *I believe that the information in this book will provide you with the clearest, most comprehensive blueprint on Internet marketing and business available.*

HOW TO USE THIS BOOK

As you read and absorb the contents of part one, understand that this information represents far more than one man's success story. It contains your future success story as well. My biography is there to show just how average a guy I really am, but it's not the focus of this material. You'll learn about my ups and downs on the road to success, and—all right—I'll even brag a little bit. However, I don't want you to think for a second that the business principles discussed in this book only worked *for me.* These are core principles and systems that work for everyone. My story is there only to highlight this fact: if I can achieve success, you can too.

If I can achieve success, you can too.

What follows in part two is a step-by-step Million-Dollar Blueprint for unlocking the wealth of profitable opportunities awaiting you on the Internet. Whether you are starting a new business from scratch without any experience or you're looking to boost your profits, this book takes you through the basics of setting up and running a profitable Internet business.

WHAT IS AN INTERNET BUSINESS?

The few differences that exist between offline and online marketing come down to speed, cost, and ease of execution. Internet marketing is typically easier, quicker, and more cost-effective for the average person.

Essentially, an Internet business is any business that offers products or services on the Internet. Potential customers visit your Web site and purchase your products online rather than by visiting a physical location. The Internet is also a marketing medium. Almost all the universal business and marketing principles that apply offline are applicable online. The few differences that exist between offline and online marketing come down to speed, cost, and ease of execution. Internet marketing is typically easier, quicker, and more cost-effective for the average person.

You also need to know that the Internet is an information highway, and this is one of the main reasons people go online. They want to find information that solves their problems, educates them, or affects them personally. An

POINTS TO REMEMBER #1

INTERNET MARKETING IS TYPICALLY EASIER, QUICKER, AND MORE COST-EFFECTIVE FOR THE AVERAGE PERSON THAN OFFLINE MARKETING.

information-based business is like any other business, except the product focus is primarily on intangible goods such as e-books, software, membership or service-based sites, etc. In other words, we'll focus more on the marketing of digital as opposed to physical goods. What matters, though, is not so much the product you're selling as the medium you're selling it in—the Internet. Whether you want to sell e-books or tennis shoes is nearly irrelevant in the long run. The important thing to understand is that Internet-based marketing is driven by information. Fundamental marketing principles apply, but they are executed in a slightly different fashion. We'll talk more about the information aspect in subsequent chapters.

The important thing to understand is that Internet-based marketing is driven by information.

THE MERCHANT AND THE AFFILIATE

There are more than a few different models for Internet business. However, there are only two core models in the transaction of online business itself:

1) Direct proprietor, also known as the merchant or product owner

2) Third-party proprietor, otherwise known as an
   affiliate marketer

So, in other words, if you are selling your own product and handling all of the payment processing, customer service, delivery, etc., then you are the merchant. If you are selling someone else's product via referral—meaning you refer customers to the merchant's sales page but play no role in the completion of payment or product delivery—then you are the affiliate. The reason I point out the differences between these two models is to show you that there is more than one way of making sales (and earning income) online. You do not need to have your own products in order to go into business online. However, you'll ultimately want to build your business based around both models, as this is where your income can truly soar. The principles you'll learn in this book apply to both models.

There is more than one way of making sales (and earning income) online.

WHAT THIS BOOK WILL TEACH YOU

Every successful entrepreneur has at least some business training. This training may come from past jobs, educational courses, mentors, or simply from jumping in head-first and learning along the way—but there is always a time when training comes into play. Whether you are starting your first business or already have some experience under your belt, *How I Made My First Million on the Internet ... And How You Can Too!* will train you in exactly how to research, create, and profit from an Internet-based business from an information-marketing perspective. Here's an overview of some of the things you will learn:

- **MARKET RESEARCH**

  What are people looking for online? What do they want to buy?

- **MARKET SELECTION**

  Which market will be easy to break into? Which market holds the most promise in terms of profit potential?

- **PRODUCT SELECTION**

  Which products can I deliver as solutions to meet market needs and demand?

- **OFFER TARGETING**

  How do I position my offer correctly within the market?

- **TRAFFIC**

  How do I get my offer in front of the market?

- **LEAD GENERATION AND FOLLOW UP**

  How do I capture prospects (potential customers) from my market onto an e-mail list? How do I present my offer to them once I have their attention?

- **BACKEND**

  How do I create a "backend" system of additional offers that will boost my income and assist in the long-term profits and growth of my business?

- **AUTOMATION**

  How do I place the majority of my business on autopilot so that it runs and makes money for me without too much additional work?

- **DUPLICATION**

  How do I start a second or even third business so I can multiply my total income?

studying this material, and then putting it into practice in the real world without hesitation. You are already halfway there, and I'm ready to guide you the rest of the way. Let's get started!

PART ONE

My Story—and Yours

CHAPTER 1

The Journey Begins

I was born on June 25, 1973, in Singapore into a middle-class family of four. My parents worked very hard to provide the best for our family, but their own union was a troubled one. Sadly they were unable to reconcile their differences and had decided to separate by the time I was in elementary school.

It was then that I decided to get my first job, and I started working part-time after school. This helped instill in me a strong work ethic and taught me the value of money early on. Even though I was a bit of a workaholic—and still am—I realized that I needed something more. I wanted to be able to enjoy my work and be wealthy from it at the same time.

When the time came to enroll in college, I chose to attend the Singapore Institute of Management, where I earned a BS in management, with honors.

I figured I'd work my way up the chain at some big company and that even if I didn't get rich right away, I'd still make a good, middle-class income for my family. Little did I know where life was about to take me …

RAGS BEFORE RICHES

Flashback to 1997: I was fresh out of college and had just taken on a sales and marketing job at Sony Music Entertainment (Singapore). I was at the job for about a year before moving on to MobileOne, which is one of the top telecommunications service providers in Singapore. I'd recently married during this period as well and was very happy to be supporting my new family. I also found myself spending a lot more time on my hobbies. I am an avid guitar player and love to write songs. So I started thinking about marketing some of my compositions.

> *I figured I'd work my way up the chain at some big company and that even if I didn't get rich right away, I'd still make a good, middle-class income for my family. Little did I know where life was about to take me …*

The Internet was really starting to take off in 1997, and it seemed logical to me that I could reach a wide audience with my music by putting it online. In other words, I was interested in Internet marketing but wasn't actually thinking about starting an online business at all. It wasn't until I began visiting different Web sites in an effort to learn how to market my songs that I came across some information about potential money-making opportunities.

"Could this be my chance to get rich?" I wondered. Well I don't do anything halfway, so I dived right in. From 1997 to 2002 I spent all of my time after work trying to learn how to make money on the Internet. This meant getting up at 7:00 AM to go to my full-time job, then locking myself away from 11:00 PM to 3:00 AM while I did everything I could to get a business going.

Unfortunately my first few years in business online did not result in the rags-to-riches miracle I'd dreamed of so vividly. Not by any stretch of the imagination. The fact is that I had no idea where to start, nor what kind of business I wanted to run.

For five straight years, I juggled long days and sleepless nights and barely had any time to spend with my family. The first few "business ventures" I got involved in scammed me out of several thousand dollars. Still, I refused to give up and continued pouring more and more money into different ideas. I bought all of the how-to e-books and courses, hoping someone would finally reveal the secret to making money online.

"Could this be my chance to get rich?" I wondered. Well I don't do anything halfway, so I dived right in.

Do you want to guess just how much money I blew? Make sure you're sitting down for this … I spent close to US$50,000 trying to unearth the key to that door I was banging my head against in a desperate effort to gain financial freedom … and I charged most of that $50,000 to credit cards. My wife was *not* happy with me, to say the least. All of those credit-card bills were rapidly gaining interest, and we were impossibly behind on payments. The situation was truly grim beyond words.

My self-confidence was fading rapidly, and I was desperate to prove to everyone—but especially to myself—that this "Internet thing" wasn't just a dream. I spent many nights alone, often in tears and feeling shut out by everyone around me. I asked myself over and over, "Why? Why can't I make this work? What am I missing?"

THE POWER OF FOCUS

It is often in our darkest moments, though, that we finally see clearly …

My turning point came one night in 2002. I was up burning the midnight oil again and asking myself how I could get out of the mess I'd created. A part of me was ready to throw in the towel, but I'm simply too stubborn to give up—even in the face of what looked like total disaster. I had to admit that not all of that $50,000, five-year-long "education" was totally worthless. In fact I'd gained many valuable skills and learned almost everything there was to know about the main models of Internet business.

> *Then it finally hit me: "I'm not missing anything!"*

I knew, for instance, that I needed to target a viable market. I knew I needed to deliver solutions to that market. I understood that I needed to drive market traffic to my offer and that I had to have a lead-capture and follow-up system in place.

Then it finally hit me: "I'm not missing anything!" In a flash, I realized that I knew what I was *supposed* to be doing, but I just wasn't *doing* it. Instead of putting in the hard work of applying my knowledge, I was still buying into all the hype about overnight riches. A part of me still wanted to believe that all I had to do was put up a Web site, push a few buttons, then wait for the customers to come flooding in by some invisible, magnetic force. Now the truth is that it *can* be this easy when you already have a successful business. Once you've put in the hard work up-front to build an existing customer base, you've got it made. But you have to treat your business as a real business first.

This was my problem. I'd been playing at my business like a hobby. I'd failed to implement the most fundamental concepts of Internet marketing—like having a target market, a clear strategy, and, most importantly, following a proven system. It wasn't the system that was failing me; it was *my* failure to follow through.

What I lacked was focus. I realized that all I'd ever needed to do to succeed was focus and commit to taking action on what I'd already learned. The thousands of dollars worth of material I'd read over the years had revealed all of the proven business models. I just needed to choose one and stick to it. Armed with this insight, I renewed my commitment to succeed. I decided then and there that failure was not an option.

I settled on affiliate marketing as the business model to focus on and started applying myself with concentrated energy and dedication. It wasn't long before the tide began turning in my favor. I made my first online sale. Believe me, your first sale will give you the greatest feeling in the world once it comes, especially if it has been years in the making! Well, then I made another sale, and another. It was a slow trickle at first, but I finally had my proof. No one could doubt my ability to make sales online anymore—not even me.

I decided then and there that failure was not an option.

MY SUCCESS STORY—AND YOURS

After that moment of truth in 2002, I became unstoppable. By focusing and applying a proven system, my income continued to soar. Just how far have I come since the days of debt?

First, I've been the top-earning affiliate in almost every Internet affiliate program I've promoted. I've created dozens of my own information products too and have seen them sell like crazy. I currently own and run over ten active money-making Web sites, including the following:

You can also check out these:

- http://www.MyFreeWebsiteBuilder.com

- http://www.AutopilotProfits.com

- http://www.SuperAffiliates.com

- http://www.WorkingFromHome.com

Each of these Web sites continues to pull in profits for me on autopilot, to the tune of about five figures per month. None of this happened overnight, either. Each of these sites represents a point in my learning curve, and each is the result of taking an idea and seeing it through to completion. Some of these sites sell individual products, and some of them are membership sites that generate recurring income. I'll let you in on a secret: not a

I'll let you in on a secret: not a single one of these sites, on its own, could ever generate the income I have right now. It is the cumulative income generated by of all of these sites over time that creates a five- to six-figure monthly income.

single one of these sites, on its own, could ever generate the income I have right now. It is the cumulative income generated by of all of these sites over time that creates a five- to six-figure monthly income.

Now let's look at some of my other credentials. I've become an in-demand speaker on the Internet-marketing seminar circuits, and I regularly travel around the world giving presentations to newbies and experienced insiders alike.

At the World Internet Marketing Summit held in Singapore in 2006,
I netted five-figure online sales ëliveí in just three days.

I was also presented with the first-ever World Internet Challenge trophy at the 2006 World Internet Marketing Summit held in Singapore, where I set up a business without preparation and from scratch in front of a live audience of a thousand individuals ... and proceeded to generate five-figure sales from it in just seventy-two hours!

Subsequently I was invited to be the only local featured speaker at the World Internet Mega Summit held in Singapore in May 2007. This was the world's biggest Internet business event, attended by over 3,500 participants.

Here I was given a standing ovation and voted best speaker by the audience! It's not all business success, either. I am driving—yes—the luxury car.

Me and my BMW 523i

I know I look like a typical Internet marketer showing off here! I was very happy on the day I purchased that BMW, though, because it symbolized the results of years of hard work and struggle. I wanted something to remind me just how far I've come, and I am reminded of my journey to success each time I get behind the wheel.

Another benefit of success is that my wife and I are able to travel almost anywhere in the world. We finally had the chance to visit Universal Studios in Hollywood last year when I went to California for a marketing seminar. And whenever we need to get away from our everyday routine in Singapore, we can vacation somewhere with a different climate and culture.

With my wife, Irene, on the ski slopes of Lucerne in Switzerland in June, 2005.

Most importantly, though, my family has *security*, and my wife and I have more time to spend at home with our kids.

Celebrating my birthday with Irene and our sons, Clayden and Coen, in June 2007.

We've achieved wealth beyond our wildest dreams, and we owe it all to the Internet business.

The crazy thing is I've managed to achieve all of this while marketing to predominantly English-speaking consumers, and English is not even my first language. I've shown you just a fraction of what I've been involved in—we haven't even addressed how I achieved my first million-dollar product launch yet. We'll get to that soon. What I want you to absorb right now is that these same results are possible *for you*.

Maybe a car or luxury holidays are not the status symbols you would choose, but I'm sure there's something you've always wanted. A new house? A fancy, flat-screen television? A jacuzzi? Or perhaps

We've achieved wealth beyond our wildest dreams, and we owe it all to the Internet business.

Maybe a car or luxury holidays are not the status symbols you would choose, but I'm sure there's something you've always wanted.

something less tangible, like a better education for the kids? Time to pursue a sporting or artistic dream? A comfortable early-retirement plan? You could have any of these things in due time when you focus on building a solid business. The unfolding of my story in the next chapter could well be yours in the making too.

CHAPTER 2

The Million-Dollar Day

During my Internet marketing journey, I saw the depths of despair and carried the burden of debt. I was ripped off, scammed, and lied to countless times. But I didn't give up. Step by step, I climbed closer to seeing my first million from Internet sales—and I'm about to tell you how it all happened.

FROM AFFILIATE TO SUPER AFFILIATE

When I finally got serious about business, I chose affiliate marketing. The first year or so, I would say I was an average affiliate. I made a decent income, but I certainly wasn't a top performer. I was still getting used to really applying the systems and strategies to my marketing. I did a lot of

> *I came to understand that people are looking for solutions, not just products.*

tracking and testing of results, seeing what worked and what didn't. The better I got at the basics, the more freedom I had to test new ideas. In fact, the more I understood and applied the basics of marketing, the easier it was to come up with new and creative approaches.

I started focusing much more on building my opt-in lists and on forging a solid relationship with my list subscribers. It was through their feedback that I learned just how important it is to provide value and information. I came to understand that people are looking for solutions, not just products.

In other words, the more value I could provide up-front, for free, the more referrals I made down the line. Just this one shift in attitude saw my commissions go way, way up. I was getting really competitive, and I started winning even more in commissions and gifts for my efforts. I was becoming a super affiliate and often beat out other affiliates to become the top earner in the programs I was involved in.

FROM SUPER AFFILIATE TO PRODUCT CREATOR

Success always brings people to your door in search of answers. Keep in mind, my primary niche has always been Internet marketing. As a super affiliate, I was selling lots and lots of "How to Succeed on the Internet"-type products. Naturally, many of my subscribers had questions for me:

"Ewen, should I buy this product?"

"Ewen, this looks great, but I'm a total newbie! How will this help me if I don't even know how to build my own list?"

"I enjoy your newsletters, but how can I be sure you aren't just conning me like everyone else? You say this is easy, but look—you generate huge amounts of traffic!"

It wasn't enough just to tell the people who put their trust in me, "Hey, I've been there." The fact is that I wanted to see my subscribers and customers succeed just as well as I had. I naturally enjoy teaching and mentoring others, sharing what I know. I did what I could to address these questions as they came in.

It wasn't enough just to tell the people who put their trust in me, "Hey, I've been there." The fact is that I wanted to see my subscribers and customers succeed just as well as I had.

However, there came a point when the volume of questions was just too overwhelming. I realized I needed to start teaching others on a larger scale, and the only way to do this was to become a product creator myself. As luck would have it, this decision actually brought about another huge leap in income for me.

One of my early smash hits as a product creator was a little e-book called *Mini e-Book Secrets*. It was designed to teach people how to become the top affiliate in any affiliate program. The secret was in first understanding the fundamentals of marketing:

- You must find a target market.

- You must offer a solution to that market.

- You must drive market traffic to your offer.

- You must capture leads onto an opt-in list in order to follow up on your offer.

The second secret was in understanding the affiliate's role as a middleman or information value provider. These short reports, or mini e-books, could be written on any niche topic for which one had a relevant affiliate program to promote. The overall system relied on driving targeted traffic to an opt-in page where people could download the mini e-book, consume the information,

> *The overall system relied on driving targeted traffic to an opt-in page where people could download the mini e-book, consume the information, and then click-through the affiliate links contained within it.*

and then click-through the affiliate links contained within it.

Although this is not the complete picture, it contains the seeds of the system I now teach to people—and it represents a very good summary of the methods I've continued to build upon through subsequent product launches. Almost every product I've created since then has been a variation on this theme, but the depth of the material has grown as my knowledge has grown. At the same time, I continue to add new tactics into my marketing with each new product I create.

I realized there was no need to choose between being an affiliate marketer and being a product owner. I could have it both ways. And it was really this desire of mine to have it both ways that led to my first million in online earnings, with the launch of a product called the Super Affiliate Cloning Program.

THE SUPER AFFILIATE CLONING PROGRAM

On April 29, 2007, Singapore's national paper, the *Sunday Times*, ran a feature story on me in its "Me & My Money" section. The headline proclaimed, "He's Made His First Million on the Internet."

The interview focused a lot on my background and my personal money-management style but didn't mention how, exactly, I'd made that first million. The fact is that my income had steadily progressed

The Super Affiliate Cloning Program generated $1.497 million in sales in thirty-six hours!

into high five figures. I didn't waste that money, either. I leveraged it back into all of my businesses and put much of the rest of it into savings and investments. What pushed my income to the $1 million mark was the launch, on August 22, 2006, of a product called the Super Affiliate Cloning Program. The Super Affiliate Cloning Program generated $1.497 million *in sales* in thirty-six hours! It was a unique mentoring program that contained my entire life's work on affiliate marketing. I put my heart and soul into the product, laying out absolutely everything I'd learned about what it takes to succeed in Internet business.

The sales letter began like this:

On the eve of my semi-retirement from affiliate marketing I want to leave my legacy...

"How Can You Learn The Closely Guarded System For Consistent 6... Even 7 Figure Income...Delivered ONE Time Only By The World's Undisputed #1 Affiliate Marketer... But Only If You Qualify!"

Click Here To Become A Super Affiliate Now!

Exclusive for present and future Stars and Superstars. There's NEVER been a program like this in the history of Affiliate Marketing. This is your ONLY chance to get my personal guidance and rapidly transform into a "Super-Affiliate" money machine!

To see the letter in full, visit http://www.EwenChia.com/supercloner. The response was insane. I had so much traffic to this offer that both of

☞ What made people so desperate to grab this incredible offer?

my servers crashed before I'd even officially gone live. It was a time-limited offer, and people were coming to the site, constantly refreshing the page so they could secure their spot before the offer disappeared. In just a matter of hours, my Alexa traffic ranking jumped to 386, meaning I had 2,850 people out of every million Internet users all trying to get to my site at once. What made people so desperate to grab this incredible offer?

1) Perhaps it was that the Super Affiliate Cloning Program represented my legacy and semiofficial retirement from affiliate marketing.

2) Perhaps it was that, given that this was my legacy, I had over delivered on value like never before.

3) Perhaps it was due to my reputation and brand.

4) Or maybe it was my army of thousands of affiliates, all promoting the Super Affiliate Cloning Program to their lists.

5) Maybe it was the fact that I'd never presented such a comprehensive course in such a personal format, complete with audios, teleconferences, and personal mentoring.

6) Or was it *all of the above,* coupled with the power of the very system I teach working its magic right then and there?

In my view, the answer is number 6: all of the above. I've spent years teaching others how to become super affiliates. My expertise has helped turn my customers into super affiliates. Yet none of this would have been possible without having first mastered the fundamental components of Internet business. This, my friend, is what you are about to learn.

Whether you want to be an affiliate marketer, a product owner, or both, there are five core components that undergird every successful Internet business, and you must master them above all else if you want to make your first million on the Internet. These five components are as follows:

1) Market

2) Offer

3) Traffic

4) Backend

5) Duplication

Whether you want to be an affiliate marketer, a product owner, or both, there are five core components that undergird every successful Internet business, and you must master them above all else if you want to make your first million on the Internet.

That's it. These five deceptively simple concepts built the foundation of all my success. So, are you ready to learn, focus, and commit to your business? I hope so, because I'm about to take you through the big picture of how the components work together, as well as discuss the guiding philosophy behind each component's role in creating a solid foundation for your business.

CHAPTER 3

The Fab Five

Every successful Internet marketing system comes down to five components:

Market + Offer + Traffic + Backend + Duplication

COMPONENT #1: YOUR MARKET

Every business serves a target market. Your market forms the foundation of your potential customer base. Therefore it is crucial that you identify your market correctly before you go into business. What are you looking for, exactly? You want to choose a market that satisfies the following criteria:

- Hungry for a solution

- Willing to spend disposable income on solutions

> ☞ *If you don't target a strong market from the beginning, you could do everything else right in your business and still fail.*

• Easy to reach

In other words, a good market consists of a large number of people with a common need who have enough spending power for you to profit from serving them. Let me emphasize the point here: if you don't target a strong market from the beginning, you could do everything else right in your business and still fail.

Another way of talking about markets is to ask the question, "What niche do I want to go into?" Do you want to target golfers, home buyers, musicians, fitness fanatics? These days, the terms "market" and "niche" are nearly interchangeable in most people's minds. You'll hear other business owners talk about being "in the health and wellness market" or "in the financial market," and so on. However, there is an important distinction between the two that you must note: every market represents a niche, but not every niche represents a viable and profitable market. In other words,

> ☞ *Every market represents a niche, but not every niche represents a viable and profitable market.*

it is not enough to say that you want to target "golfers" or "fitness fanatics" or "the computer software market." This is far too broad. There is no universal golf market or fitness market.

Likewise, you cannot create markets where they don't exist. "Cold" markets always result from improper targeting, whether too broad or too narrow. You also risk running into a nonexistent market if you launch your solution prior to doing your research. For example, let's say you are a musician and have also recently learned some tricks for raising your credit score. One day you think to yourself, "I could write an e-book on credit repair for musicians!" You may think you've come up with a winning product idea. After all, many musicians are on fixed budgets and this impacts their ability to obtain credit. There's also the chance that a fellow musician would enjoy learning about finances if someone who shares the creative mindset presents the information. The problem with this type of

Product targeting is really secondary to market targeting. Pay attention to your market above all, and the rest will follow.

reasoning is that you don't *know* for sure if the market actually exists. It's a classic example of putting the cart before the horse and trying to force the market to fit the product.

Proper targeting, however, always works in reverse. You must target the market first, determine its needs, and then either create or locate a product to address those needs. Product targeting is really secondary to market targeting. Pay attention to your market above all, and the rest will follow. There is nothing wrong with brainstorming ideas, but market selection should be governed by real research and hard data.

COMPONENT #2: YOUR OFFER

Many business owners believe that their product is synonymous with their offer. While this is true on the surface, it is far too simplistic and shortsighted an idea to hold if you want to generate a serious income from your business. You will be years ahead if you memorize this one concept: people do not buy products—they buy solutions. Shift your focus away from the details and features of your product. Look instead for the problems it can solve. The solution is your offer. This is true whether you are selling downloadable information

People do not buy products—they buy solutions.

A strong offer consists of more than just the primary solution. It also includes intangible benefits and a focus on presenting the solution to the customer as "the right solution at the right time and the right price."

or physical goods. Think about this for a moment: even a pair of roller skates is a solution. A good pair of roller skates can solve a child's boredom problem as well as his parents' frustration problem. Note within this discussion the underlying idea of multiple solutions within your offer, or multiple benefits. A strong offer consists of more than just the primary solution. It also includes intangible benefits and a focus on presenting the solution to the customer as "the right solution at the right time and the right price."

For example, let's say you want to sell a set of videos about dog training. Your offer goes beyond the content, beyond the information contained in the videos. Why? First, keep in mind that your customer knows what she is trying to achieve on a very basic level: she wants to train her dog. Your offer, if it is to be powerful, must address all of the unspoken criteria hiding in the back of her mind. This means putting an emphasis on things like the following benefits:

- It will be so much easier to learn how to train her dog by watching live examples on video.

- Video allows her to rewind, pause, fast-forward, etc., so she can digest the information at her own pace, and it is always available for her to review.

- This learning format will make it that much easier and quicker to train her dog, which will get her what she really wants (an improved pet/owner relationship) much faster.

- She can order right away and download the videos immediately.

- She can opt to have the videos shipped to her for a small extra fee.

- She's protected by a money-back guarantee.

- This is the lowest price she'll find anywhere for this level of quality information, and she'll save hundreds over hiring a local dog trainer or taking classes.

- She gets a free, one-on-one consultation with you as a bonus.

- The sooner she takes action the better—because behavioral problems only worsen with time and become harder to break.

Study the above list carefully. What if, instead of including these points in your offer, you simply advertised "dog- training videos for $29.95"? There's a big difference, isn't there? Limiting your offer to telling people what your product is and how much it costs is far less effective than telling them the tangible and intangible benefits:

- How much better they'll feel when they have the solution

- How easy it is to implement the solution

- How easy and inexpensive your solution is compared to the customer trying to solve her problem alone

- How safety, confidence, and satisfaction are built into the solution

- How the purchase of this solution may solve additional problems, as well as prevent existing ones from worsening or new ones from developing

No matter which market you go into, you must position your product as a solution, and you must market it as a solution

I hope this makes clear just how much more robust and complex your offer to your market can (and should) be. No matter which market you go into, you must position your product as a solution, and you must market it as a solution.

COMPONENT #3: TRAFFIC

Driving traffic to your Web site is much like luring potential customers into a brick-and-mortar storefront. If no one shops in your store, you go out of business. If no one visits your Web site, you go out of business.

Let's extend this metaphor a bit. Everyone who visits your site has an agenda. A certain percentage of your visitors arrive knowing exactly what they want, and they'll purchase right away. A larger percentage will require more time and persuasion to make a buying decision. They need the equivalent of a sales associate to assist them. Finally, the remaining percentage of traffic walks back out the door when they realize they're in the wrong place.

Now, while you cannot control your visitors' ultimate agendas, you *can* control the percentage of visitors coming to your site who are open to your efforts at turning them into customers. In other words, you can improve your sales by generating targeted traffic so that you minimize the amount of window-shoppers coming to your site, while boosting the number of immediate customers and prospective customers.

You should know before you get involved in Internet business that the majority of your traffic, no matter how well targeted it is, will consist of prospects—potential customers. You can celebrate those visitors who purchase from you during their first visit, but just keep in mind that this is a rarity. The core of your revenue is going to come from the targeted prospects you've collected onto an opt-in mailing list and converted into repeat customers.

It is just as important to get your offer in front of the right people as it is to make the right offer to them.

So, what is targeted traffic? A visitor is considered targeted when he can be identified as a member of your target market. In order to generate and direct targeted traffic from your market to your Web site, then, you must be able to locate sources of market-specific traffic. Targeted traffic plays just as large a role in the conversion process as your offer and your sales copy. Why? Because it is just as important to get your offer in front of the right people as it is to make the right offer to them. If you are selling tennis rackets, you obviously don't want any visitors who are searching for baseball bats. A subtler example would be that if you are selling an e-book on how to play the electric guitar, you don't want too much traffic from people looking for acoustic-guitar lessons. Even visitors within your overall market can be untargeted. If you were advertising electric-guitar lessons to acoustic-guitar players, you might get some "general interest" sales, but nothing near like what you'd get putting your offer for electric-guitar lessons in front of electric-guitar players. Make sense? There are markets within markets, or niches within niches. You must identify the specific segment of your market that will be most interested in your offer, then generate traffic by advertising to that segment of the market.

You must identify the specific segment of your market that will be most interested in your offer, then generate traffic by advertising to that segment of the market.

Identifying market-specific traffic sources will be easy once you have learned how to conduct market research. Your prospects will virtually target themselves for you via the keywords they use for Web searches, and this information ultimately leads you to all of your market's online "hideouts." In my blueprint, I will teach you the specific tactics to use for generating this traffic to your site. For now, keep in mind the following points about targeted traffic:

- Targeting is necessary to convert visitors into customers.

- Targeted traffic is traffic that comes from within your target market.

- Proper market research will reveal to you who to target and where.

COMPONENT #4: BACKEND

"Backend" is a strange term, isn't it? At least, I always thought so until I learned what this bit of marketing lingo actually means. The backend refers to the offers you make as follow-ups after an initial sale. In case you were wondering, marketers also use the terms "front-end" and "midlevel" when discussing the different points along a sales funnel (the plan or actual achievement of converting prospects into sales).

The front-end refers to the lead offer or lead product. Your lead offer is what you advertise or promote to your market from your Web site—the offer that initially draws them to your site and onto your opt-in list.

The midlevel is another way of referring to the classic up-sell—trying to persuade the customer to buy a more expensive product or a related additional product at a discount. Midlevel offers are presented to the customer prior to completing the front-end sale.

The only levels you need to focus on for now are the front-end and backend. In fact, you could say that these two types of offers are the sole offers made in any sales funnel, because the midlevel is really just an optional upgrade to the front-end offer.

The majority of your income is going to be generated by backend offers.

Now that we are clear on all of the terms, let's look more closely at the backend and why it is important. As stated earlier, your lead offer gets your customer through the door. However, these front-end sales are not where you'll earn the bulk of your income. The majority of your income is going to be generated by backend offers.

Let's look at an example. Pretend for a moment that you are an affiliate promoting a $27 e-book. It's a great book, you have a great offer, the low price tag makes for easy sales, and easy sales mean a larger portion of your opt-in list gets converted from prospects to existing customers.

Now, two things should be evident right away:

- You aren't going to get rich off of the commissions on a $27 e-book.

- Existing customers are much more likely to buy from you again if you present them with another offer.

Here is where the backend comes into play. If you want to earn a real income from your Internet business, you must follow up with existing customers. Once someone has purchased a product through you, they are very likely to purchase another and another ... if you follow up with relevant offers! The key, though, is that your backend offers up the ante, so to speak. Follow-up offers are almost always for products or services that carry a higher price tag than the lead product or differ in terms of the product's format. For example, you could follow up the $27 e-book with an offer for a $47 piece of software that nets you double the commissions. Then follow up with yet another offer for a membership site or similar product that generates recurring revenue.

Let's look at what would happen if you knew you were guaranteed one hundred sales per month on any offer. We'll say you get twenty-five new sales of the lead offer each month, twenty-five on your first follow up, and fifty on your second follow up. If your commission structure were as follows:

1) Lead product—$15 per sale

2) Backend #1—$30 per sale

3) Backend #2—$9.95 per month (recurring)

… then your total monthly income would be $1,622.50, with over $400 of that coming from a passive (recurring) income source. Now, if you didn't have a set of backend offers built into your business, then you would have to rely solely on generating new sales of your lead product each month. At only $15 per sale, this wouldn't get you very far.

I hope it is clear now why you cannot rely on front-end (or I should say "one-time") sales alone. A successful business model requires that you maximize the lifetime value of every customer by including a solid backend follow-up series in your sales funnel. Otherwise you're just leaving money on the table.

COMPONENT #5: DUPLICATION

Many people's systems end at component #4, but this should not be the case. The final step, always, is to duplicate your existing business model/ system into other markets or into horizontal product lines within the same market. Once you've established yourself successfully with your current business (and put the business on autopilot), you can hunt down new opportunities and repeat these same steps:

Find a market → Create an offer → Drive traffic to the offer → Present backend offers

Duplication has been one of the major factors in my ability to build wealth. Duplication allows you to explode your overall profits by creating multiple streams of income. Having more than one income

Many people's systems end at component #4, but this should not be the case.

stream is crucial for a variety of reasons. First, there's going to come a point when you're squeezing about as much as you can from your first business. While you might be able to generate a few extra thousand here and there, what you really want is to double your income. Duplication allows you to do this over and over again, in as many markets as you like.

With this snapshot of the five components of a successful Internet business, I'd now like to give you some background to the Internet in general and to Internet marketing before you come with me on a guided exploration of my Million-Dollar Blueprint.

CHAPTER 4

Understanding
Internet Marketing

You can duplicate my success (or enjoy something very close to it) provided you have the mindset I talked about in the introduction—the unwavering focus and motivation to succeed—and my indispensable Million-Dollar Blueprint. Before I take you through the blueprint, however, we'll need to take the time to understand the unique qualities of the Internet as a business medium. Think of this chapter as a quick tour of Internet marketing. A little Internet know-how goes a long way.

THE MERCHANT AND THE AFFILIATE

In the introduction, I mentioned the two core business models: the direct proprietor (also known as the merchant or product owner) and the third-party proprietor (also known as the affiliate marketer). It is easiest for newbies to go into business online as affiliates first. This is because you don't need to have your own product; you earn commissions selling someone else's product via referral to the merchant's sales page. As you know from reading my story, I have been on both sides of this equation. I began my business strictly as an affiliate marketer. Once I mastered affiliate marketing, I started creating my own products for sale and added the merchant model to my business.

Think of this chapter as a quick tour of Internet marketing. A little Internet know-how goes a long way.

WHAT IS AFFILIATE MARKETING?

Affiliate marketing is based on the idea of revenue sharing. The affiliate marketer links (via an affiliate link) to the merchant whose program he is affiliated with and earns a commission whenever the visitor he sent through his link purchases the referred product. So, you ask, how does the merchant know that you referred a particular customer? All the traffic you generate to the merchant's site flows through your affiliate link. An affiliate link is a special URL (uniform or universal resource locator—a Web address) that uniquely identifies you as an affiliate. For example, if you are promoting a product at http://www.xyz.com, your affiliate link will usually be some longer variant of this address, such as http://youraffiliateid.xyz.com/ or http://www.xyz.com/product.html&aff=your

affiliateid, etc. Affiliate links redirect the visitor to the correct page on the merchant's site while simultaneously setting a tracking cookie that contains your affiliate information.

Let's look at an example. ABC Company (the merchant) sells e-books through its own Web site. A customer who visits the site through a regular, nonaffiliate link buys an e-book for $47. In this scenario, ABC Co. has made a direct sale and earns $47. Now, let's say that ABC Co. wants more traffic and more sales. They decide to start an affiliate program that pays affiliates 50 percent of every sale they refer. You decide to join the program and start promoting ABC Co.'s e-books through your own Web site. Now, your visitor will go through your affiliate link to ABC Co.'s Web site. When that visitor purchases that same $47 e-book, *you* pocket $23.50, and ABC Co. keeps the other $23.50. In effect, you've both earned money through a revenue-sharing model.

As the affiliate, you've paid for all the tools needed to generate that referral (Web hosting, autoresponder, etc.—more about these in the next chapter). All you have to do to stay in profit is keep referring more sales, as long as the money you spend generating those referrals does not exceed what you earn back in commissions.

Your merchant, meanwhile, must do all these:

- Pay for all these same tools

- Pay any fees associated with their payment processor

- Deliver the product to the customer

- Issue refunds if requested

- Answer customer service and support questions

- Pay any other ad costs

- Pay out affiliate commissions

This isn't to dissuade you from being a merchant at some point; as I mentioned earlier, putting both models into operation will boost and secure high-end profits. I am just illustrating how much easier and cheaper it is to start your first business as an affiliate. You don't have nearly as much overhead cost, you don't have to create the product, and you don't have to deliver it. Instead, the majority of your work involves being an effective information provider. What kind of information? Well, let's take an in-depth look at it right now.

UNDERSTANDING THE INTERNET MEDIUM

In the introduction, I explained that the Internet is a vast information highway. People go online searching for all kinds of information—let's take hobbies, for example. The type of information people want on their hobbies could be anything from how-to guides to product- or price-comparison shopping. People are willing to pay for this information, even when they can find much of it for free. The reasons for this are myriad; here are some:

- Laziness—They don't have time or don't want to bother with searching too much to find what they need.

- Urgency—They need information right now and don't have time to find it themselves.

- Perceived value—Packaging information into a product gives the impression, true or not, that the information is comprehensive and high quality, more so than could be found for free.

- Passion—In certain niches, the customer base is rabidly devoted to their special interest and will spend money on almost anything related to this passion, even if it's similar to something they already own.

So the nature of the Internet as an information provider gives us its value as a business medium. If information is the number-one product on the Internet, your value to the marketplace is as an information provider. If you want to earn your first million online, you must become an information provider. The demand for information exceeds that of any other item you could sell.

If you want to earn your first million online, you must become an information provider. The demand for information exceeds that of any other item you could sell.

Think about the types of information you tend to search for online. You're usually looking for a solution or an answer to a problem, question, or concern, right? It might be something like this:

- How to get started in Internet marketing

- Home-decorating tips

- How to fix a car

- The fastest way to lose weight

- Learning some new magic tricks

All of the above represent the kinds of how-to information people search for and for which information products offer solutions! In fact, the examples I just gave you are all from existing information products.

WHAT IS INFORMATION MARKETING AND WHAT IS AN INFORMATION PROVIDER?

Information marketing is a combination of affiliate marketing and e-mail marketing.

Affiliate Marketing + E-mail Marketing = Information Marketing

The ultimate way to succeed as an affiliate marketer is to act as an information provider, or middleman between the customer and the merchant, rather than as a salesperson. Why? Because people value information and solutions over products. Value is the yardstick against which all your information should be measured. If you focus on truly helping people and providing real value, you can't fail.

Affiliate Marketing + E-mail Marketing = Information Marketing

People can see through inferior products, no matter how good the sales hype. Even if you manage to convince someone to buy a shoddy product, you'll pay for it later. A reputation for poor quality is *not* what you want! Having a reputation for quality, on the other hand, means more referrals and lots of repeat customers. Quality is what separates *average* affiliates from *super* affiliates.

Value is the yardstick against which all your information should be measured. If you focus on truly helping people and providing real value, you can't fail.

THE AFFILIATE AS MIDDLEMAN

Let's say that a potential buyer is looking for information on weight loss. He will use the search engines and come across thousands of Web sites that offer diets, exercise tips, and weight-loss tips. This potential buyer's main concern is, "Which solution is best for me?"

Here's where you come in as the middleman. You've researched the weight-loss market and all of the major solutions and products available in it. You decide that http://www.burnthefat.com/ offers one of the best solutions for the money. Your job, then, is to connect with that buyer and show him why Burn the Fat is an ideal solution to invest in. You connect with the buyer, then connect that buyer to the seller of Burn the Fat. In order to do this, you first have to capture that buyer's personal information—name and e-mail address. This allows you to follow up with him on his expressed interest in weight-loss solutions.

WHERE E-MAIL MARKETING COMES INTO PLAY

In order to connect with that potential customer as an affiliate, you must do the following:

1) Attract him to your Web site, where you have set up an opt-in landing page that presents him with an information offer.

2) Have an opt-in subscription form on your page so that this visitor can take you up on your information offer by subscribing to your e-mail list.

3) Follow up with that subscriber by providing more information that, you hope, will convince him to click through your affiliate link to the merchant's site.

When you follow up, you essentially provide your leads with the information they need to make a decision. In our weight-loss example, this

It's a lot like making an introduction between strangers in the real world.

would entail educating the subscriber on weight loss in general, as well as showing him the major benefits of the Burn the Fat solution, specifically.

It's a lot like making an introduction between strangers in the real world. You're introducing the prospect to a product he may not have seen before. Think about all of the factors people weigh when they first meet someone new. First impressions are *crucial*. There's always an implied transaction involved. People gather information about each other in order to determine whether and how a relationship will proceed.

The same thing is at play when it comes to introducing people to new products and services. Just as you would, in the real world, introduce two people by sharing their names, background, status, and so on, you introduce people to new products by name and by providing details about the products' features and benefits. Benefits are a lot like shared interests. People are usually more comfortable when they have things in common with each other, right? Your job as an affiliate is to help foster that sense of connection, that sense of "this product sounds like the right solution for me."

I hope you're starting to get the picture—are you beginning to grasp the enormous business potential out there on the Internet? You might be saying, "Great, Ewen. What else do I need to get started?" I'm glad you asked. We're getting to that right now.

CHAPTER 5

Tools of the Trade

E very business needs certain tools to run effectively, and your Internet business is no exception. These tools are necessary not just to get the job done but also to improve your marketing. Improvements in the marketing process always lead to bigger and better profits. For an affiliate marketer, especially, the following four tools are required:

1. A Web site with your own domain name

2. An autoresponder

3. Link-tracking software

4. Link-cloaking software

Let's go over each to discover why these tools make such a difference to every affiliate's bottom line.

A WEB SITE WITH YOUR OWN DOMAIN NAME

A serious affiliate marketer must own his own Web site and domain name. The reasons for this are numerous:

1) More control over the presentation of marketing materials and product offerings

2) Dedicated lead generation

3) Branding and visibility

4) Control over the flow of Web site traffic

5) Ability to interact with and respond to visitors

When you run your own Web site, so much more is available to you in terms of control. If you don't have your own site, think of what happens when you generate traffic and direct it toward someone else's Web site? You lose the ability to influence those visitors. You are at the mercy of the merchant's ability to sell the product. When you have your own Web site, however, *you* get to capture those visitors first. This means that you can present a given product to a visitor in the manner *you* believe is most likely to lead to a sale. You get to capture that visitor's name and e-mail address and grab repeat business from her. You can even survey her to find out what she really wants.

Improvements in the marketing process always lead to bigger and better profits.

Let's say you own a domain called http://www.best-deal-on-nike.com. Through the effective use of branding and visibility, your site could well become the first one people check out when they're looking to buy Nike shoes. Not so if you simply link

It all comes down to freedom and control. Your site is the engine that will power all of your marketing strategies.

(in an advertisement, for example) to http://www.nike.com. Sure, your affiliate link might be embedded behind that URL, and you might earn a commission, but whose brand recognition will go up a notch?

I'm sure you're beginning to see my point. I could list dozens more examples to support the importance of owning your own site. It all comes down to freedom and control. Your site is the engine that will power all of your marketing strategies.

AN AUTORESPONDER

This is the second most important tool to have in your arsenal. Actually, I should probably say that it is just as important as your Web site. However, it is very difficult to run a proper autoresponder campaign without a Web site, so I won't belabor the point here.

An autoresponder is just a software program, hosted either on your Web site or on the autoresponder service's Web site. You've probably seen an autoresponder in action already if you've spent a significant amount of time online. Let's say a visitor arrives at your Web page. He sees your newsletter subscription box (it may be embedded on the page, or you might present it to him inside of a pop-up window) asking for his name and e-mail address. He decides to join, so he goes ahead and enters his information and clicks on the Subscribe button. Behind-the-scenes programming puts his information into your database, then sends out your first e-mail message to the address the visitor entered.

If you've set it up for this, you can have your autoresponder send that visitor messages automatically with prewritten content that you've created. You can also send separate messages (for example a newsletter or a quick update) without interrupting the flow of the other messages.

The autoresponder is a really powerful tool because it allows you to accomplish one of the most important tasks faced by any marketer: following up with your prospects. Better yet, it lets you do this hands-free. If you didn't have an autoresponder at your disposal, you'd have to follow up with each prospect individually, typing out your messages every single time—totally overwhelming! This one tool alone will save you much time and money. Don't leave home without it!

LINK-TRACKING SOFTWARE

Link-tracking software (or even simple do-it-yourself link-tracking methods—more on that in a moment) is another key component of successful marketing. What does link-tracking software do? Link tracking means keeping tabs on the URLs you've placed in advertisements, pay-per-click campaigns, e-mails, and articles. Every single link to one of your Web pages—on- or offline—can and should be tracked, because you need to know where your Web traffic comes from. You need to know which advertisements perform and which ones are duds. You do this by measuring action, where the desired action is that a click is generated. The

> *You need to know where your Web traffic comes from. You need to know which advertisements perform and which ones are duds.*

prospect reads your e-mail or Google ad or whatever it is and is motivated to click on the link you provide.

Now, you might be thinking, "But, Ewen, my Web host offers a Web statistics program—isn't that good enough?" Absolutely not! Regular stats programs do provide valuable data, but they do not offer you the control and flexibility of pinpointing the exact source of your traffic. Let me illustrate the level of control that a link-tracking solution offers you.

Let's say you want to promote a new e-book. The merchant's URL is http://www.abc.com. Your affiliate link is (I'm just making this up) http://joeaffiliate.abcbook.hop.clickbank.net. Now, let's say you're doing some testing via Google Adwords. You create two separate ads that are almost identical, except for their headlines. You want to know which headline pulls best. Both of these ads need your affiliate link attached to them. But what happens if you place http://joeaffiliate.abcbook.hop.clickbank.net, as is, into each ad? How can you tell which advertisement was actually clicked on, when the hits are recorded as coming from "joeaffiliate" every time? You can't! And that's bad, because you won't know which headline got more results.

Now, let's say you get wise and find a way to track those links. This time, you have two separate specially encoded links. They both lead to the desired destination, but this time you know which ad got clicked on! Your two links might look like this:

http://joeaffiliate.abcbook.hop.clickbank.net/?tid=adwords1

http://joeaffiliate.abcbook.hop.clickbank.net/?tid=adwords2

"Adwords1" will correspond to the ad with your control headline, and "adwords2" will correspond to the other headline you're testing. Now, when you check your tracking stats, you'll see something like this:

Google Ad 1: 27 Clicks from adwords1

Google Ad 2: 39 Clicks from adwords2

Notice now that you have far more information and control than before. Tracking in this way allows you to keep tabs on (and test) everything. It doesn't matter which element you're testing, and it doesn't matter if you're testing Adwords, e-mails, or articles. You can create a special link for every single case and know *exactly* what's going on. So remember this: link tracking is crucial and a very big part of what separates average affiliates from super affiliates! Invest in software that will allow you to track your links.

So remember this: link tracking is crucial and a very big part of what separates average affiliates from super affiliates!

LINK-CLOAKING SOFTWARE

Link cloaking isn't always a necessity, but it's a good practice to follow. Before we delve into the reasons for this, let's talk about what link cloaking does. Link cloaking involves the manipulation of a URL from its original form into a different URL while still permitting both to lead to the same destination. Even link shortening is a type of link cloaking. Maybe you have seen URLs such as this before:

http://www.tinyurl.com/eagv9

Clicking on that URL should take you to http://www.EwenChia.com. I just took my URL and cloaked it here as an example. TinyURL and other services like it can handle (and were designed for) far longer URLs than my sample URL. But I wouldn't recommend relying on third-party services like

TinyURL to cloak your links, because you have no control over how long your link redirect will last. Instead, invest in software that will do the job reliably and for however long you need it to. An excellent product is the Affiliate Cloner, which you can check out at http://www.EwenChia.com/clone.

Why bother with cloaking links at all? Think about affiliate links for a moment. Often these links are very long and ugly, kind of like this:

http://www.abcsite.com/shopping/cart.asp?$lang=true$affid=76394

Yikes! Now imagine sending an e-mail out to your subscribers with a link like that. The link itself might break or wrap in some people's inboxes, requiring them to copy and paste it. If they're lazy, they won't even bother. You could lose commission just because your affiliate URL isn't convenient enough for some of your subscribers.

Others might recognize the "affid=" part on the end and say, "Aha! An affiliate link! I don't want anyone making money off of me, so I'm just going to erase that part and make sure no one gets a commission when I purchase that product." In this scenario, you would lose commission from intentional URL alteration.

Both of these lost-commission scenarios present solid reasons for cloaking your links. Yes, there will be some situations where cloaking is not necessary. That said, however, a good rule of thumb to follow is: when in doubt, cloak it.

There are a lot of different link-cloaking tools available, and some are fancier than others. For example, the hot thing now is the "recommends" script that can take a link like this:

http://affname.merchant.hop.clickbank.com

and turn it into this:

http://www.yoursite.com/recommends/product

To summarize, then, these four tools really are the engine behind the majority of communication that will take place between you and your customers:

1) A Web site with your own domain name

2) An autoresponder

3) Link-tracking software

4) Link-cloaking software

They are the key technical components of your sales funnel.

With some background marketing know-how and your trusty toolkit under your belt, let's now start turning that money-talk into reality, shall we? Let's move on to the meat of my Million-Dollar Blueprint, starting with market selection.

PART TWO

The Million-Dollar Blueprint

CHAPTER 6

Your Market

Part two of this book is dedicated to an in-depth look at each of the Fab Five, the essential components of a successful Internet business system. Together, these chapters make up my Million-Dollar Blueprint. With this book you will have everything you need to launch your own Internet business and see your profits skyrocket like never before. To begin, we must understand the process of selecting a market.

There is a formula I use when deciding whether a given market is worth my time and effort. I call it the APO formula—affinity, profitability, and opportunity.

MARKET AFFINITY

When you begin brainstorming ideas for a target market, think about the things you have an interest in. What do you love? What are your hobbies and interests? What type of specialized knowledge do you possess that might be of use to others?

☞ *Strike a balance between profit and desire.*

Affinity marketing is about doing what you love. You've heard the old adage, "Do what you love, and the money will follow." Nowhere is this more relevant than in business. That said, there are many marketers out there who disagree with this idea and will argue vehemently against choosing your market based on your own interests. They do have some valid points. For example, you might have very narrow or specialized interests in an area where there's not much of a marketplace to speak of. Alternatively, you might love something so much that you'd have a hard time making objective business decisions. It's important to keep these points in consideration. You need a profitable market. But what I'm urging you to do is strike a balance between profit and desire. Even a profitable market may prove difficult for you to break into if you've no interest it or choose it based purely on profit potential alone. The absolute best place to be is to have a business in an area that's both profitable and enjoyable. Now let's take a look at some other aspects of affinity marketing.

☞ *The absolute best place to be is to have a business in an area that's both profitable and enjoyable.*

What you need to look for is a niche market. You must target your products and services toward a well-defined group of consumers. In other words, the market you're going after is clear and can be named.

But don't forget: you must let the needs of the market dictate your product offerings, not the other way around! Here's a random list of very broad, potential niche markets to give you a better idea of what I'm talking about:

- Car buyers

- First-time home owners

- Exercise fanatics

- Model-train builders

- Golfers

- Newlyweds

- Computer programmers

- New moms

- Restaurant owners

- Guitar players

- Investors

- Graphic designers

Notice how each potential market I listed is a subset of people who may have specific product needs based on their careers, hobbies, circumstances, etc.? Each of these market groups represents a potential niche.

However, it is not specific enough to say that you intend to target "guitar players" or "investors." The question becomes: *which segment* of the guitar-player or investor market are you going to target? There are markets/

niches within the categories above. For instance, some guitar players are looking for guitar lessons, while others are looking to purchase equipment. Likewise, some investors are beginners looking for how-to information, while others are experts looking for advanced information to give them an edge. One of the main reasons for doing market research is to determine which of these segments is expressing the most need. You simply must not attempt to launch a marketing campaign until you determine what your market wants and how badly they want it! You might assume that there are plenty of guitar players, for example, looking for online guitar lessons. As it turns out, this *is* an example of a currently viable market, but it would be foolish to dive into it without first verifying these factors:

1) Need/Demand

2) Profitability

3) Competition

This goes to the heart of your most important and very first step, which is to understand the following principle:

A niche business consists of a business idea that is centered around a highly targeted market group.

Read that again and really think about it. When you zero in on a niche, what you're really doing is zeroing in on the following:

1) The audience or target market you would like to serve

2) The core mission and unique selling proposition of your business

3) The core product line of your business

4) The realities of the market—which guide every aspect of how you structure your business, how you advertise and promote your business, and how you manage the long-range growth of your business

To find a niche and create a business based on that niche is to stare marketing reality in the face. It's the difference between having a concise business plan and no plan at all.

A lot of people don't get niche market identification right the first time.

One maximizes your chances for success; the other is an almost certain road to failure. So as you read this and begin to think about niches and niche businesses, keep these points in mind. Niches are not magical, newly discovered entities. They are simply markets within markets—markets that are hungry and eager to buy.

A lot of people don't get niche market identification right the first time. They choose a market that is either inappropriate relative to their skill and resources or far too general and broad. I believe one of the reasons this happens is that those of us who teach Internet marketing have neglected to explain our hidden thought processes. In other words, it is one thing to tell you to go look up some keywords at Wordtracker or Google and quite another to explain how to evaluate the market potential represented by those keywords. So I'm going to do the best job I can here, right now, to show you how I make my own value judgments about whether a market is worth entering and whether it merits further research in the first place.

☞ It doesn't always begin with keywords!

First, it doesn't always begin with keywords! You'll hear a lot of marketers, myself included, tell you to use keyword research tools like Wordtracker, Google AdWords, various software programs, and a host of other keyword research tools. Why? Because this is the quickest way I know of to find an online niche market. There is an assumption behind this, though. The assumption is that you have a starting point or idea already in mind when you run these searches. You need a broad keyword to start with—something that defines the industry you intend to research. If you have no clue which industry you're interested in, then I'd be doing you a disservice to tell you to use keyword research as a starting point. You'd be forced to sit at your computer just randomly entering words like "cats" or "coffee cup" into these research tools, hoping to see something interesting pop up.

So, first things first—do research and brainstorming via other sources, and get your markets of interest (your affinity markets) nailed

☞ Do research and brainstorming via other sources, and get your markets of interest (your affinity markets) nailed down to start.

down to start. You see, I've already defined my market. I know that Internet marketing is my area of expertise. Hence, I have a standard vocabulary in mind that I can use as the starting point for my niche research.

Where are *you* in this step? Are you starting totally from scratch? If you are, then pay close attention to what follows next. I'm going to give you a crash course on how to perceive the landscape of salable products the way a businessperson perceives it.

So, let's say you are starting totally from scratch … The first thing you need to be aware of is that your mind is habituated to seeing the world from a consumer's point of view. There is nothing wrong with this. You should keep this ability intact, because it's going to help you relate to your customers. However, this way of thinking (when done without awareness) can also blind you to the profit opportunities staring you in the face.

The niche marketer thinks in terms of both existing products as well as products that haven't been introduced to the market yet.

The average person thinks in terms of products that already exist. The niche marketer thinks in terms of both existing products as well as products that haven't been introduced to the market yet. How does the niche marketer see opportunities where others don't? It's simple:

- He pays attention to what people are already buying.

- He pays attention to trends and the latest hot industries.

- He keeps up with national and world news.

- He is a voracious reader.

Now, how do you apply this so that you can come up with your own list of potential target markets to research? Ask yourself the following questions:

1) What products am I already consuming?

2) What issues have been in the news lately that might connect to a need for a particular product or type of information?

3) What have I read about in books or magazines lately that might point to a potential market?

Now, write down everything that comes to mind. Examine your answers and pull out anything that looks like the simplest one- or two-word description of a broad niche. Examples: the software industry, the clothing industry, relationship advice, the latest advances in allergy treatments according to that story I saw on the news last night …

Now, pick out a couple that really grab you, and get ready to do some serious reading and research. You'll want to start out just surfing the Web for sites related to the broad keywords you've selected. See what you can find in terms of existing products, services, and content (e.g., articles, message boards, etc.) related to your niche topic. The questions you want to answer during this process are as follows:

1) How many visible submarkets does my market break into?

2) What are the products and services being sold?

3) What range of prices are people charging?

4) How are these products and services being delivered?

5) What information is the market seeking out?

6) What topics are currently hot items of discussion?

7) What is the market's "inside vocabulary"?

This is going to give you a much better big-picture view of market opportunities while also helping you zoom in on the details and get away from overly broad definitions of the market in question.

Let's put it all together with an example. Let's say you choose "clothing" or "fashion" to describe your interests. I really like this example because most people would react by saying, "Clothing? I don't want to sell physical goods! You said that information marketing is where it's at. What kind of information could people possibly be looking for about clothing?" It's true that there are plenty of Web sites out there selling shirts, pants, shoes, and belt buckles—and some of them even run affiliate programs. This, however, does not indicate a market preference. Clothing represents a lot more than "functional items to put on so you won't be naked."

Think about all the other ideas that circle around clothing:

- Fashion, fashion modeling

- Dressing to express personal style

- Dressing to look thin

- Dressing for a business interview

- Dressing for a first date or to attract someone

- Finding affordable clothing via thrift stores or learning how to make your own clothes, sewing, etc.

- Care and cleaning (e.g., stain removal), tailoring

- Clothing worn only on special occasions (e.g., wedding gowns, Halloween costumes, etc.)

Notice how many related concepts I generated right off the bat? Also, did you notice how each idea can be broken down further, sometimes into entirely new niches? Did you notice how each of these concepts represents a potential information market? For example:

Fashion → Fashion modeling → Modeling as a career → "How to Get a Career in the Fashion and Modeling Industry"

Is there an existing market for that information? You bet there is, and there are people out there right now selling that information to the market. Why not you?

Now that you've a better idea how to brainstorm potential markets, let's move on to explore the crucial vetting process that must take place before you finalize your market selection. You see, it is not enough to go into a market based solely on the presence of preexisting products or competition. You must also determine whether the market will be profitable for *you* and whether you can afford to enter that market based on your current budget and resources.

MARKET PROFITABILITY

Market profitability is based on two factors:

1) The market has plenty of disposable income.

2) The market is known to buy. In other words, the market is willing to spend a fair share of disposable income on products or services that address needs.

So, the first thing you look at is the overall financial health of the market. In some cases, you'll be able to make an intelligent guess at this information. For example, it is common knowledge that members of certain professions (e.g., medical professionals, law professionals, etc.) tend to have a good deal of disposable income. This is a quick and easy guide when you know you're going into a luxury market or following a business-to-business sales model (where you market to businesses instead of individuals—e.g., you provide technical expertise to other companies or professionals such as doctors).

However, you cannot guess at the profit potential of an average market simply by looking at the average income of your target market, as this is hard to determine except in all but the most exclusive cases. You would be surprised at how much money people will spend on their hobbies, even when they nearly go broke in doing so. Think, for example, of people who build model trains or those who love to collect the latest movie memorabilia.

These passions cut across many demographics. Everyone from the clerk at the corner store to the CEO at a huge corporation may share an interest in collecting stamps, playing golf, or some other type of hobby. So, the profitability of any given market comes down not to how much one type of individual is willing to spend, but to the following factors:

1) Are there preexisting products or services in the market that sell well?

2) What is the average price of these products and services?

3) How much demand for these products and services is being expressed?

In other words, what you really want is a healthy amount of competition, and where there's a wide variety of price points. Be wary of markets where it appears no one is selling anything. There's often a good reason for it! Also be wary of markets in which there's not much variation in product type or quality. The best type of market allows you to promote everything from entry-level, low-priced products to higher-ticket items.

Be wary of markets where it appears no one is selling anything. There's often a good reason for it!

The surest and easiest way of getting the big-picture view of your market is to examine the advertising that's already targeted to that market. Look to television, radio, newspapers, and market-related magazines. You can, for example, take a trip to your local bookstore or library and find the specialty magazines that your market reads. Try to gather up several months' worth of issues, if possible. Search for advertisements throughout these publications. You'll usually find the bulk of them in the back of the magazine. What types of products are being advertised? How much do they cost? Most of all, how many of the same advertisements are repeated month to month? The running of certain advertisements again and again in a particular publication indicates that the advertiser is making money. Study these advertisements and the products they promote. You can glean a lot about your market. You can start classifying the types of products your market is spending money on. This will help you later on when you begin looking for your own products to promote to that market. There are several online resources you can use as well to perform these profitability checks and get a better idea of the types of offers and products your market is looking for.

PROFIT CHECK #1: IS THIS A MARKET WHERE PEOPLE ARE ALREADY BUYING?

Use the resources listed below to discover the markets people are already spending good money in:

1) http://www.eBay.com

2) http://www.YahooShopping.com

3) http://www.Amazon.com

4) http://www.Magazines.com

5) http://www.Bookspots.com

When you visit any one of these sites, you should look for the following indicators:

- **WHAT'S POPULAR**

    See if you can spot trends. Make note of what is currently popular versus where there is long-term or cyclical demand (e.g., the annual markets for Valentine's Day, Halloween, Christmas, etc.)

- **TOP LISTS**

    Most of these sites have top lists showing which products or subjects are currently selling the most. Book lists are especially helpful in putting your finger on the pulse of a market.

- **RELATED ITEMS**

    On sites like Amazon and eBay, you can uncover some very useful information about a market's interests. On Amazon, for example, scroll past the editorial review for any book, and you'll see a section titled "Customers Who Bought This Item Also Bought"—where you'll see the other titles people have purchased.

- **NICHE MARKET IDEAS**

    This is one way to narrow things down and find a niche within your market. The titles of various books, especially, can give you clues to what new spin is being put on old subjects.

PROFIT CHECK #2: ARE YOU TAPPING INTO CURRENT OR FUTURE HOT TRENDS?

These sites can give you a sneak peek at growing trends in popular culture and society:

1) http://Pulse.eBay.com

2) http://50.Lycos.com

3) http://www.Trendwatching.com

This is a good check to use against any affiliate products you're considering, too. See whether your market is heating up or cooling down. Also, make sure that you have the right affiliate products with the right spin. This is most important when targeting a market where opinions change quickly and people are prone to following the latest fads. A good example of this is the weight-loss industry, where fad diets come and go on a regular basis.

PROFIT CHECK #3: WHICH MARKETS ARE WRITTEN ABOUT?

You can visit the following article directories and search for articles targeted to your market:

1) http://www.Ezinearticles.com

2) http://www.Goarticles.com

3) http://www.ArticleAlley.com

4) http://www.IdealMarketers.com

5) http://www.Searchwarp.com

The reason for doing this is simple: popular subjects (and people) get other people talking! In a good market, you should find plenty of articles covering a wide range of topics. The more questions, problems, and concerns the market has, the better—because this means a greater demand for solutions. It also suggests passion. Any time people care enough to read, write, and relate around a common interest, you can be sure there is a need just waiting to be filled. There is, in other words, a demand for information.

Any time people care enough to read, write, and relate around a common interest, you can be sure there is a need just waiting to be filled.

PROFIT CHECK #4: VALIDATE YOUR MARKET WITH FREE KEYWORD RESEARCH TOOLS

To validate your market through keywords is to verify that your market is present on the Internet and hungry enough for information that they search for it online. This is crucial. If your market isn't going online to search for information, then you have nothing to offer them. This is because a search for information always implies an unanswered question. Questions indicate needs. Needs demand solutions, and your solutions make up your offers!

So, your next step is to make use of the following tools:

1) http://www.Featuring.com/wtt

2) http://Adwords.Google.com/select/ KeywordToolExternal

Start by entering some broad keywords related to your market. For example, let's say you want to validate the market demand for relationship advice. The key phrase

To validate your market through keywords is to verify that your market is present on the Internet and hungry enough for information that they search for it online.

"relationship advice" would be a good starting phrase to check out, but you'll also want to run an even more general inquiry on just "relationships" or "love." What this will do is return a whole host of related searches containing those words, as in the sample results below:

27,090 searches (top 100 only)	
Searches	Keyword
2523	relationship poems
2023	relationship quizzes
1519	relationship compatibility
1176	relationships
874	troubled relationships poems
826	relationship advice
749	sagittarius men relationships
633	free relationship quiz
576	free relationship compatibility
563	relationship compatibility by names
520	ways to end relationships
511	end relationship quiz
498	compatibility relationship test
468	troubled relationship poetry

What you see in the above screenshot is just a portion of the total results returned when I entered the word "relationships" into Wordtracker's Free Keywords Tool. Wordtracker pulls its results from the databases at Metacrawler and Dogpile. Each item in the list represents an actual search phrase people are typing into those two engines. The numbers you see to the left represent how many times those words or phrases were used in a search in the past month. Keep in mind that these numbers are only for those two engines! We haven't even scratched the surface yet.

For the bigger picture, we need to run this same inquiry on Google's Keyword Tool, too. This time we have the option of pulling in some synonyms related to our search, so we'll do that. Here's a small portion of the top results Google gives us:

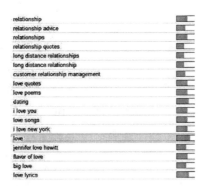

Unfortunately, we don't get to see the exact numbers for the search volume here, but the blue bars indicate that we're probably looking at numbers similar to what we saw with Wordtracker. This is good because it means we've got a healthy amount of market presence across the Web. Remember: these are the top searches for just one month. Although these results will fluctuate slightly from month to month, we can view them as representative of the average. Why? The topic of love and relationships is universal. Therefore our results are less likely to be artificially inflated by seasonal concerns (with the exception of a spike in searches around Valentine's Day) or by stories in the media.

We can also see that the market's hunger for information centers quite clearly around help and advice targeted primarily toward romantic relationships. Advice for family relationships appears to come in a close second.

When you run this type of search yourself, you'll be able to get the actual numbers. Google does provide that information, but you have to download your keywords into a file in order to get to it. Other research tools, like Wordtracker, will display the search volume right next to your results. That said, here is a useful rule of thumb when it comes to evaluating search volume: Weigh your keyword(s) search volume against the number of indexed pages reported by Google as natural search results and by the number of sponsored advertisements being run by Google PPC advertisers.

Weigh your keyword(s) search volume against the number of indexed pages reported by Google as natural search results and by the number of sponsored advertisements being run by Google PPC advertisers.

So, for example, if the bulk of your niche market's keywords average five hundred searches per month, while Google reports that it has indexed over a million pages containing those keywords, you may have some market saturation on your hands. It all depends on the nature of the million results. If you see some commercial Web sites in the natural results, but little to no sponsored advertising, you may have hit an untapped niche. However, if there are no commercial Web sites at all and zero sponsored advertising, you're likely looking at a dead market.

Conversely, what if you find a niche with a lot of competing advertisers? Competition is good. It means the market is alive, and highly profitable for some people. It may or may not be profitable for you. In order to find out, you will have to look at what the existing advertisers are paying per click to run their ads. We'll talk more about that in the chapter on traffic generation. Meanwhile, if you can say with certainty that a demand for information exists within the market, it's a good bet that you may also profit by providing that information. It's simply a matter of determining the best way to build your business within the niche and doing so within your means.

After you have validated your market ideas, choose your *top three* potential markets, and make your final selection after you have investigated the market opportunities within each.

MARKET OPPORTUNITY

Market opportunity has to do, in a sense, with breadth. In other words, how many opportunities are there for you to capitalize on the market? This is in large part influenced by competition, or other players in the market.

You want your market to have some established businesses already there serving it. Why? Because these businesses may give you a leg up with opportunities for partnerships and joint ventures. They're also going to be big sources of additional traffic to your Web site. Market opportunity is also about the breadth of product offerings. In other words, how much room in the market is there for selling a variety of products? Are you limited to selling just one genre of product, or is there an opportunity to roll out new formats and capitalize on new trends?

For example, some markets get flooded with e-books and not much else. But you want to be able to go a step beyond that. You want to be able to offer audio and video products, software, and even home-study courses. Think of it like selling video cameras, for example. You'd do all right just selling cameras, but you'd really rake in more money when you can offer tripods, cases, tapes, lenses, and the like. In other words, market opportunity is mainly about how many options you have for creating profitable, backend follow-up offers.

So, let's say that you've performed all of the necessary steps so far, and you've come up with the following three main market ideas:

1) Love and relationships: advice/help

   Potential (sub)targets: singles, couples, families

2) Fishing: tips, tricks, secrets

   Potential (sub)targets: bass fishermen, fly-fishing

3) Car repair: how-to, do-it-yourself

   Potential (sub)targets: used cars, foreign cars

At this stage, what you're really looking for is how many profitable offers you can target to your market. As an affiliate, you especially want to look for residual or passive income programs, programs with a variety of products (at all price points), as well as the breadth/depth of available products and solutions for your market.

For example, if you went into the relationships market, you'd have a ton of programs to choose from:

- E-books that cover everything from dating to weddings to parenting to breakups

- Books, audios, and videos that teach attraction secrets

- Matchmaking sites that charge members a monthly subscription fee for full access, on which you can earn recurring commissions

Again, because relationships are such a universal topic, there is a wealth of market opportunity. Products are out there that address the needs of just about any demographic you can think of when it comes to love. There are hundreds of unique spins on the subject. The more related products there are to fill out your backend system, the better. You'll want to have a ready store of potential offers and bypass the chore of having to create your own products for now.

The completion of this step requires research into the available products, and there's a particular set of criteria I want you to use for that. It is closely related to the process of creating your offer, which is the next step.

CHAPTER 7

Your Offer

7A

FINDING AND KNOWING
YOUR PRODUCT

Recall that powerful offers require you to hold a clear understanding of market needs. Although your offer may be customized in many ways as discussed earlier (bonuses, guarantees, time limits, etc.), product selection is still of utmost importance. We're going to look at the process of aligning offers to markets from the standpoint of affiliate marketing, as it is the easiest to demonstrate (because the products are already created).

FINDING A PROFITABLE AFFILIATE PRODUCT

The first thing to do is find a profitable affiliate product within your market. When offering affiliate products as solutions, it's important that the product is a winner for you and your customer at once. Not just any product will do. What you need to find is something I like to call a *mega* affiliate product. Mega affiliate products may be high or low in price but share the following qualities:

- They pay out high commission percentages (50 percent and above).

- They have a proven conversion rate.

- They are hot, timely, or in demand year-round.

- They are backed by a merchant affiliate program that provides solid support to affiliates.

You should choose at least three products to start out with. These products should differ in price and commission type; you'll want one low-ticket item, one higher-ticket item, and at least one product that earns you residual (recurring) income. The first product will be the lead product that you are going to promote from your opt-in page and first e-mail series.

The second product will be the backend product that you promote to your list of existing subscribers or customers. This is typically done in the second e-mail follow-up series. The backend product should be somewhat higher priced than your lead product and pay out at least a 50–75 percent commission.

The third product should be a residual income product—a product that will earn you monthly, recurring commissions. These types of products are things like subscription-based services and membership sites.

Remember that the products you recommend will influence your reputation. In fact, your reputation will also be affected by the merchant's behavior, even though you have no control over the merchant's actions.

Look for products through affiliate program directories like these:

> http://www.AssociatePrograms.com
>
> http://www.AffiliatePrograms.com
>
> http://www.AffiliateFirst.com

Look for products through natural search engine results at these sites:

> http://www.Google.com
>
> http://www.Yahoo.com
>
> http://www.MSN.com

Look for physical product programs at sites like these:

> http://www.CommissionJunction.com
>
> http://www.LinkShare.com
>
> http://www.ShareASale.com

Look for digital product programs here:

> http://www.ClickBank.com
>
> http://OneNetWork.DigitalRiver.com

Look for residual income programs here:

> http://www.lifetimecommissions.com
>
> http://www.AffiliateGuide.com/residual.html

Many of these sites are organized by category. You can browse through directory-style listings by marketplace—for example, categories for health and beauty, electronics, etc. You can also usually perform searches for specific products or companies, but note that some of these sites don't support searches as well as they should. Clickbank, for example, often won't return the results you think it should; sometimes it won't even return products you already know are there. In that case, it is better just to browse through each category.

Likewise, sites like Commission Junction will let you sort within categories and arrange the listings according to factors like which products are converting the best for affiliates, which products are paying out the highest commissions on average, which programs offer residual income, and so on.

STUDYING THE AFFILIATE PRODUCT AND SALES COPY

When you locate a mega affiliate product, you must take the time to sit down and really study it. I recommend, if you can afford it, that you actually buy the product. You really need to know your product inside out in order to sell it effectively. Also, take time to study the sales copy on the merchant's page. Notice some of the elements there that make you want to buy the product. What you should aim for in this step is to turn yourself into the number-one expert on that product. You should also look for indicators to how well this product will convert for you. Is it a suitable offer for your market? Here are some of the things to look for:

You really need to know your product inside out in order to sell it effectively.

- **COMPELLING COPY**

  Are you pulled into the sales letter and able to read it all the way through? Even better, do you feel convinced of the product's ability to solve your problem even before you finish reading?

- **CLEAR BENEFITS**

  Does the sales letter do a good job of highlighting the product's benefits? Do you understand clearly what you'll gain by owning the product?

- **POWERFUL OFFER**

  Does the merchant make a powerful offer and a call to action in the sales letter?

- **EASY TO BUY**

  Has the merchant made the product easy to buy, with well-placed order buttons, a money-back guarantee, etc.?

- **EASY AFFILIATE PAYMENT**

  Is the merchant using only *one* payment processor or affiliate program? This is very important. You don't want to promote any product where the customer has the option of making payment through an alternative service that doesn't credit you as the affiliate.

Each of the above factors is very important to your conversion rate. Make sure everything is in place before you dive in. If you find anything lacking—say the merchant hasn't done a very good job of highlighting benefits in his sales copy—then you'll need to make up for this when you write up your own version of the offer. In other words, you'll need to lay out those benefits to your prospects so that they have a clearer idea of the value of the product before they visit the sales page.

NOTING INTERESTING POINTS AND BENEFITS

As you review the product and its sales page, *write down* what stands out to you. What makes the product unique? What are the most compelling benefits this product has to offer? How and why is it the best solution to your market's needs? This step is very important because you're going to use what you've written down later on to help you craft your offer.

In this discovery process, you get to pull out additional benefits that your market might respond to, and this allows you to speak to their needs even more effectively.

Also, if you purchase and study the product, you'll probably discover some benefits or points that aren't mentioned in the sales letter. This is because the sales letter was written from just one person's perception of the product. You, on the other hand, might notice or value an entirely different aspect of the product. Maybe you notice an ease of use that wasn't emphasized in the sales letter or a really eye-opening piece of information that the merchant doesn't mention. In this discovery process, you get to pull out additional benefits that your market might respond to, and this allows you to speak to their needs even more effectively.

Here's an example. Let's say you've decided to promote an e-book that shows people how to cure their acne in just days. You've read through the sales letter and written down some of the points the merchant brings up as well as the claims he's making:

- Skin problems can be cleared up without pills or creams.

- You can eliminate most acne in a matter of days.

- Most people believe that junk food contributes to skin problems, but this is not true.

You've also written down the benefits stated in the sales letter:

- Gain confidence from knowing your skin looks great.

- Acne is easily cured; it doesn't take a lot of work or expense.

- Eliminate acne permanently.

- Experience a "new you" in as little as three days.

So, what you have at this point is everything that the merchant felt was important to emphasize. Next, you read through the product information—maybe you even try it out yourself—and you come up with a list of points and benefits the merchant left out:

- The cure is based on a little-known scientific discovery.

- It does more than clear up acne; it also improves overall skin tone and texture.

- It works for all ages and ethnicities, regardless of skin type, hormones, etc.

- It is also a treatment for old acne-related scarring.

- Your healthy glow and increased self-esteem has improved your interactions with other people.

Now, you see, you have even more material to work with—and you've come up with additional selling points (a fuller solution) that could make a real difference in crafting an offer that speaks to your market.

MARKET CAPTURE AND LIST BUILDING

Once you've identified your target market, your next step on the way to profit is to capture that market's prospects. As mentioned earlier, a prospect is anyone who might be interested in what you have to offer. A prospect is a potential customer. In order to capture a prospect, you need to entice her to give you personal information: her name and e-mail address. What you're really doing here is building market share. Imagine that at any given time, there are 100,000 people searching online for your product (as evidenced by the search volume data for your niche keywords). If you can entice 1,000 of those people to give you their names and e-mail addresses, you've captured a 1 percent market share. It seems really elementary, but this is one of the easiest ways online marketers can measure their share of a market. Your bottom line comes down to how much of the market you're able to contact, at will, any time you choose. It doesn't matter how much money you throw at advertising and promotion—if you allow prospects to click away from your site without grabbing their contact information, you're essentially throwing advertising dollars down the drain.

> *Your bottom line comes down to how much of the market you're able to contact, at will, any time you choose.*

Why is list building so important? A targeted opt-in list is the heart of your business because it allows you to follow up with potential as well as existing customers. Maybe you've heard this statistic before: it usually takes seven to twelve exposures to a message before a prospect will take the bait and make a purchase. You simply can't afford to allow prospects to get away from your sales message. You need them on an opt-in list so that you can presell to them as many times as needed. You need them to remain on your opt-in list, too, so that you can sell new products to them down the line. It is much easier to grab a repeat sale from someone who knows and trusts you than it is to get a sale through a stranger. For an affiliate:

repeat customers = repeat, lifetime profits

In addition to building your list, you must do everything possible to make sure that your opt-ins are targeted. In other words, you want your list members to want to be on your list, to be interested in what you have to offer, and to be "hot" (ready to buy).

But how do you accomplish this? Remember when we discussed market selection in the previous chapter? List building is another instance where market alignment comes into play. You want to make absolutely sure that you've targeted the correct market to begin with on several levels, that you've done the following:

repeat customers= repeat, lifetime profits

- Established the market's level of interest and profitability

- Located the correct affiliate product for that market

- Targeted the correct keywords for that market on that product

Each of the above three rules should be checked and double-checked for compliance every step of the way. If you don't correctly target your market and the products for that market, then you're going to see very poor lead conversions.

You must generate market-specific traffic, firstly, by targeting the correct keywords. You

You must generate market-specific traffic, firstly, by targeting the correct keywords. You also need to make sure that all of your other traffic generation methods are targeting the market correctly.

also need to make sure that all of your other traffic generation methods are targeting the market correctly. This means the following actions:

- Advertising only on relevant and noncompeting Web sites

- Advertising only in relevant and noncompeting e-zines

- Writing articles correctly targeted to the market

- Aligning with the correct joint venture partners for your market

- As a merchant, making sure your affiliates are correctly targeting your market

- Testing and tracking all of your traffic

You'll know whether you've correctly targeted market traffic by monitoring your conversion results. If you generate one hundred unique visitors to your site and not one in that hundred converts, then you likely have a problem somewhere in the chain. You're either targeting the wrong traffic or you've improperly targeted your offer.

Now, what does the total market capture optimization task look like? There are three elements:

1) **Keyword optimization**

    Make sure the keywords you use to lure in prospects are a good match for what you're selling. For example, if you're selling an e-book on allergy cures, then you should target phrases such as "allergy cure," "relieve allergy symptoms," etc. But you wouldn't want to target phrases like "allergy pill" or "allergy doctor." They're only marginally related and hence not targeted enough.

2) OPTIMIZED COPY

Copy optimization picks up where keyword optimization leaves off. How? Well, someone could come to your site looking for, say, information on food allergies, but your allergy cure is targeted toward things like hay fever or mold allergies. So, you'll use your opt-in page copy to clarify the specifics of your product. Let the prospect know exactly what they're opting in for, what they'll receive, and why you should be viewed as a trusted source for the information they seek.

3) LIST CLEANING

Over time, you'll notice certain unresponsive segments of your list. Some prospects might have used a fake e-mail address or simply changed e-mail addresses. Others might be tire kickers or freebie seekers who never open your messages and have never purchased. It's a good idea to do some list cleaning every six months or so. Delete any dead or bouncing e-mail addresses. See if you can make a final offer to the nonresponders and then delete them from your list if they don't bite.

BUILDING A RELATIONSHIP WITH YOUR LIST

In keeping with your role as an information provider, it is crucial that you build your relationship with your list by providing as much timely, useful information as possible. This means going above and beyond the reviews contained in your product-specific autoresponder sequences. The key is to always have some form of information in front of your list, especially between the gaps in each autoresponder sequence and often in the middle of an ongoing sequence.

> *The key is to always have some form of information in front of your list, especially between the gaps in each autoresponder sequence and often in the middle of an ongoing sequence.*

There are two ways to do this. First, you can insert informational e-mails or newsletters in between autoresponder sequences. Second, you can also use your autoresponder to broadcast one-time messages to your list at will.

What type of information should you send to your list in these follow-ups? Any type of content that helps build a deeper, more responsive relationship with your subscribers and that exceeds their expectations in terms of *quality*. Here are some ideas:

- Longer articles

- Videos

- Gifts, such as free reports that your subscribers can download

For example, let's say that you've created a helpful video you want your subscribers to see. You can upload and post this to your site, then e-mail your subscribers to let them know it's available for them to view. The reason for doing this is partly to keep subscribers on their toes and paying attention but also to build up a sense of real value in being on your list. You see, if you just keep sending them the usual follow-up messages, they're going to get bored. They're going to be starved for more information. As someone who makes a living off of being an information provider, the one thing you don't want to do is leave your list hungry! You've got to satisfy their hunger for more. You've got to provide them with as much value as they can handle. This all goes toward building a feeling of goodwill between you and your list. Try to think about where you can fill in information gaps.

What do your subscribers need? What would really help them? Then create this content and give it to them for free.

YOUR OWN BLOG: THE BEST PLACE FOR RELATIONSHIP-BUILDING CONTENT

Now we're going to put a twist on the follow-ups. When you send out these informational messages in between autoresponder sequences, I want you to post these messages to a blog.

A blog (short for *Weblog*) is just a type of Web site publishing platform that allows the site owner to post his content onto his site without having to use HTML, the markup language used to create documents on the Web. The pages are generated dynamically (they aren't static HTML pages), and the posts are usually arranged all on one page from newest to oldest.

You'll still send out an e-mail, but the e-mail will contain a link to your blog post. We do this because people usually don't read long e-mails; if you're sending them a lengthy article, a blog is the best place for them to read it. Secondly, you're going to have some extra revenue streams on your blog, so you'll want to get your subscribers there to interact with you.

As someone who makes a living off of being an information provider, the one thing you don't want to do is leave your list hungry!

So, let's say that you've just written a very long informational article for your subscribers, and you've also created a free PDF report you want them to download. You'll first post the article to your blog along with the link to download the bonus report. Then you'll send out an insertion message to your list, telling them to go read your blog and grab their gift. For example:

Hi First Name,

Do you know the top 10 tricks to making money online? If you want to know, I've just written an article for you on this very subject. It's posted over at my blog: http://www. yourblog.com/

Make sure you read the whole article, because I also tell you how you can grab a FREE gift I've created for you. You don't want to miss it.

Now, your subscriber will have to take action to satisfy his curiosity. This is a good thing. You need to pull your subscribers out of e-mail mode every so often and get them clicking around and paying attention.

For a step-by-step tutorial on how to set up your own blog using Blogger, please refer to bonus chapter 11 of this book.

PRESELLING

Building a relationship with your list through your autoresponder sequences and your blog also helps you presell your product. Preselling is the process that allows you to overcome the prospect's objections and overwhelm her with benefits. It makes buying the obvious choice. If you've ever subscribed to an opt-in list, you've already seen preselling in action. The following case study shows you what it looks like when the average prospect experiences this most effective of marketing tactics:

It's a dark and stormy night. Joe Customer switches off his TV (the weatherman predicted a few more hours of heavy rain), switches on his computer, and logs on to the Internet to check his e-mail. After wading through a few spam mails and notes from friends, his eyes land on a subject line that makes him sit up and take notice: "Joe, do you know the real reason you can't fall asleep?" "No," he thinks, "but I would love to know why. In fact, I'd pay good money right now if I could just find a way to get to bed by midnight. I've got a huge presentation tomorrow."

As he opens the e-mail, he remembers who it's from. He visited the site last week around 3:00 AM. They were selling a "sleep solution." Joe wasn't sure if he believed they had the answers, but they did offer him a free e-book on relaxation techniques, and he had applied those with some success before bedtime. The latest message reads as follows:

Dear Joe,

It's been one week since you subscribed to *The Sleep Easy Solution* newsletter and downloaded your free copy of "Ten Tips to Relax before Bedtime." Have you benefited from the tips so far? I certainly hope so. As you know, insomnia is like a waking nightmare. I suffered from it for over ten years until I discovered the powerful information available only in *The Sleep Easy Solution*.

In fact, I remember two life-changing facts presented in the book that put me to sleep fast the same night I read them. Did you know there are a grand total of two reasons most people can't fall asleep at night? That's it. A measly two issues that stand between you and a good night's rest. One of them concerns your overall health. The other is a psychological trigger—and it's so powerful you'll be rolling on the floor when you find out what it is.

Joe, I can't recommend this product highly enough. It will truly revolutionize your life. Sleep is the fountain of youth, after all. You can visit http://www.thesleepsolution.com/ again for all the juicy details and place your order over a secure server. You can download the solution instantly after payment and be fast asleep an hour later.

Yours Truly,

Jim Marketer

Joe is inspired to visit the site yet again. He rereads the sales copy and discovers a few choice benefits he hadn't noticed before. He checks the price: $49.95. It doesn't seem too bad. After all, he might pay the same for a book down at the local bookstore. Joe decides to go for it. He clicks on the Order button and whips out his credit card. If you were Jim Marketer, you could congratulate yourself now for making a 75 percent commission (that's $37.46) while you're out at the movies with your spouse. A bell just went off to signal more money headed to your bank account, and you aren't even at home in front of the computer. That's the power of effective affiliate preselling in action!

> *Preselling is an under-the-radar method of sales that primes your prospect to become a customer*

As you've probably worked out, preselling is an under-the-radar method of sales that primes your prospect to become a customer. Essentially, you're softening the target so that you can persuade him or her easily when you ask for the sale. Why is this important? First, here are the facts:

- **MOST PROSPECTS DO NOT MAKE A PURCHASE WHEN THEY FIRST VISIT A SITE.**

In fact, it may take several repeat visits from the prospect before you get the sale. There can be any number of reasons for this. The prospect may be short on time, viewing your site from work, or simply not have the funds to buy at that time.

- **PEOPLE GENERALLY DISLIKE BEING "SOLD" IN THE OBVIOUS WAYS.**

  Educating and informing the prospect (giving something of value before asking for the sale) goes a long way. This is especially true online. Keep in mind that your potential customer sees dozens of offers per day. He is bombarded with spam, banner ads, and other intrusive media.

- **PRESELLING = FOLLOWING UP.**

  Following up is proven to increase conversion. Remember the ratio of visits to first sales. If your prospect visits your site and you do not follow up with him, your chances of making a sale are very low. When you do follow up, however, you have the ability to keep your offer in front of him and keep the lines of communication open so that you can earn his trust and sway him to your recommendations.

- **BETTER YOU CAPTURE THE PROSPECT (AS AN AFFILIATE) BEFORE THE MERCHANT DOES.**

  One of the worst things you can do as an affiliate is to send a prospect to the merchant's sales page before you've captured his name and e-mail address! It is likely that the merchant will end up capturing that person's name and e-mail, instead. Also, consider what happens when the merchant's sales copy is less effective than yours.

If you aren't preselling, you are losing prospects and losing sales.

Preselling guarantees you the maximum odds for optimizing all elements of your affiliate campaign—from your traffic budget to the integrity of your tracking data. If you aren't preselling, you are losing prospects and losing sales.

THE THREE STEPS OF PRESELLING

There are three basic (but crucial) steps to preselling:

1) Building a landing page

2) Collecting e-mail addresses

3) Sending your follow-up material

Each step is a link in the sales chain. You need to make sure each of your links remains strong and effective.

The **landing page** is the first page your prospect ever sees, and for this reason, you need to write the most solid and attention-grabbing copy that you can. Your job on the landing page is to snare the prospect's attention immediately and get her interested—more importantly, make sure she keeps reading! Your task is to capture the maximum number of prospects into your affiliate sales funnel and turn them into rabid, ready-to-buy subscribers. E-mail opt-in lists are proven sales generators for affiliates. It is far more effective to capture your visitors onto a list and follow up with them about the product than it is to try and convert them on the front page of your site.

A landing page can be as simple as a headline with a brief list of benefits and a subscription box, or it can be a full-length sales letter in its own right.

What you are selling here are the benefits of joining your list to learn more about the product. Actually, you're selling the benefits of learning more about the subject to which the product relates. It's a basic problem–

The job of your landing page is to acquire the customer's e-mail address!

solution setup: the prospect arrives with a desire or a problem, and you hold out the carrot of a solution in exchange for joining your list.

Remember this: the job of your landing page is to acquire the customer's e-mail address! This is so important that it cannot be overstated. Too many affiliates make the mistake of sending their prospects right back to the merchant's site through a link on their landing page without getting the addresses. Don't make the same mistake!

To collect e-mail addresses, there is a tool you need to acquire. It's called an autoresponder, and you read a little about

Collect e-mail addresses.

it in an earlier chapter. An autoresponder is a powerful list-management software product. It can be remotely hosted through a service such as http://www.monsterresponse.com/ or you can purchase a license to a product like AutoResponsePlus and host it on your own site.

An autoresponder allows you to send automatic replies to everyone who joins your list. You can also schedule periodic messages and time them to broadcast by the hour, day, week, or month. Your autoresponder service (or software) will generate for you a subscription box, which is just a piece of HTML form code that you paste into your landing page. This is where the prospects will enter their name and e-mail address. Once they hit the Submit button, the software handles the rest, and *voila!*—you have a new subscriber.

If you want to convert more prospects to subscribers, you need to sell your list benefits effectively in your copy and offer prospects some "bait" in exchange for joining your list. Let's talk a bit about the list-building bait.

> *You should offer your prospects something of value in exchange for joining your list.*

You should offer your prospects something of value in exchange for joining your list. This can be a free e-book download, a piece of software, or perhaps an informative e-course. You can choose just about anything, but it needs to be a subscriber-only bonus, and it needs to have value in the prospect's eyes.

Imagine, for example, that you are promoting a weight-loss e-book. What are some of the bonuses you could use to lure in more subscribers? Well, how about these:

- Calorie-counting software

- Menu-making software

- A short e-book on the dangers of yo-yo dieting

- A collection of tasty, low-fat recipes

Any of these bonuses would be suitable as bait. Here's a side benefit to this tactic: when you create the material yourself, you can embed your affiliate link again! You can also embed links to other sites and products you'd like to promote. Not only that, but if people happen to share the material with others, you'll have a viral effect in motion, which will send more visitors to your site for free. Your opt-in list is the powerful link in the chain. So *do not bypass this step*. Get your landing page and your autoresponder set up first thing, and start collecting prospects' addresses.

Your **follow-up material** should be exclusive content that the subscriber can't find anywhere else. You'll send him periodic mailings (the timing is up to you) that sync with the subject matter of the product you're promoting.

Let's return to our weight-loss e-book example. Each mailing you send could contain unique information on some aspect on weight loss, healthy eating, or even general health. This information will be placed in context by either expressing or implying that the subscriber is sampling "just a taste" of what she can find out when she buys the product. *This is very important.* You do want to share something of value with your prospects. You can reveal a few choice pieces of information from the product, but don't give away the farm. Your job is to give content that arouses curiosity—which in fact raises more questions than it answers—and whets their appetite for more. The reaction you want your subscriber to have is, "Wow! What a great message. This is fascinating. I really need to buy this product so that I can get the full story." Make sense?

Although it requires more work, the ideal approach for you to take is to buy each product for which you are an affiliate. You need to familiarize yourself with the product in order to sell it effectively. Live it and breathe it. Once you do this, you'll be able to create your own content for the presell and for your bonuses.

If you aren't up to creating all of the content on your own, consider hiring someone to do it for you. You can find ghostwriters for cheap at sites like Elance and FreelanceWarriors. You can also look into the public domain for tons of free content you can reprint or even format into your own e-books. The best sites for public-domain material are Archive.Org, Project Gutenberg, and Creative Commons.

Your follow-up material should be aimed at educating and informing the prospect. There are no hard sales tactics going on here. This is the time to slip under the radar, into the subconscious, and build desire. You are also taking the time to build trust and credibility so that the prospect feels more comfortable purchasing from you.

WATCHING THE SALES ROLL IN

The last step in the presell chain is the moment when the customer decides he's been effectively swayed and reaches for his credit card to buy the product through you. This is the moment all affiliates dream about. You have set up a system that, once in place, works on autopilot. All of your follow-up message are loaded in your autoresponder and go out like clockwork without you lifting a finger. This leaves you a lot more time to focus your efforts on traffic generation and campaign analysis, two elements that are sure to increase your bottom line.

There's really no lazy man's way out. You do need to create landing pages, collect e-mail addresses, and work the system of preselling to your prospects. Believe me when I say that it is worth the effort.

If you want to win in the affiliate game, and in online business overall, you must understand that there's really no lazy man's way out. You do need to create landing pages, collect e-mail addresses, and work the system of preselling to your prospects. Believe me when I say that it is worth the effort. Your commissions will skyrocket, and you'll wonder why you ever did things any other way.

7B

MAKING AN
IRRESISTIBLE OFFER

So you've studied your product, built a list of prospects, and are ready to make them your offer. In order to capture leads and convert those leads into customers, you need to create and present your front-end offer *from your own Web site.* In other words, your Web site is the platform from which you present your offer. It doesn't matter whether you're selling your own product or selling a product as an affiliate, your Web site is the first link in the chain of your sales system.

You see, your Web site is basically like your storefront. When you start advertising and generating traffic, you'll be directing that traffic to your Web site so that you get your offer in front of people by either presenting them with the sales page for your product or presenting them with a page that encourages them to opt in to your e-mail list, where you'll present your offer again (and again) via e-mail follow-ups. This is a multistep process that rests on the quality and value of your content and on the power of your copywriting.

CREATING YOUR OPT-IN LANDING PAGE

When I discussed preselling in the previous chapter, I talked about the importance of the landing page, or opt-in page, a simple Web site designed to collect your customers' information (name and e-mail address) so that they are subscribed to your opt-in list. Now we're going to look at an example of an effective opt-in page, one that enhances the effectiveness of the offer it carries. I'm showing you the opt-in page at http://www. PassiveIncomeSecrets.com:

Believe it or not, the rule with both offers and opt-in pages is: the simpler, the better. Your opt-in page does not need a lot of fancy graphics, and your

> *Believe it or not, the rule with both offers and opt-in pages is: the simpler, the better.*

offer does not need to give away so much information about the product that people know exactly what it is. In fact, the less you reveal, the higher your opt-in rate will be. Would you believe it if I told you that the above squeeze page converts, on average, 75 percent of my visitors into subscribers? Well, it's the truth—and the page has only four things:

1) A headline and the subheadlines, which draw attention to my offer

2) The subscription form

3) Standard legal disclaimers and privacy notices

4) My name

What is it about this approach that works so well? Why do I *not* need to give visitors a lot of information or fancy graphics to persuade them to opt in? First, *the key conversion tactics are compressed*. To understand what I mean, you first need to understand the five most common conversion-boosting tactics used on squeeze pages:

1) **A COMPELLING HEADLINE**

   Your headline must grab and hold the visitor's attention so he keeps reading your page.

2) **A TIME-SENSITIVE OFFER**

   Response rates go up whenever people perceive the risk of loss. This perceived loss can be anything from the opportunity to buy the product itself to losing out on a price break or a special bonus package.

3) **A CLEAR OFFER AND CALL TO ACTION**

   It doesn't matter whether you're making an offer via e-mail follow up or on your squeeze page; conversions are improved when people understand what they are getting and are told explicitly what they need to do to get it.

4) **BONUSES**

   Bonuses and freebies are a type of bait that compels people to take action.

5) **BUILDING TRUST**

   Visitors are more likely to opt in when you explain your privacy policies to them. Let them know your list is opt-in only and that you do not spam or sell their information to a third party.

As you might imagine, it is easy to create a very long squeeze page incorporating these five elements. Some marketers do this, and it works all right. However, the effect on the visitor is far more powerful when you group all of these elements together and keep them compressed in her immediate field of vision! Instead of having to scroll down the page and read a lot of text, she's shown the bottom-line offer right away and in a minimum amount of time.

> *The effect on the visitor is far more powerful when you group all of these elements together and keep them compressed in her immediate field of vision!*

You see, you've really only got a couple of seconds to capture your visitor's attention. After that, you've only got a minute or so to make the offer clear and convince him to opt in. The simple squeeze page model makes this a snap by integrating your offer, your conversion elements, and your call to action into a series of attention-grabbing headlines. Let's go over the page once more so you can see what I mean:

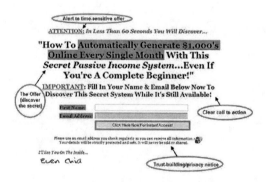

It is simple and effective. You can read the whole thing in about sixty seconds. This is really ideal, and it saves both you and your visitor a lot of time. The only trick you'll have to master in order to create this type of page is good copywriting skills! You don't need to learn how to create fancy graphics, but you will need to practice writing good headlines that integrate these conversion-boosting elements—in as few words as possible.

The second reason my squeeze page succeeds so well is that *the general offer is clear, but details are ambiguous.* Conversions are boosted by curiosity. Notice that the general offer is clear. I'm inviting the visitor to discover how to generate thousands of dollars *easily* using a *secret* passive-income system … that runs on autopilot (again implying ease).

So, while I'm telling the visitor *what* he'll learn, I'm not letting on about the details. I don't reveal the name of (or link to any information about) this secret passive-income system. To do so would be to throw the opt-in away, as the visitor would simply leave to investigate it for himself.

Also, I made a point of pushing some psychological triggers by using power words ("secret," "easy," "passive," "autopilot"), which serve to raise curiosity even more while also implying benefits. It is the equivalent of walking up to a complete stranger and saying, "If I told you I'd give you $10,000 just for telling me your first name, would you do it?" Most people are going to say, "Yes!"

This leads us to the third reason my copy works. *There are only two choices: yes or no.* Your visitors will make their decisions quickly in the first place, but this format pushes them to do so even faster.

> *Basically, there's nothing to do on the page other than read the offer and make a decision.*

There are no long, bulleted lists to read through. There are no affiliate links or any links to other Web sites. Basically, there's nothing to do on the page other than read the offer and make a decision. It's just enough to intrigue the visitor but not enough to satisfy him. Even

The ultimate advantage you gain with this simple squeeze-page method is the ability to turn the larger portion of your traffic—the "Maybe" visitors—into resounding "Yes!" subscribers.

if he's sitting on the fence about opting in, he won't find any other clues on the page to help him make that decision. It comes down to yes—join the list, or no—and hit the Back button. There's nothing you can do about the people who intend to say no regardless of how hard you try to persuade them. Likewise, it's easy to get super targeted visitors to say yes. The ultimate advantage you gain with this simple squeeze-page method is the ability to turn the larger portion of your traffic—the "Maybe" visitors—into resounding "Yes!" subscribers.

So, to summarize, here are the seven points to follow in crafting a simple, effective opt-in page and offer that converts:

1) **DO YOU HAVE A COMPELLING HEADLINE?**

   This is the first thing your visitor will notice when she reaches your site. Your headline needs to grab her attention right away and raise her interest enough to keep her reading the rest of your page.

2) **DO YOU HAVE A CLEAR OFFER?**

   Your visitor needs to see why and how opting in to your list will benefit him. What will he receive when he joins? What will he learn? How will your information help him?

3) **DO YOU HAVE A CALL TO ACTION?**

   Tell your visitors exactly what to do in order to join your list. Let them know they must provide their name and e-mail address by filling out and submitting the subscription form on your site.

4) **DO YOU HAVE THE SUBSCRIPTION FORM DISPLAYED PROMINENTLY?**

Keep in mind that your visitors may not have the time or inclination to read all of your opt-in page. So you need to place the subscription box as high up the page as you can rather than burying it at the end of your copy.

5) **DO YOU HAVE A PRIVACY NOTICE AND E-MAIL NOTICE?**

Remember to use trust-building elements. Always alert your visitors to your opt-in policies, and let them know that their information will be kept private. Also, it's a good idea to alert them to the necessity of providing a valid e-mail address and to check that e-mail account for their confirmation/welcome message.

6) **DO YOU HAVE OPT-IN BAIT, SUCH AS A BONUS OR TIME-SENSITIVE OFFER?**

These two elements should be considered part of your overall marketing strategy, and you need to have them in place if you intend to use them on your squeeze page. In other words, your claims need to be true. You can probably get away with stretching the definition of what constitutes a time-sensitive offer, but don't promise a bonus if you don't have one to deliver!

7) **DO YOU HAVE GOOD RULES OF FORMATTING FOR YOUR WEB SITE?**

You will want to make sure that your Web site is simple and appealing to the eye. Clean, consistent opt-in pages convert much better. Avoid clutter and the overuse of fancy graphics.

CREATING A THANK-YOU PAGE

This is the page that your subscribers will see after they have opted in to your list (from the opt-in page) by entering their name and e-mail address. (You'll learn how the subscriber gets directed to this page when you study the section on setting up your autoresponder. It's important that you have this page created first, though.)

There are two types, or models, of affiliate thank-you pages:

- **AN AUTOMATIC REDIRECT THROUGH THE AFFILIATE LINK**
  Your subscriber is automatically redirected to the merchant's sales page via your affiliate link after opting in. This is the easiest to set up, as you've no additional Web pages to create.

- **A CUSTOM THANK-YOU PAGE**
  Instead of redirecting the subscriber to the merchant, you direct him to your own, custom thank-you page. This allows you to thank the subscriber for joining your list, as well as promote your backend affiliate products right on the page.

The first model (affiliate link redirect) is only recommended for what I call "affiliate review" sites, where the opt-in page consists of a full-length product review. The second model—what you're going to learn to create— is the recommended model to pair with the simple opt-in page you've learned about here.

Notice that this page is also very clean and simple, just like the opt-in page you saw earlier. Here, though, we can get away with using a few more graphics, as this is a more appropriate venue for introducing product images and other branding elements.

What is the purpose of the page? A custom thank-you page is a highly versatile tool, but to understand how and why to use it, we first need to take another look at your subscriber's mindset. *Buyer's remorse*—a phenomenon existing in varying degrees of intensity—describes the state of mind people fall into after they've purchased a product outside of their comfort zone in terms of price, practicality, etc. This nervousness and uncertainty following a purchase sometimes leads to returning the product, especially when the consumer encounters difficulty using the product. In order to soothe and counteract buyer's remorse, the merchant has to follow up in some way after the purchase. This is one of the main reasons that big-ticket items (and even some smaller ones) are backed by warranties, guarantees, customer-support hotlines, and, in some cases, more personal forms of post-sale follow-up. Now, although your subscriber has not purchased anything from you (yet), he is still susceptible to a similar phenomenon—let's call it *subscriber's remorse.*

When your subscriber first opts in to your list, she knows nothing about you. You are both relative strangers to each other. While she expects to receive the information you promised her on the opt-in page, she also hopes to see information that puts her at ease and validates her decision to give you her personal information. In other words, getting a visitor onto your list is only half the battle. You've got to follow up with her on your thank-you page in a way that consolidates the new relationship and builds instant rapport. Rapport is critical to building a responsive opt-in list, and the process of building this mutual trust needs to start right away.

> *Rapport is critical to building a responsive opt-in list, and the process of building this mutual trust needs to start right away.*

BUILDING RAPPORT

Your thank-you page will be far more effective when you include the following:

1) **A THANK-YOU HEADLINE**

    Just seeing the words "thank you" lets your subscriber know immediately that his subscription request has been completed successfully. You can instill further peace of mind by confirming the delivery of the information promised on the opt-in page. This is why my headline says, "Thank you, read on for full details about the secret passive-income system you can use now!" rather than just "Thank you."

2) **TRANSPARENCY**

Notice that I've placed a picture of myself on the page, alongside my name. This instantly personalizes the relationship and boosts rapport and trust up another notch. Your picture should be tasteful and professional, but it doesn't have to be too formal. I wear a casual business suit in mine because I'm presenting myself as an authority on a business opportunity. You might wear something more casual depending on the niche you're targeting. For example, you wouldn't want to wear a suit if you're telling people how to get a free vacation in Hawaii!

3) **PERSONALIZATION AND LANGUAGE OF WELCOME**

Notice that I opened my welcome message with the words "Dear Valued Subscriber." This is a good generic greeting to use. It's safe and unlikely to offend. You can formulate other types of greetings as appropriate. For example, if you have an opt-in list devoted to guitars, you could open with, "Dear Fellow Guitar Enthusiast." Finally, notice that I also weave in a bit of personal history and experience into my presentation. This helps to further my authority on the topic of passive income as well as shape the subscriber's perceptions about why I'm promoting the system.

4) **PROVIDE THE GOODS**

My opt-in page promised to reveal the passive-income secret to the subscriber. Notice that I waste no time delivering on that promise. I've placed multiple links to the system early on in the welcome message and made sure those links are prominent. Make sure you do this as well. Nothing irritates a new subscriber more than having to scroll and search through your thank-you page in order to find what you promised him.

DELIVERING BONUSES

Now, let's look at the second function of your thank-you page—delivering bonuses and promoting your affiliate offers. As mentioned earlier, it is best to deliver your opt-in bait right away. If your bonus can be delivered only via e-mail, then make sure you inform your subscriber of this fact on the thank-you page. If your bonus consists of downloadable material, such as an e-book, audio file, software program, etc., then make sure the download links are provided right away and formatted to draw the visitor's attention to them.

There's no rule saying you have to save your affiliate offers for your follow-up e-mails. You can (and should) promote some of your offers right on the thank-you page.

A powerful but often-overlooked feature of thank-you pages is that you can also use them to promote your affiliate offers. There's no rule saying you have to save your affiliate offers for your follow-up e-mails. You can (and should) promote some of your offers right on the thank-you page. Look again at the screenshot (a couple of pages back) of my thank-you page, where I'm promoting one of my affiliate offers. What I want the subscriber to do here is purchase the PIPS (Plug-In-Profit System) business opportunity through my affiliate link. However, notice that I'm not presenting the real offer to him directly. Instead, I attempt to focus his desire and attention onto the Passive Income Secrets Teleclass.

The teleclass is actually a product I created for use as a promotional tool. It is technically not for sale at all. (This is something you can do too, when you feel ready to create your own products. If you wanted, you could even grab some private-label or public-domain products to use in creating a similar promotional tool.) Here's the best part, though: the teleclass product is designed so that its perceived value is greater than the cost of the PIPS product. In other words, I present my bonus as being worth more than the affiliate product I want the subscriber to purchase! This technique of minimizing the primary offer works amazingly well. Who wouldn't want to get a $197 product thrown in for buying one that costs less than half that? But don't think this is all there is to it.

In order to pull this technique off effectively, you must understand some of the additional conversion factors that are at play:

- **THE VALUE OF THE OFFER IS REINFORCED BY THE MERCHANT.**
  If you read the PIPS sales page (http://www.SuperAffiliates.com/pips), you'll see that the product offer is very high on perceived value as well. The merchant offers an overwhelming amount of bonus material and support relative to the price.

- **THE BONUS PRODUCT IS COMPLEMENTARY.**
  The teleclass is designed to complement the PIPS product and actually add even more value to it.

- **THE BONUS OFFER IS TIME-SENSITIVE AND REQUIRES ACTION.**
  You can see that the bonus offer is limited to seven days. The subscriber must follow my instructions in order to receive it. This requires, at minimum, clicking on my affiliate link to visit the PIPS sales page. Hence, I'm able to expose the subscriber to my offer even before he receives the first follow-up e-mail about it!

You should develop your own solid system like this one for promoting your affiliate offers from the thank-you page. It should work well as long as the bonus you're using is aligned to complement the affiliate product and provides real value.

If you aren't able to create a bonus product like this on your own, there are still some other tactics you can use:

- GET PRIVATE-LABEL RIGHTS (PLR) TO COMPLEMENTARY PRODUCTS

  A PLR product can be used as is, or you can edit it yourself. This lets you have a complete product without doing all the work to create it. Also, with PLR products, you're allowed to brand the product as if it were your own, then sell it or give it away.

- CREATE YOUR BONUS IN ANOTHER FORMAT

  You aren't limited to just e-books or teleclasses. You can also create audio, video, or software products—and there are private-label rights sites for these, too.

- OUTSOURCE

  If your budget will allow it, you can hire a freelancer to create a bonus product for you. Visit http://www.elance.com or http://www.rentacoder.com.

Lastly, you don't have to have your own bonus offer for all promotions. In fact, you don't have to use this tactic at all; but I do urge you to implement it as soon as you can, because it does increase conversions. Meanwhile, if necessary, you can start out just advertising or reviewing your affiliate products on the thank-you page. This can take the form of anything from simple banner ads or text links to a full-fledged review.

CREATING FOLLOW-UP E-MAILS IN

YOUR AUTORESPONDER

Remember all of the information you collected when you studied your product and its sales letter? It's now time to pull that information together to create a series of follow-up e-mails to send to your opt-in list. The purpose of this sequence of e-mails is to educate and presell your prospects, effectively presenting your offer to them from as many angles as possible. You also want to continue to build your rapport and relationship with your subscribers.

Your sequence can be as long or short as you want, but the recommended number of messages is at least five to seven. Any fewer than that and you really don't have a chance to give your subscriber enough information. That said, your first follow-up message is almost always a welcome message, where you thank the subscriber for joining your list and provide them links to any of the list bait bonus materials (e.g., a free e-book download) you may have promised them at the opt-in page offer. The welcome message can also be the point where you introduce the product/solution.

The easiest way to learn how to compose good follow-up messages is by example; try to model what I've done in the first five messages from the autoresponder sequence I use for http://www.PassiveIncomeSecrets.com:

E-MAIL #1

> Subject line: %%FNAMEFriend%%, passive income secrets
> …
>
> Hi %%FNAMEFriend%%,
>
> My name is Ewen, and I want to sincerely thank you for opting in to receive more information on this passive

income system …

You can click here to see this system:

=> http://www.PassiveIncomeSecrets.com/pips

Just like you, I've been searching for a proven method to easily make multiple streams of passive income online. More specifically, I was looking for a system that will work for the ordinary person regardless of his or her level of experience …

And I've finally found it in the Plug-In Profit Site (PIPS)!

This system now earns me huge passive income on complete autopilot 24/7, and I HIGHLY RECOMMEND it …

Make sure you click here to check it out immediately:

=> http://www.PassiveIncomeSecrets.com/pips

I'm also going to give you a very special bonus worth $197 valid for the next seven days only—see the details here:

=> http://www.PassiveIncomeSecrets.com/welcome.htm

Thanks, and I look forward to hearing the good news of your success. You will also be receiving more helpful passive income information and tips from me, so look out for them in your e-mail …

To Your Success!

Ewen

P.S. If you don't want to receive more information and tips to help you out, you can scroll down to the end of this e-mail for details on how to unsubscribe.

E-MAIL #2

Subject line: %%FNAMEFriend%%, you can do this easily ...

Hi %%FNAMEFriend%%,

How are you doing? Ewen here with a quick reminder ... Hope you had a good look at the Plug-In Profit Site system:

=> http://www.PassiveIncomeSecrets.com/pips

By the way, the special bonus just for you is almost gone, and there're only five days left for you to grab it ...

=> http://www.PassiveIncomeSecrets.com/welcome.htm

This system really works. And you can do this easily ... The best thing is, it makes you unlimited passive income automatically! Yes you read that right—you will make *six* instant streams of passive income with this system automatically *at the same time.*

This is because you get a *marketing system* built in for massive leverage—and leverage is one of the key secrets to passive income success.

Check it out here:

=> http://www.PassiveIncomeSecrets.com/pips

To Your Success!

Ewen

P.S. There're just five days left for you to grab your Passive Income Secrets Teleclass special bonus ... Here's how you can secure it immediately:

=> http://www.PassiveIncomeSecrets.com/welcome.htm

E-MAIL #3

Subject line: Who are you %%FNAMEFriend%%?

Hi %%FNAMEFriend%%,

I've a number of subscribers asking me, "Ewen, who are you?" So I thought today's a good chance to introduce myself more; it's always better to know whose e-mails you've been reading. :-)

Well I'm a full-time Internet marketer from Singapore and have been doing business online since 1997. After many years of trial and failures, I finally discovered how to get real consistent income from this Internet business ... And I promise to show you the way with real tips and information as well. One of my major income sources is this passive system I shared with you earlier:

=> http://www.PassiveIncomeSecrets.com/pips

This really works. In fact it doesn't matter where you are from or how old you are. The Internet is a level playing field, and anyone who's serious *will* become successful. For example, I'm from Singapore. Jeff Casmer, a member from the United States, has this to say about the passive- income system:

"Thank you! Two years ago I lost my job, had a baby on the way, was drowning in debt, and had no idea where and who to turn to. Today I am earning over $4,000 every month from this program and the figure is growing each month ..."

You can read about his results, plus many other real-life stories here:

=> http://www.PassiveIncomeSecrets.com/pips

I highly suggest you get started immediately!

To Your Success!

Ewen

P.S. The Passive Income Secrets Teleclass special bonus will be available for just another *48* hours. Get it now ...

=> http://www.PassiveIncomeSecrets.com/welcome.htm

E-MAIL #4

Subject line: Last 24 hours %%FNAMEFriend%%!

Hi %%FNAMEFriend%%,

Just a quick reminder about the Passive Income Secrets Teleclass bonus … It will be removed for good in just 24 hours.

So if you haven't grabbed it, this is really your last chance. Here's the link with the details:

=> http://www.PassiveIncomeSecrets.com/welcome.htm

To Your Success!

Ewen

E-MAIL #5

Subject line: %%FNAMEFriend%%, thanks again …

Hi %%FNAMEFriend%%,

Thanks again for reading my e-mails for the past week; I hope you enjoyed them. I'll be sharing with you a lot more tips and information to help you in your Internet business, so make sure you look out for my e-mails and keep reading.

If you're new to this business, here's a little something from me that may be helpful to you.

=> http://www.InternetBusinessForNewbies.com

I'll talk to you soon ...

To Your Success!

Ewen

SETTING UP YOUR AUTORESPONDER ACCOUNT

We talked earlier about the function and importance of an autoresponder in building your list and managing your follow-up e-mail sequence. Here's where we talk about setting up your autoresponder account.

Professional autoresponder services such Aweber and GetResponse (pro version) will cost you about $19.95 monthly. You can also get a professional autoresponder from http://www.monsterresponse.com. Once you have your autoresponder account, you'll need to log in and fill out a couple of details:

- LIST NAME

   Create your first list (autoresponders allow you to run more than one list) and name it. Note that the name you give it will not be visible to subscribers. It's just for your own reference.

- "FROM" ADDRESS

   Most autoresponder services allow you to cloak their address with your own. For example, if you're using Aweber, you can change yourlist@aweber to yourlist@yourdomain.com.

- "REPLY TO" ADDRESS

   You can also specify the address you want your subscribers to respond to if they have a question or comment about your e-mail newsletter. This can be the same as your "from" address, but it is usually better to just route those replies to another address.

- SIGNATURE FILE

  Your autoresponder should have a tab for global list settings, and this is where you should find a place to type in your own custom signature to be appended at the end of each e-mail. You can use this space for your sign-off and name, as well as links back to your Web site, blog, or current offers.

- THANK-YOU PAGE URL

  Even if you've yet to upload your thank-you page to your server, you should know ahead of time what the Web address will be.

Finally, you will need to input the actual e-mail sequence you created into your autoresponder. Each message should be a separate e-mail. After you have input your series of e-mail messages, the next thing that you will have to do is to plug in your opt-in form into your opt-in page.

Your opt-in form is actually a block of HTML code that is generated by your autoresponder. Your account should have a menu item that says something like "Generate Code," "Get HTML," or "Form Generator." We'll run through this step-by-step, using Monster Response as our example autoresponder.

If you have a Monster Response account, then you'll see a button that says Form Generator, and this is where you want to go once you've set up the basics of your list and input your e-mail series. Make sure you've selected the Single Subscription option, and put a check in the boxes for the Name and E-mail Address fields. Next, scroll to the bottom, and you will see a field labeled Thank-You Page. This is where you will enter the URL to your thank-you page.

Now, just click Generate Form, and you should be taken to the next screen, where you'll be able to copy the actual form code:

Notice that at the top you're shown a preview of what your actual subscription form will look like. Below that is a scrolling window that contains the code you need to copy and paste into the HTML of your opt-in page.

TESTING THE WEB SITE AND E-MAIL BEFORE YOU LAUNCH

Before you move forward, it's time to double-check everything and make sure your autoresponder is working properly. What you're looking for is assurance of the following:

- The opt-in form is working properly and does not generate any errors after you've clicked the Submit button. (Try entering your own name and e-mail address into your opt-in form, and click Submit.)

- The opt-in form redirects the visitor to the right location. (Make sure you are redirected to the thank-you page.)

- You are able to receive your first automated e-mail after opting in. (Check your e-mail to make sure you receive the first message of the series.)

- You continue to receive each message in your sequence as scheduled. (Just make sure to keep an eye on your inbox over the next few days.)

That's it! If everything is working properly, then you are ready to move on to the next step! If any step of the process fails, however, double-check to make sure of the following:

- You entered your e-mail address correctly.

- Your e-mail provider or program is not filtering your messages out to the "Trash" or "Spam" folders.

- You entered the correct link to your thank-you page in your autoresponder settings.

  Tip: If you own more than one e-mail address through different providers (Yahoo!, Gmail, AOL, etc.) it's worth testing your system for each of these. This allows you to see if your messages get incorrectly filtered by these services and also lets you see how your messages appear (in terms of formatting) to your subscribers.

BUILDING A RESPONSIVE OPT-IN LIST

You don't just need a list; you need a super responsive list. You need a group of people who are thrilled to be a part of your list, who look forward to each newsletter you send, and who take action on the offers you send to them. It may not be pretty, but it's the truth: getting people to join your list is only half the battle. It's really what you do with those subscribers once they're on your list that counts. You must begin the process of building the list relationship from the moment a subscriber signs up.

Here are the top seven rules for building a super responsive list:

1) FOLLOW UP IMMEDIATELY

Proper list management and commonsense marketing strategy dictates that you follow up with a new subscriber immediately. If you've promised a bonus, an e-course, or a newsletter issue upon subscription, then you need to set up your autoresponder to send that content out as soon as the subscriber confirms his opt-in. You risk losing that subscriber if you don't follow up right away. How would you feel

> *You must begin the process of building the list relationship from the moment a subscriber signs up.*

if you confirmed your opt-in to a list, and then heard absolutely nothing for days or weeks afterward? You'd doubt the list owner's commitment and power to deliver. By the time that list owner actually e-mails you, you might not even remember signing up for his newsletter in the first place. You may not even care anymore, as the initial excitement you felt over his offer has long since waned.

2) FOLLOW UP FREQUENTLY

In order to maintain your subscribers' interest, you need to stay in touch with them on a regular basis. You need to send some type of content out to your list at least once a month. Once a week is even better. Remember that every new subscriber is a person who is new to you. You need to make sure they remember who you are. You also need to train them to expect from you a consistency of content and a consistency of delivery of that content. A regular mailing schedule builds rapport. Your subscribers come to expect news and offers from you on this schedule, and they look forward to it. It's a lot like receiving a magazine or newspaper subscription.

3) KEEP YOUR CONTENT BALANCED

You must make sure that you keep a balance between your regular, free content and your offers, endorsements, and other sales efforts. Too many sales pitches, and your subscribers will feel used. They'll unsubscribe fast, because you aren't offering them anything of value. Too few offers and, of course, you won't make any sales. Have no fear of marketing to your list; you have every right to do so. The key is to establish balance between the free content messages and the sales messages. What's the proper ratio? Well, it depends on the nature of your list. Only you can judge for sure. However, a safe average is about 1:6—one sales-driven offer to every six pure-content mailings. You may need to adjust this higher or lower, depending on your results. There's no harm, either, in mixing the two types of content on occasion. For example, you may send out an informational, educational message that ties in with a particular product you're promoting.

4) WRITE AUTHORITATIVELY

I can't stress the importance of this enough. If you want your subscribers to listen to what you have to say and believe you when you say it, then you must write with a tone of authority. Position yourself as the teacher and expert on your subject matter. The language you use should be present tense, active, and confident.

Don't: "I admit I'm not much of an expert on Google Adsense, but here some tips you might like …"

Do: "As your trusted source for the latest, greatest affiliate marketing tips and tricks, I've got some killer Google Adwords tips to share with you today."

See the difference? The *Don't* example started off with me completely giving away my power. I just admitted to my list that I don't know what the heck I'm talking about, but I ask them to listen to me anyway. Never undermine your own authority in this way! The second example is much more powerful. I buy your trust immediately, simply by telling you that I am privy to the best information. Notice that the language is eager and even a little exaggerated. The tips are "killer." I'm your "trusted source." I've got the goodies for you!

5) **ELIMINATE PASSIVITY**

One problem with the majority of mailing lists is that the subscribers are placed in a passive situation, trained to just sit and read your messages and maybe click on links if you're really persuasive. You need to go a step beyond this and train your subscribers to take action. The simplest way to do this is by making your list more interactive. There are lots of ways to get your subscribers up off their proverbial behinds and engaging with you. One way is by setting up a blog to which you post each of your newsletter messages. You send only the link to the blog out to your list. They must click on it if they want to read your message. Of course, you will want to summarize the topics covered and do so in an interest-leading fashion, like so:

First name,

The latest edition of "Dog Secrets" is now online, and you can read it by clicking on the link below:

http://www.dogblog.com/issues/080106.html

You don't want to miss this latest edition of the newsletter. I'm going over some TOP SECRET dog-training tips:

How do you house train an older dog?

What's this new device on the market that can keep your dog in his yard?

A hidden danger in microchipping: is your dog safe?

If you want the answers to these questions, you'll have to visit the blog. That link again is:

http://www.dogblog.com/issues/080106.html

Notice a few things about that message?

- It's short and to the point.

- It generates interest and curiosity by mentioning the topics to be covered without giving away too much about them.

- It keeps the message short and easy to read.

- It keeps your link visible and primary. There's no real choice other than to click on it!

Now, what are some other methods you can use? You have a lot of tricks at your disposal:

- Set up surveys, games, or Q&As. Have your subscribers participate in the creation of your newsletter.

- Make frequent use of multimedia presentations. Send out video tutorials to your subscribers.

- Consider setting up a blog and message board where subscribers can interact with you and with each other.

- Consider sending long newsletters out in PDF format. Give them the feel of "special reports."

- Always keep your subscriber bait fresh. You need to pamper your subscribers on a regular basis with freebies and specials.

- When possible, hold teleconferences! Get your subscribers on the phone with you (and maybe a couple of related niche experts) for a full-on, value-packed Q&A teleseminar. Make audio recordings of the call available in MP3 format as well as in transcribed e-book format.

- Similarly, you might also consider holding Web chats where you and your subscribers can meet up to discuss the latest niche news.

6) KEEP OFFERS HOT

When you do e-mail offers to your list, make sure the offer you're sending is hot. Hot offers are not junk offers. They are not offers for old, worn-out products, either. Hot offers share these characteristics:

1. They include the newest, most worthy products.

2. They are high-value packages, priced to be incredible deals.

3. They are often time sensitive, meaning the subscriber has a limited window of time to act on the offer before it disappears.

4. They may be offers not available anywhere else; only you are able to offer the product, the special pricing, or the additional bonus packages.

And don't forget, your own ability to write sales copy factors into this as well. You must be able to describe the implicit value and benefits of the offer. You must be able to create a sense of urgency in the subscriber's mind as well. Learn to create truly hot offers as well as compel subscribers to act upon them.

7) CLEAN YOUR LIST

At some point, you'll want to do some list cleaning. As we discussed in the section on building a list, it's important to keep your list clean and up-to-date. This means going through and removing all of the dead or bouncing e-mail addresses from your list. You might also send a mailing out to your least active subscribers asking them to reconfirm their subscription to your mailing list. This isn't so much a global responsiveness-building tactic as it is a tactic for getting your list organized. Once you've pared your list down to only the most responsive subscribers, you'll get a lot more value from your tracking and click-through data.

CHAPTER 8

Easy Traffic

8A

THE TRAFFIC GAME

You're already familiar with the term *traffic* and the importance of targeting the traffic to your site, that is, of getting your product in front of people who are looking for precisely that product. A lot of newbies—and even some seasoned pros—allow themselves to be far too intimidated by the task of generating targeted traffic to their Web sites. This is in part due to some of the hype surrounding the many how-to guides that promise to "solve your traffic problems for good." Think about that statement for a moment. It implies

> *The only real traffic-generating "secrets" are just methods you haven't learned about yet.*

that traffic generation is hard, problematic, and confusing. I want to demystify that idea right now. The only real traffic-generating "secrets" are just methods you haven't learned about yet. Once you understand the basic rules governing how people find Web sites, you will never again be at a loss for traffic-generating ideas.

RULE #1: EVERYTHING IS CONNECTED

The Internet consists of millions of Web servers. While not all of these servers are linked directly to one another, they are inevitably linked within their own "mini nets." What does this mean, exactly? Well, people discover new Web sites in three main ways:

1) By inputting keywords into a search engine like Google, Yahoo!, MSN, etc.

2) By clicking on links in articles or advertisements on well-known Web sites

3) By word of mouth—online (e.g., mentions in forums or chat rooms) or offline (e.g., via business cards, stickers, classifieds, radio/TV spots, etc.)

Almost everyone knows about Google, Yahoo!, MSN, AskJeeves, eBay, AOL, CNN, MSNBC, and so forth. Those are some of the most popular search engines right off the top of my head. Most people have the addresses memorized and know how to get to them without searching for them. Sites like Google and Yahoo! are the first places people go when they want to perform a specific search. Sites like MSN and AOL are often set as "start pages" or "home pages"—meaning they are the first sites a person's Web browser goes to when they get online. So these types of sites represent major hubs of Internet activity—like the airports or bus stations of the Internet. A majority of people start from there but can pursue an unlimited number of destinations because these sites are heavily linked sources of information. You can click on a news article, a search result, an advertisement ... and suddenly you find yourself at a site you may not have seen before. This "new" site will also be linked to other sites, which link to other sites, which link to ... you get the idea. You can start in a familiar place and keep clicking link after link until you arrive at a Web site you've never seen before. This brings us to the next principle.

RULE #2: IT'S ALL ABOUT LINKS

In order for someone to get to your site, they need to hear it, see it, or write it down and then type it into the address bar of their browser; or they could click on an active hyperlink (this can be a text link or graphical link) from another Web site or from within an e-mail. It follows, then, that what you need to do to generate traffic to your site is get your URL on as many other Web sites as possible. You do this in the following ways:

- Advertising (buying text or banner ads on other sites)

- Creating content (e.g., articles, press releases, viral reports, etc.)

- Networking with other site and list owners

- Linking to your site within forums, newsgroups, testimonials, classified ads, product reviews, blog comments, videos, etc.

The possibilities are limitless. The key point is that there are opportunities all around. There's always a way to get more links back to your site. The more links you have out there, the more traffic you're going to get.

RULE #3: EVERY MARKET HAS A HUB AND A MINIHUB

Sites like Google, Yahoo!, MSN, and so on, are considered portals. In other words, they are gateways to a broad range of information targeted at the widest possible audience. Your market will also have portals (hubs) that are more targeted in nature. Let's look at the category of sports, for example. A site like ESPN is a market-specific portal for the sports world.

However, you can often shrink your market's target portals down even further to find sites that have medium to high traffic and are authoritative—but are not quite as large or competitive (meaning it will be easier for you to get your links published in some form).

Let's look at an example in the gardening niche. As a test, I went to Google and just typed in "gardening." Out of the top ten results, I decided to visit a site called "Dave's Garden" (http://www.davesgarden.com). The first thing I noticed was a link to the "Community" section. Two resources stood out right away: the discussion forums and the gardening blogs.

These resources should stand out to you right away as prime opportunities for gaining visibility and posting your Web link in a high-traffic venue

The forum community had over 332,374 members. In the blogs section, some 1,519 members were hosting their blogs on site. These resources should stand out to you right away as prime opportunities for gaining visibility and posting your Web link in a high-traffic venue.

The site was also displaying Google Adsense advertisements. You could get your link pulled in there if you ran site-specific targeting in your Google Adwords campaign. Lastly, the site owner offered exclusive advertising opportunities. You could place a text or banner ad directly on the site where it would be visible to the largest number of visitors.

Determine whether it is possible to get your link in front of people somewhere along these paths!

Whenever you find a site like this, keep clicking through any interesting links you find. More than likely, you're going to end up at another market favorite Web site—which will have links to still more niche-specific sites—and you'll usually find advertising opportunities at each one.

Why bother clicking through? Because you want to follow as many of the same paths that other visitors might take. Note how each site is set up, where it links to, and which portion of the site seems to capture the most attention. Then determine whether it is possible to get your link in front of people somewhere along these paths!

Can you advertise on a site? Can you submit articles that include a link back to your site? Can you place your link in a forum signature? Can you be listed as a partner site in a "Resources" section? Can you post a comment on their blog?

Just find one or two new sites per day that hold potential for giving you more exposure.

Keep digging for these types of opportunities at every single market-specific Web site you can find. You'll be very pleased with the results. The best part is that this is relatively easy to do, and you can take it slow—just find one or two new sites per day that hold potential for giving you more exposure.

TARGETED TRAFFIC

Now, in order to make sales, you need contact with real people who will take action on your offer.

No traffic = no people = no action.

As discussed earlier, this traffic must be *targeted*. The person who visits your site must be searching for the solution you offer. Traffic generation is both an art and a science and is accomplished through a combination of both free and paid advertising methods. The bulk of your paid traffic will come from pay-per-click (PPC) campaigns—more about this and other traffic-generating methods in my next chapter—that you run on search engines like Google (Google Adwords), and any additional banner or text link advertisements you purchase on market-focused Web sites. Free methods of generating traffic are centered primarily on content. This means using methods like:

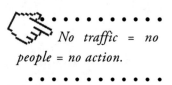
No traffic = no people = no action.

- Writing and submitting articles to article directories

- Writing and submitting press releases

- Writing and distributing free viral reports

- Participating in market-focused groups, forums, bulletin boards, etc.

- Making use of Web 2.0 (e.g., social networking, blogging, using video, etc.)

Traffic generation is not difficult, but it does require that you put in the necessary effort to learn the correct techniques. It's just like a school subject.

If you learn and apply the methods, you *will* get traffic. Before we discuss the specifics of each method, we must look at the relationship between keywords and targeting, because the primary means of targeting visitors is through keywords. It doesn't matter whether your visitor is coming to you from one of the search engines, via a link from an article, or anything else; you must learn how to use keywords in order to attract market-specific traffic to your advertisements and content.

Keyword selection always begins during the initial market research phase. As you research your market and begin zeroing in on a niche, you should keep a running list of relevant keywords and phrases.

First, let's discuss what it means for a set of keywords to be targeted, or properly reflect your offer. Take the key phrase "buy a laptop online" as an example. You can be pretty sure right away what someone is looking for when they type this into a search engine, right? If you are selling laptops from your Web site, then any advertising you do around this key phrase should draw in a highly targeted visitor. However, if you were to advertise or otherwise attract visitors to your site from the key phrase "laptop repair"—and you aren't offering advice or repair tips on your site—then that visitor would be untargeted. In other words, what you're offering is *not* what he's looking for.

So, how do you know which keywords or phrases will drive the kind of traffic you need? The kind of traffic that sees your visitor's desires aligned with your offer? Keyword selection always begins during the initial market research phase. As you research your market and begin zeroing in on a niche, you should keep a running list of relevant keywords and phrases. You'll be able to refer to these later on as well as use them as input in keyword search tools to find even more targeted phrases.

SHORT-TERM VERSUS LONG-TERM TRAFFIC

Another strategy to think about is the type of traffic you'll use based on where you are in your business launch. In terms of timing and effectiveness, there are two types of traffic: short term and long term. Short-term traffic is traffic that you can generate really quickly but that may only bring you visitors for a short period of time. The short-term aspect can be inbuilt into the tactic itself, or it may be by your own choice. We can clarify this with some examples.

Short-term traffic is traffic that you can generate really quickly but that may only bring you visitors for a short period of time.

Let's say you send an e-mail to your subscribers asking them to visit a new Web site you've put up. You'll get a quick, but short, boost in traffic to that site when your subscribers visit it. The traffic is short term there because it is limited to your list. Of course, you can periodically send out messages to your list about the site(s) you want them to visit (and get repeat traffic), but it isn't an ongoing source of totally new visitors. Also, let's say that you run a Google Adwords campaign to promote a new site. The length of time you receive traffic from that method is entirely dependent on how much traffic you're willing to pay for. If you're working with a small budget, then you might just run your ads for a short while.

Long-term traffic methods, on the other hand, usually require some time to pass for your momentum to build; but once it does, you get steady streams of new and repeat traffic without having to invest extra time or money. A good example of this is the use of articles as traffic generators. Good articles will circulate across the Internet for months, sometimes years—and you'll continue to receive traffic from those articles for as long as people come across them in the search engines, via e-zines, article directories, etc.

The most important thing to realize is that traffic comes down to either time or money. In other words, you can generate traffic by paying for it, or you can generate traffic by putting in the necessary work of writing articles, submitting press releases, optimizing your Web site for natural search-engine results, and so forth—taking a content-focused approach. All traffic generation methods fall into three categories of action:

1) Buy the traffic

2) Attract the traffic

3) Steal the traffic

You can **buy traffic** using things like pay-per-click, e-zine advertising, buying advertising space on other high-traffic sites, classified advertising, and so on. **Attracting traffic** is a matter of generating content. Some methods include writing articles, submitting press releases, participating in forums and groups, and using viral reports and videos (Web 2.0). **Stealing traffic** is not what it sounds like. What I mean by *stealing* is actually leveraging the traffic that other site owners have generated. For example, you can post comments on high-traffic blogs to get links back to your site. You can do joint ventures

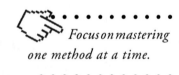

Focus on mastering one method at a time.

with other list owners to grab a share of the action from their subscribers. You can even offer up your own products and reports to other marketers to give away as bonuses on their big product launches. It is all about finding ethical ways to capitalize on other people's resources.

As you study the traffic tactics laid out in the next chapter, there are a couple of things to keep in mind. Most of all, you'll want to focus on mastering one method at a time. Pick just one tactic and get started on it *today.* Pay close attention to your results. Second, pay attention to your conversion rate. In other words, how many people (coming from a certain traffic source) become customers or subscribers? The standard formula for calculating conversion rates is X sales out of one hundred visitors, or X actions taken per one hundred visitors. If you make, for example, five sales out of every hundred visitors to your

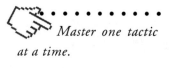
Master one tactic at a time.

site, then you've got a 5 percent conversion rate. Five new subscribers to your list out of every hundred visitors means you've got a 5 percent opt-in rate, and so on. On that note, make sure that your efforts are leveraged toward getting subscribers onto your opt-in list. Subscribers will be your number-one source of repeat sales and traffic.

8B

FOURTEEN TACTICS TO BOOST YOUR TRAFFIC

We'll move on now to specific traffic tactics, starting with the most common and then going on to some advanced strategies. Although this will strike you as a very long chapter—because I've gathered *all* the traffic-generating tactics I can think of in one place—you mustn't feel overwhelmed by the amount of material we're covering. As I mentioned in the last chapter, the trick is to *master one tactic at a time.* Make sure you put it into action right away, monitoring its effectiveness as you go along.

Here are some of the most frequently used and well-known tactics for generating traffic:

- Pay-per-click advertising

- Article marketing

- Advertising in forums or groups via your signature file

- E-zine advertising

- Viral reports

The information in this chapter will be arranged according to which methods bring you traffic most quickly, without regard to cost. We'll also analyze how effective each method is over time. As I mentioned in the previous chapter, some traffic methods are short term, meaning they provide you with a quick surge of visitors that quickly dies down unless you repeat the tactic on a consistent basis. Long-term traffic methods, on the other hand, can continue to bring in a steady stream of visitors to your site for months (sometimes even years) after implementation. There are also some methods that fall into a gray zone, and we'll look at those as special cases.

The quickest way to get traffic to your site is through paid advertising

The quickest way to get traffic to your site is through paid advertising in the following forms:

1) Pay-per-click

2) Banner and text-link ads on market sites

3) Advertising in market-specific e-zines or newsletters

Methods #2 and #3 are speedy but generally take longer than pay-per-click. This is because of competition and publishing schedules. If you advertise in a competitive e-zine, for example, there may be several advertisers ahead of you. Depending on how many advertisements the publisher allows per issue, you may have to wait a couple of weeks before your ad is featured. Pay-per-click, however, is instantaneous. Once you set up your campaign, your ads will appear within minutes. In this case, the competition is between you and the other advertisers running ads on the same keywords. The time it takes for you to see actual clicks on your ads will depend on the quality of your ad and your placement in the sponsored search results—which depends on how much you've bid per click for a given keyword.

TRAFFIC TACTIC #1: PAY-PER-CLICK ADVERTISING

Pay-per-click (PPC) advertising can be both a long-term and a short-term strategy. This is because you can control your campaign at will. It all depends on your budget. If you're profiting from your campaign, you can leave it running indefinitely. If you're on a tight budget, you can run the ads for as long as your budget will allow, then pause your campaign at any time (and, of course, you can turn it back on, too, when you're ready).

Pay-per-click advertising is often referred to as performance-based advertising. In other words, you pay for results and not for exposure. To put this in context, think of traditional newspaper classified ads where you are usually charged per word to run your ad. Similarly, you may have come across some Web sites that will let you run a banner advertisement for a specified amount of time when you pay upfront. The problem with that form of advertising is that you've no guarantee of results. You could spend hundreds on pay-upfront advertisements and end up going broke if your ad performs poorly—no one responds, no one clicks on your link, etc.

The PPC model of advertising, however, gives advertisers like you the advantage by letting you control costs. Instead of being charged for publication or ad exposure, your ads are run for free. You don't actually pay anything until someone clicks on the link to your Web site—hence the term "pay-per-click."

PPC ads are delivered by pay-per-click search engines like the following:

- GOOGLE—THE GOOGLE ADWORDS PROGRAM
  (HTTP://ADWORDS.GOOGLE.COM/)
  Google Adwords is the current leader in the pay-per-click industry. It has the highest volume and traffic quality. However, it's also the most competitive and the most expensive.

- YAHOO!—THE YAHOO! SEARCH MARKETING PROGRAM
  (HTTP://SEARCHMARKETING.YAHOO.COM/)
  This program includes all of the engines formerly participating in the Overture program. There is high volume and traffic quality, but careful research is still required to find the cheapest clicks.

- MIVA
  (HTTP://WWW.MIVA.COM/US/CONTENT/ADVERTISER/PAY_PER_CLICK.ASP)
  An excellent program that is currently underutilized. Your competition will be lower.

- MSN—THE MSN ADCENTER
  (HTTP://ADCENTER.MICROSOFT.COM/)

This program is Microsoft's attempt to muscle away some market share from Google and Yahoo!. Still relatively new, so there are lots of opportunities for cheap traffic.

These are the four major players that affiliates focus on in the beginning. However, there are also a handful of smaller PPC engines (with slightly lower volume) that offer high-quality traffic and super cheap clicks:

- Enhance (http://www.enhance.com/)

- GoClick (http://www.goclick.com/)

- 7Search (http://www.7search.com/)

You should use a mix of PPC engines in your traffic campaign, especially if you want to get the most traffic possible for your budget. Don't rely only on one PPC engine. Also, make sure you use both the large and small networks. The best thing to do if you're new to all this is choose just one of the major players, like Google, and one of the smaller players, like 7Search. See what kind of results you get, and then decide if you want to run your campaign on additional engines or drop one from your campaign to save money.

> *You should use a mix of PPC engines in your traffic campaign, especially if you want to get the most traffic possible for your budget. Don't rely only on one PPC engine.*

PPC advertising uses short, classifieds-style advertisements, which appear next to regular search-engine results. You'll usually see a heading that says "Sponsored Results" above pay-per-click ad listings. Here's an example from Google:

Those were just a portion of the sponsored ads that came up when I typed in the search phrase "affiliate marketing." There are several things to make note of here. First, realize that these ads were triggered by the search phrase "affiliate marketing." This means that the advertisers behind these ads chose specifically to target people searching for "affiliate marketing." How? By bidding for that phrase. Remember, this is pay-per-click, so the bid represents the amount the advertiser is willing to pay each time someone clicks on the ad link to his Web site.

If you're totally new to PPC advertising, this can be a bit confusing at first, so let me give you another example. Let's say you are an affiliate promoting e-books related to cooking (how-to tips, recipes, etc.), and you want to drive traffic to your opt-in page. Obviously, you want to target people who are looking for information about cooking, recipes, and so on.

During your market research, you should have generated a large list of terms that your market is keying into search engines. These terms will be your targets for pay-per-click advertising.

For example, let's say a portion of your keywords list looks like this:

curry recipes

chicken curry

Indian recipes

Indian cookbook

South Indian vegetarian recipe

how to make samosas

Now, if one of your affiliate products is an e-book of Indian cuisine recipes, then the above key phrases are ideally targeted to your offer, and you would want to run pay-per-click advertisements for each targeted key phrase. In other words, you would have an ad that runs on the phrase "curry recipes," one that runs on "chicken curry," one for "Indian recipes," and so on. Each key phrase (most of the time) should get its own advertisement, like so:

Curry Recipes
Delicious red, green, and yellow curry recipes. Complete Indian cookbook. $47.

http://www.your-site.com/

Indian Cookbook
Includes all the most popular dishes. Download free sample recipes today.

http://www.your-site.com/

etc.

So, in the example above, the first ad would go with the key phrase "curry recipes," and the second ad would go with the key phrase "Indian cookbook."

Note that you do not always need to write separate ads when bidding on groups of similar keywords. For example, you could use the "curry recipes" ad alone for several key phrases, including "how to make curry," "recipes for curry sauce," etc.

Now, when you are ready to run your ads, you must specify a maximum bid amount for each keyword or key phrase.

Now, when you are ready to run your ads, you must specify a maximum bid amount for each keyword or key phrase. Note this is different from the minimum bid, which is the minimum amount you must bid in order for your ads to run at all. Minimum bid amounts are affected by how much competing advertisers are bidding on the same key words. Your maximum bid is the most *you* are willing to pay per click on your link. This amount is not necessarily the amount you will have to pay, but it affects your advertisement's placement or "rank" within the listings.

For example, let's say that you're using Google Adwords and find that the current minimum bid amounts for your key phrases are as follows:

"curry recipes"—10 cents per click

"chicken curry"—5 cents per click

"Indian recipes"—5 cents per click

"Indian cookbook"—11 cents per click

"South Indian vegetarian recipe"—5 cents per click

"how to make samosas"—3 cents per click

So, in order to run your ad on the key phrase "chicken curry," you must bid at least 5 cents per click. This gets you in the game. However, it may not get you as high a placement among the competition as you want. Let's say you want the number-one position in the sponsored listings. As a new advertiser, you will have to bid at least 6 cents per click. If this is what you know you can afford, then 6 cents per click becomes your maximum bid.

If you have the budget for it, however, you could also try to lock out some of your competition by setting your maximum bid much higher. For example, you could bid 10 cents per click. The key here is keeping all of this within your budget. Most PPC sites allow you to set a maximum daily spending limit, which serves as a cutoff point for how much money you spend each day on clicks.

For example, with Google Adwords, you could specify a daily budget of $10. Google will keep serving your ads until you've received enough clicks (on any ad) to total $10. Once you hit your maximum, your ads will stop running until the next business day.

When **writing PPC ads**, the following tips should come in handy:

- Your headline is the most important part of the ad. Make sure it captures attention. The general wisdom on this is that you should try to incorporate all or a part of the search terms into your headline.

- Test out different conversion factors that might affect your click-through rate and the quality of the leads arriving at your site. For example, you can mention the price of your lead product. Likewise, you can mention free reports or other bonuses you are offering for download.

- Realize that you have only so much space. Typical PPC ads allow you about twenty-five characters (including spaces and punctuation) for your headline and thirty-five characters per line for your subheadlines.

- Emphasize the information/offer on your opt-in page rather than trying to advertise the lead product explicitly.

TRAFFIC TACTIC #2: BANNER/ TEXT-LINK ADVERTISING

Banner/text-link advertising can be done on a short-term basis or on a continual basis if you have the budget for it. This form of advertising can also bring you very good, highly targeted sources of traffic *if* the sites where you advertise do a good job of attracting targeted traffic from the market. There are two ways to find banner and text-link advertising opportunities:

1) On targeted, market-specific Web sites where the site owner has implemented these advertising opportunities on site (meaning you'd usually negotiate ad space and rates with the site owner).

2) By targeting sites that participate in ad networks. In this case, the ad network manages the relationship between advertisers and participating sites in the network.

Let's go over some examples of each type of opportunity, beginning with the first case of negotiating directly with the site owner. Remember the example site we came across earlier, called Dave's Garden? This site offers us an example of in-house advertising. In other words, the site owners or operators run their own advertising program, rather than allowing it to be managed through an ad network. If you visit the advertising link at Dave's

Garden (http://davesgarden.com/aboutus/advertise/), you'll see they've set up a contact form. The phone number and e-mail address for the director of sales are also given. This is a good example of what you'll come across when looking for site-specific advertising opportunities. Sometimes the "advertise with us" page will contain information on the types of ads available, along with their rates. In other cases, you will need to e-mail or call someone to negotiate rates, ad types, and scheduling. Much of this depends on the site owner's needs and preferences. He may have strict quality guidelines in place in terms of the types of advertisements placed on site.

There may be other issues to work out as well, including the following:

- When your ad can be run

- Whether you want front-page placement or context-specific placement (e.g., running your ad on a page containing a relevant article)

- Size and type of ad (Some sites will accept both banner and text-link ads, while others may prefer to run only one type due to how their site is designed, i.e., making the best use of space.)

It is much more common these days to run banner and text ads through what is known as an *advertising network.* Ad networks are much like affiliate networks. Many Web sites prefer to have a third party run their affiliate program rather than doing it themselves. So, they sign up with companies like Commission Junction or Linkshare or Clickbank. Why? It just makes life easier, especially for large sites that offer a lot of products and foresee themselves having many affiliates to manage. The same is true for sites that want to implement advertising across the board. It's a lot of work to negotiate rates and placement with individual advertisers. It also takes a lot of time to go through and publish each advertisement. Third-party advertising networks allow site owners to have a steady stream of different advertisers running ads on their sites, without having to deal directly with those advertisers. All the site owner needs to do is join the network, specify the requirements, and then paste some code into her Web pages that will pull in (and rotate) advertisements on autopilot. It's a win-win situation for the publisher and the ad network, as both share in the revenue paid in by advertisers. It also benefits advertisers like you, because you can find targeted opportunities in one central location, effectively eliminating the need to search for opportunities site by site.

The following is a list of some of the most popular advertising networks, with a brief description of the opportunities each one provides:

- **@dVenture**

  Large range of options, and you can target by site, category of interest, or targeted demographics across all sites in the network.

- **Aaddzz**

  A performance-based network for pay-per-click advertising. Automatic site targeting.

- **AdAce**

  Targeted advertising services. Focus on smaller online businesses.

- **Ad-Net**

  Participating publishers have a choice between centrally served ads (delivered by Ad-Net) or site-hosted ads (the Web-site owner chooses which advertisers from the network he wants to work with, then publishes those ads himself).

- **ADSMART.NET**

  Boasts a large inventory of sites that attract highly
  targeted audiences.

- **BURST! MEDIA**

  Focused on providing ads for special-interest and niche-focused
  Web sites. Claims over three thousand publisher members.

- **DOUBLECLICK**

  Serves some of the most heavily trafficked sites on the Web. A good
  option to test once you've got some experience under your belt. Not
  recommended for newbies, though.

- **GOOGLE ADSENSE**

  Advertise with banners, text links, and even video! Many options
  for site-specific targeting.

- **VALUECLICK**

  Guarantees to buy 100 percent of advertising space on host sites.
  Performance-based pricing for advertisers.

- **WEBCONNECT**

  Ad placement service. Delivers highly targeted advertising coverage
  in a variety of market areas on the World Wide Web.

As a newbie, your best bet may be to start out with Google's Adwords program. This is because Google now offers advertisers a range of options beyond standard pay-per-click. You can target specific sites within Google's content and Adsense networks, using a variety of ad formats including banners, video, and text. Your advertising costs will follow a model similar to pay-per-click. On some networks you may be charged for the actual click on your banner or link. In other cases, you may be charged on a cost-per-impression basis. In other words, you bid a specified amount of money (say, $X) per number (say, 1,000) of displays (impressions) of your ad, regardless of whether visitors actually click on it.

As a newbie, your best bet may be to start out with Google's Adwords program. This is because Google now offers advertisers a range of options beyond standard pay-per-click.

For *text-link only advertisements,* you can follow the traditional pay-per-click model when writing your ads. Just a short classifieds-style ad will usually suffice. With *banner ads,* there are more options. There are two types of Web banners: static and animated. I'm sure you've seen these in action before. A static Web banner contains an image and text that remain unchanged while displayed on a site. There are no special effects; what you see is what you get. An animated banner, however, can utilize special effects. It can display different images and different snippets of text as the animation cycles through. If you aren't familiar with this style of animation, I recommend trying out this free resource: http://www.animationonline. com/. You can create your own banners and see them in action!

For the most part, banner sizes have been standardized by the Web advertising industry. You'll encounter about nine sizes as you explore your options through the ad networks:

1) Full banner—486 x 60 pixels

2) Full banner with navigation bar—392 x 72 pixels

3) Half banner—234 x 60 pixels

4) Square button—125 x 125 pixels

5) Large button—120 x 90 pixels

6) Small button—120 x 60 pixels

7) Micro button—88 x 31 pixels

8) Vertical banner—120 x 240 pixels

9) Vertical tower or "skyscraper"—160 x 600 pixels

If you don't have graphic- design skills, you'll need to get your banners created by someone who does. Again, sites like http://www.elance.com and http://www.rentacoder.com will have plenty of freelance graphic artists you can hire to create great-looking banners for you. When you send your requirements to your designer, make sure your ads follow all the principles about branding that we've discussed and that they shoot for attention-grabbing images and text.

TRAFFIC TACTIC #3: E-ZINE ADVERTISING

You can advertise in e-zines as often as you like, but I call it a short-term traffic tactic because what usually happens is you get a quick rush of visitors when your advertisement first appears. It's not usually a technique for generating a continual flow of traffic. Some will say that e-zine advertising isn't what it used to be. This is only partially true. You see, back when e-zine advertising was all the rage, nearly everyone offered advertising opportunities in their newsletters. This was great in terms of finding ad opportunities for any niche—but it also made it hard to determine which e-zines had a truly responsive subscriber base. In other words, a lot of people started up lists just for the sake of being able to sell advertising.

Today, you can still find quality e-zines to advertise in. The only question is whether you can find some within your particular market. It's pretty easy if you're promoting business opportunities or products relating to Internet marketing, but you may have to do a little digging to find good opportunities within your niche. The easiest way to start looking is still via regular Web search, typing in your niche keyword plus "e-zine" or plus "newsletter." For example, you would go to http://www.google.com and type in something like "guitar e-zine" or "guitar newsletter" if you were looking for guitar-focused e-zines.

E-zines and newsletters that actively solicit advertising will almost always have a link on the site that says "Advertise." If you don't see such a link, go ahead and sign up for the newsletter. Get a feel for the author's focus, content, and attitude. Then, send a personal e-mail to inquire about his interest in getting paid to send out one of your solo ads or make space for a small classified ad within his newsletter. If you aren't having any luck finding good newsletters this way, there are a couple of other resources you can use:

- **http://www.ezineadvertising.com**

    A comprehensive search engine and directory for e-zine advertisers. Requires subscription.

- **http://www.onlineforsuccess.com/ezine-marketing-directory.htm**

    Freedom to browse and search. Provides data on list size, frequency of mailings, and cost.

- **http://www.ezine-dir.com**

    Free resource. Browse by category. Quality score assigned by subscriber reviews. Unfortunately, this site does not list whether advertising opportunities are available for each e-zine, so you'll have to visit the sites yourself.

- **http://www.ezinelisting.com**
  Similar to http://www.ezine-dir.com, but you can never have too much variety!

- **http://www.oclc.org/firstsearch/periodicals/index_title.asp**
  This is the search database for serial periodicals that have chosen to obtain ISSN numbers through the Library of Congress. Note: use the LOC ISSN as a last resort or advanced tactic. You won't find very many mom-and-pop- style e-zines there (though there are a few). However, you will definitely find very high-quality publications that do offer advertising opportunities. The only barrier will be cost, as many of these publications run in both print and Web versions. For example, one newsletter I found called *The Guitar Review* sells ad space the way a traditional magazine would—with inside-back-page ads, quarter-page ads, etc., and prices ranging from $148 to $825.

Typical formats for e-zine and newsletter ads include the following:

- **SOLO ADS**
  A solo ad is sent separately from the regular e-zine or newsletter. You can think of this type of advertisement as similar to sending a promotional e-mail to your own list. The benefit to running a solo ad is that you have more space (words) to describe your offer, and you have no competing advertising or content. As you might imagine, though, solo ads are often the most expensive type of e-zine advertisement. Competition for solo-ad placement is generally fierce.

- MINI-ADS WITHIN THE E-ZINE

  The remaining formats differ only in terms of their placement depending on how many advertisements the publisher is willing to run per issue. Publishers who run, say, three advertisements per issue will break pricing down by ad placement. For example, you'll find different prices based on whether you want your ad to run near the top of the newsletter, the middle, or the bottom.

When **writing e-zine ads**, first check whether the publisher has certain requirements or guidelines you must follow. However, the formats for both types of ads (solo and mini) are basically standardized. Mini-ads are similar to pay-per-click ads in terms of space. You'd write something like a little classified advertisement, usually in no more than one hundred words:

Tired of feeling "tired" in the morning? Discover how you can wake up refreshed each day, even on 6 hours of sleep. Guaranteed!

http://www.yourlink.com/

Solo ads will allow you more space, but there will usually be a limit on length, for example, no more than five hundred words or so. When creating this type of ad, you need to keep in mind the reputation and trust that your publisher has built with his subscribers. Also, understand that you are a relative stranger to these subscribers. You need to help them make a connection, so to speak, by aligning yourself with what's already familiar to them. Let me provide with you a sample solo ad to illustrate how this can be done:

Dear First Name,

As a subscriber to [name of e-zine or newsletter you are advertising in], I know you expect to receive only the most high-quality, cutting-edge information about [niche topic].

That's why I'm writing to you today.

My name is [your name], and I have some very important and exciting information to share with you today about how you can [solve/create/learn/succeed, etc. something related to the niche topic or problem].

And so on.

I'm keeping the example short here because it's impossible to create a template that's suitable for every niche. However, did you notice the most important points? Right from the very beginning of the advertisement, I did the following:

- Established/reinforced familiarity by referencing the name of the e-zine/newsletter

- Introduced myself

- Quickly transitioned to the point of my e-mail

These factors are key with solo advertising. You must establish trust and familiarity as quickly as possible, while simultaneously capturing the reader's interest in what you have to say.

To **get the most out of e-zine ad traffic**, note the following tips:

- Keep your objective in mind. As a super affiliate, you always want to build your list. So, your ads should drive people to your opt-in page.

- Consult first with the publisher if possible. She will know best what works with her list, and this will help you tailor the tone of your advertisement in the way that speaks best to her subscribers.

- Use an effective headline. Remember, a solo ad will go out as an actual e-mail to the list. Your e-mail subject line should be attention grabbing and designed to get people to open and read the e-mail.

- Make sure you keep track of every advertisement you've placed for every e-zine you advertise in, and monitor your click-through rates. Note: you can create special tracking links for just this purpose in your Monster Response account.

- Start small. You can microtest response rates by buying cheaper ads in a few select e-zines at first. Make sure you've optimized your ads before expanding your campaign or paying for more expensive placements.

- Keep an eye on branding. Use your name and reference your Web-site name or domain name wherever possible.

- Repetition—it's OK to run the exact same ad multiple times in one e-zine. Remember that people often need several exposures to your message before they'll take action.

- Use tested and proven copy. Although you will refine your e-zine ads as necessary, it's often useful to start with copy that has already been proven to convert. For example, you can use expanded versions of your most effective pay-per-click advertisements as a basis for writing your e-zine ads.

TRAFFIC TACTIC #4: ARTICLE MARKETING

Article marketing and the methods that follow are "slower" in that you generally don't get a rush of traffic to your site within minutes or hours of publishing the article. However, these methods are often very effective for building long-term and continuous streams of targeted traffic. Article marketing is by far one of the best ways to drive targeted traffic to your site for the long term. Why? Once your article is published, it will remain online indefinitely. Since you'll also be able to link to your site within the "author's byline" section of your article, this means that the link to your site is also sitting out there indefinitely, just waiting for a new reader to click on it.

> *Article marketing is by far one of the best ways to drive targeted traffic to your site for the long term.*

The focus of article marketing is on driving traffic to your site by providing high-quality, useful information. It is also a prime method for increasing brand and name recognition (exposure), reputation, and authority, or "expert status," within your market. The fact is that people tend to respect and listen to individuals who are published authors. The written word is a highly respected form of communication, and whether it's really true or not, people will view you as an authoritative source of information when they keep coming across the articles you've authored.

What types of information should you provide, and what should you write about? Mainly, you want go for hot topics. You can discover these using the same steps you used for market research or by looking into which keywords and key phrases people are entering into the search engines.

Articles work on several levels. They're keyword rich, they're informative, and they build credibility or "expert status" for you within your niche.

You might wonder about those last two elements. How is it that the "worthiness" of information would drive traffic? How does credibility bring in more visitors? The reason is simple. It isn't just the online presence of the article that brings you clicks. It's what's *in*

If you plan on using articles to generate long-term traffic, you need to write excellent articles.

the article that compels people to visit your Web site! You see, your article could be very well optimized in terms of key phrases and search-engine placement, but that doesn't mean that it's a great article. Your article could be, well, boring! It could be sloppy or too "sales pitchy" or any number of things that turn people off.

The point I want to make here is that if you plan on using articles to generate long-term traffic, you need to write excellent articles. Your goals should be quality and honesty at all times. Never post an article on your site or to an article directory if you know it's all fluff and filler. I'm not implying that you have to be the greatest writer on earth or write at a PhD level. Not at all. However, you do need to keep the needs of your audience in mind at all times. Whenever you're writing an article (or when you hire someone else to write one for you), ask the following questions:

- If I were to read this for the first time, would I learn something new?

- If I were to read this for the first time, would I enjoy the author's style of conveying information?

- If I were to read this for the first time, would I trust what the author is telling me? Would I want to read more about what he has to say on this topic?

Article directories are brimming with more content than you could ever possibly post to your own Web site.

If you can't answer yes to all three of those questions, then your article is not yet ready to publish.

Why is this so important, and how do articles drive traffic to your site for the long term? First, properly optimized articles grab search-engine placement in two ways. The articles you post to your Web site may show up in the search-engine listings. The articles you post to other people's Web sites (to article or reprint directories) may also show up in search-engine listings! Sometimes, you might not be able to get your site to rank on a particular key phrase no matter how hard you try. But you just might be able to get a good ranking on that key phrase if the article is posted to one or more article directories. Why? Because article directories, by their very nature, have more of what the search engines are looking for. They have content, they have inbound and outbound links, they have keyword-rich links, and (in Google) they have page rank. Article directories are brimming with more content than you could ever possibly post to your own Web site. They've got the stuff search engines look for, and more of it.

When your article is good enough to be republished, this can mean a massive boost in traffic for you. Your article will circulate across more sites and in front of more readers than you could reach on your own.

This is good news for you, because it gives you a fighting chance.

Second, when you publish your articles, you'll do so under what is called a *reprint rights license*. A reprint rights license is a disclaimer from you that grants other Web publishers and e-zine publishers the rights to reprint and distribute your article on their sites and in their e-zines. When your article is good enough to be republished, this can mean a massive boost in traffic for you. Your article will circulate across more sites and in front of more readers than you could reach on your own.

Now, at some article directories, you grant the reprint rights implicitly upon submission. At certain other venues (on your own site for example), you'll have to include your disclaimer alongside your author's byline. The author's byline is where your link to traffic comes into play. At the end of your article, you'll place a little advertisement for yourself. It might look something like this:

> Joe Smith is an expert affiliate marketer who rakes in over $100,000 annually via his amazingly simple online profit system. Learn how you, too, can break free from the 9-to-5 rut by doing what Joe does. Just visit: http://www.bigmoneyaffiliate.com/

How about another trick? Maybe you're after more e-zine subscribers rather than direct traffic to your Web site? Then, you'd do this with your byline:

> Jane Doe is an expert affiliate marketer who rakes in over $100, 000 annually via her amazingly simple online profit system. She'll teach you how to do it, too, when you sign up for her "Six Figures in Six Months" e-course via this link: subscribe@www.bigmoneyaffiliate.com.

Finally, here's one last example of how to do the author byline while including a reprint rights disclaimer:

> David Jones has been training show dogs professionally for over 20 years. Have a dog-training question? Ask David at http://www.dogtrainer.com. The author grants full reprint

rights to this article. You may reprint and electronically distribute this article so long as its contents remain unchanged and the author's byline remains in place.

That link in your byline is a pure gold traffic-generating machine.

Want to know how to **generate article topics** easily? Go through your list of keywords and pick out at least ten popular "long-tail" key phrases—phrases that include three or more words. For example, the phrase "natural allergy cure" is a decent long-tail phrase, but see if you can find phrases that are even more specific, like "natural mold allergy cure." More on why in a moment.

What you want to do is write an article centered on that long-tail key phrase. You should shoot for an article that is at least 300–500 words in length. You'll also want to work your key phrase into the article enough times so that you've got a density of around 3–5 percent (in other words, the phrase "natural allergy cure" would make up 3–5 percent of the total word count of the article). Try to do this as naturally as possible, though. You want your article to read smoothly, and avoid anything that looks like keyword stuffing.

To illustrate, here is a sample article I've created around the "natural allergy cure" key phrase:

NATURAL ALLERGY CURES: EASY TIPS FOR INSTANT RELIEF

For some of us, it doesn't matter what time of year it is. Mold, hay fever, grass, weeds, trees, smoke, and pet dander assault our immune system. Sometimes it seems as if we're allergic to daily life itself!

Many people turn to their allergy medications, nasal sprays, allergy shots, or other forms of medical treatment yet still can't find the level of relief they really need.

So, we begin to look elsewhere. Maybe there really are all-natural allergy cures available to us that we can put to use right away and that don't have to cost an arm and a leg.

The good news is that natural, effective allergy treatments are available—pardon the pun—right under your nose! You see, it's not just about nutritional support or herbal "cures." The fact is that true allergy relief begins at home, in our environment. What hidden triggers might be lurking right now in the very room you're sitting in?

To find out, run through this checklist of the most common household allergy culprits:

- AIR-CONDITIONING FILTER
  How long has it been since you changed your air-con filter? If you answered, "More than a month," you need to take action! Replace that old, dirty filter with a new one. Go for a higher-quality filter if you can afford it. It's well worth the money. Make sure you change your filter each month from now on.

- DUST MITES
  Dust mites love to live in your bedding. Washing your sheets isn't enough, even if you wash them in hot water or use generous amounts of bleach. Consider

getting dust covers for your mattress as well as each of your pillows.

- OLD CARPETS

  Are your carpets in need of a good steam-cleaning? Are they old enough that they should be replaced? Understand that allergens in the air eventually fall and settle onto and into everything, including carpets.

- POORLY SEALED DOORS AND WINDOWS

  Check the caulking and sealing around your doors and windows. Even small gaps can let in allergen-filled air from the outside.

- TAKE A DOSE OF LOCAL HONEY

  Did you know: all of the pollens carried by the bees in your area go into the honey they make? When you eat locally produced honey, you can give your immune system a natural allergy shot that helps you build more and more tolerance to those allergens over time.

Last, but not least, remember that the above is not to be construed as professional medical advice. Always check with your doctor if your allergy symptoms worsen. Meanwhile, take action on these five tips for natural allergy cures. The sooner you do, the better you'll feel!

Note these tips from my sample article and use them in yours:
- Try to work the key phrase into the article title, if possible.

- Try to work the key phrase in again within the first one or two paragraphs as naturally as possible.

- Boost the density of the overall key phrase theme by rearranging the order of words or using synonyms (e.g., "to cure your allergies naturally," "all-nature allergy cure," "natural ways of curing allergy symptoms," etc.).

- Offer real content, real information, and real tips. Your article must provide something of value to the reader if you're to inspire him to learn more from you.

Your byline will give the reader a little bit of background information on you and direct her to your opt-in page for more information.

Each article you write should have a byline. Your byline will give the reader a little bit of background information on you and direct her to your opt-in page for more information. Let's say that I promote allergy-cure products as an affiliate and have distributed an article like the one above. The byline I would create to go along with it would look something like this:

> Ewen Chia is committed to finding natural allergy cures that work for all allergy sufferers. You can learn more about his research as well as receive a free report packed with the latest in allergy relief methods by visiting http://www.link-to-opt-in-page.com.

The key to generating traffic through your articles is to make sure that your articles are published and distributed in as many venues as possible. This is easily accomplished by submitting your articles to article directories.

When you do this, you basically grant reprint rights to anyone and everyone who wants to republish your article. The article directories are prime sources for Web-site and newsletter owners looking for high-quality content they can republish without paying a licensing fee.

Don't worry about giving away reprint rights. You still retain ownership of your article, and those who republish it are required to keep your author's byline in place.

Also, more and more automated sites (blogs, for example) make use of article directories to populate their syndication feeds with fresh content. So, if you write a quality article, you stand to see it reprinted virtually all across the Web on other targeted sites. Don't worry about giving away reprint rights. You still retain ownership of your article, and those who republish it are required to keep your author's byline in place. They are also required to keep your article as is and not edit it, rewrite it, or make any other content-based modifications.

You should shoot for writing at least ten articles based around long-tail key phrases when you launch your site. You'll want to submit these right away, and then follow up with ten more fresh articles in about two weeks to a month.

The following is a list of some of the best **article directories** to use for submitting your articles:

- http://www.articlecity.com

- http://www.ezinearticles.com

- http://www.goarticles.com

- http://www.submityourarticle.com

- http://www.articlesbase.com

- http://www.articledashboard.com

And there are literally hundreds more. Do a search using the phrases "submit article," "article directory," "free articles," etc. To save yourself some time, consider investing in a tool such as Article Submitter Pro (http://www.articlesubmitterpro.com). This tool allows you to submit multiple articles to multiple directories at once.

TRAFFIC TACTIC #5: MARKET FORUMS/GROUPS

I've placed forums and groups in the gray zone because it can be difficult to predict their ability to generate speedy or long-term traffic when so many variables are in play:

- How much traffic the forum/group receives

- How quickly the discussion or threads cycle through the group

- How well the group's discussion posts are indexed by the search engines

- Whether reading of posts is open to general public or requires visitors to first register an account

Overall, you can expect a nice stream of traffic from within a forum or group, particularly forums and groups where participation is high and members are passionate about their subject of interest. Plus, you may scoop up some natural search-engine traffic if the forum or group discussions are indexed by the search engines.

The method here is very simple:

1) Find forums or groups pertaining to your market or niche.

2) Make sure these forums or groups receive a good amount of traffic and that members participate on a regular basis—in other words, lots of active discussions and new topics. Avoid any forum or group where no one has posted in months.

3) Register an account for yourself and start reading through some of the threads to get a feel for the community.

4) Introduce yourself and start participating in discussions.

5) Once you've integrated into the community, place a short advertisement with a link to your opt-in page in your signature file.

In order to find forums or groups dedicated to your target market, run a search in your favorite search engine using some of your target keywords coupled with the word "forum." For example, you can go to Google and search "sewing + forum" to find sewing-related forums or bulletin boards. Another trick you can use is to search using your market's main keyword coupled with the phrase "powered by [name of the bulletin-board software]." For example, one popular bulletin-board platform is Snitz. Others include phpbb and vbulletin. So, let's say you were looking for forums related to the topic of cameras or photography. You would type in "cameras + powered by Snitz." Try that out in Google. You'll see several very niche-focused camera forums pop up in the search results.

The idea is to build rapport, trust, and credibility as a member of the forum community, much in the way you build a relationship with your opt-in list. There is no need to post about your business or be pushy in any way. As long as you are a helpful member of the community, people will be naturally curious about you and drawn to the information in your signature file.

For example, let's say you are in the pet-training market, and in one of the forums you participate in, someone has asked a question about how to get his cat to use a new brand of cat litter. Being the "expert," you provide a helpful answer:

Cats love routine. They don't take kindly to sudden changes—and they're particularly disturbed by sudden changes to their litter-box routine. When you need to introduce them to new litter, the best thing to do is go slowly. Start by mixing ¾ of the old litter with ¼ of the new. After a few days, clean the box again and refill it with ½ the old litter and ½ the new litter. Leave this for about five to six days. Clean the box out again. This time mix ¾ new litter with ¼ old. That should do it. By the next time you clean and change out the box, you should be able to fill it with 100 percent of the new litter. Hope this helps!

-Your Name

Now, when you are using a signature file, what happens is that your posted reply will have an extra space below it, where your ad can appear:

If you're mystified by your furry friends, don't despair! You *can* learn how to "speak their language." I can help! Get your free copy of my special report, "How to Talk to Cats," just for visiting http://www.link-to-your-optin-page.com.

Anyone reading your post can see this signature. If they're interested, they'll click through to your site and, ideally, opt in to your list. This type of traffic is usually good quality because the visitors are pretargeted due to context.

TRAFFIC TACTIC #6: PRESS RELEASES

Press releases also fall into a bit of a gray zone. Well-written, relevant, and timely press releases can bring you a big surge of traffic when the press release first goes out. This is a short-term boost. However, a well-written and keyword-rich press release can often rank very high in search-engine results. In this sense, it acts more like an article and can bring you a steady stream of long-term traffic.

Your ability to use press releases as an immediate traffic generator relies upon the fact that they are syndicated. In other words, press releases are automatically distributed across a very large network of Web sites that subscribe to the press-release publishers' news feeds. The number of sites that may pick up your press release is considerable. We're talking in the hundreds, if not thousands.

Also, the quality of sites becomes a factor. A well-written press release may appear on major sites like Yahoo!, Google News, CNN.com, and more. Best of all, submitting press releases is, for the most part, free. Now, getting really broad exposure usually involves a fee. PR Web, for example, will charge you if you want your press release distributed to the really big-name sites. The upside is that your fee usually includes some editorial help with getting your press release up to the standards for publication on those big sites.

The first rule for creating solid press releases is that they must be newsworthy. A press release is not a product announcement or advertisement.

The thing to keep in mind that will help you stick to the guidelines is to ask yourself, "How can I tie my offer into a current hot or new topic or issue?" So, how do you make a product or offer newsworthy and make the press release work effectively as a marketing tool at the same time? You do it by turning the main product benefit into a news headline. It's the "solution" that is newsworthy.

The first rule for creating solid press releases is that they must be newsworthy. A press release is not a product announcement or advertisement.

For example, your headline might be, "A Simple Solution for Back Pain?" if you've found a product that offers a unique, easy solution to that problem. The second rule of press releases is that they must follow a stylized format. This format is based on journalistic guidelines employed by most news agencies. These guidelines are as follows:

- Press releases must have a headline.

- Press releases usually have subheadlines.

- Press releases contain the origin or source of the news (for example, the location).

- This is followed by the body of the press release.

- Additional and contact information may be placed at the end of the release.

Putting it all together with an example, here's a sample press release for a fictional product:

EASING LOW BACK PAIN: IT MAY BE SIMPLER
THAN YOU THINK

SUFFERERS FINDING RELIEF IN SURPRISING WAYS

PHILADELPHIA, PA—Low back pain—studies suggest at least one in five of us will suffer from an episode of it during our lifetime. For many, though, low back pain can be a chronic, debilitating condition. While many back-pain sufferers shell out money at the chiropractor, other sufferers are finding relief in surprising ways.

John Doe, author of *The Low Back Pain Cure*, has developed a series of simple, at-home treatments that have provided real relief to dozens of consumers thus far.

"John's low-back-pain cure is the first I've seen that addresses both the nutritional and psychological origins of pain ... which is something most treatments miss," says Jane Smith, a long-time back- pain sufferer.

[Note: you can pull these types of quotations from testimonials or from the benefits list you generated during your research.]

Unlike other treatments, John Doe's low-back-pain cure is not dependent on the usual back-strengthening exercises, which can take weeks to provide relief. Instead, he says, clients usually find significant relief from pain in a "matter of days."

Will the cure work for everyone?

"It will work for most types of pain," says Doe, "except in cases of very serious diseases of the spine. You should always consult your family physician first."

For more information on *The Low Back Pain Cure*, visit http://www.yourwebsite.com/your-optin-page

TRAFFIC TACTIC #7:
CLASSIFIEDS ADVERTISING CAMPAIGNS

Classifieds advertising online is similar to advertising in print newspapers, with the exception that online ads are usually much cheaper (sometimes free) and give you a little more space.

Your first step is to come up with about four to five variations of classified ads to place on different sites. As always, the headline of your ad is the most important, as it will be the link people click on to view your ad. You'll need to create a powerful, interest-grabbing headline. The body of your ad will be relatively short. The amount of space you're allocated for an ad varies from one classifieds site to another.

Here's a sample classified ad to give you an idea of what I'm talking about:

ELIMINATE CREDIT-CARD DEBT
IN 365 DAYS OR LESS?!

Are you struggling each month to pay all of your bills and just make ends meet? Credit-card debt is stressful and, for most people, it seems like an insurmountable problem.

I'll let you in on a secret, though: you can be debt-free in one year or less! No hassles or legal footwork involved and no painful budget cuts. Just a simple, step-by-step, proven system that really works.

Find out more today! http://www.link-to-optin-page.com/

In a moment, I'll give you a list of some of the **most popular classifieds sites**. However, I need to go over a unique case first. That unique case is Craigslist (http://www.craigslist.org). Craigslist receives an enormous amount of traffic, and it can be a real goldmine of free advertising for you. But you have to know how to use the service the right way. The Craigslist community is very strict about business advertising. If you place your ad in the wrong section, it will get flagged and deleted. Your e-mail or IP address may even get banned from using the site if you break the rules too many times. Also, it is very important that you direct your Craigslist traffic toward your landing page, where you're giving away free information. Linking directly to a sales page will almost always get you in trouble.

When you write your ad, keep the focus on the information you're offering (via your list) rather than on the product or offer you intend to pitch. Remember: the goal is to collect opt-ins to your list! *Then* you can follow up more intensely with regard to your offer.

Now, here's that list of the most popular classifieds sites:

- http://www.usfreeads.com ✓

- http://www.sell.com ✓

- http://classifieds.yahoo.com ✓

- http://www.adlandpro.com

- http://www.domesticsale.com

- http://www.classfiedads.com ✓

- http://www.adpost.com ✓

TRAFFIC TACTIC #8: SOCIAL NETWORKING

Sometimes you have to step outside the usual way of doing things when you want more sources of free traffic. Social-network sites are all the rage right now and provide a unique opportunity for you to clone yourself, so to speak, across the Internet. Multiple points of contact are offered at sites such as:

- MySpace

- Friendster

- FaceBook

- Tagged

- Squidoo

- HubPages

All of the above provide incredible opportunities for boosting your traffic. Although some sites differ in functionality, they all have large enough feature sets to allow you to create outposts or hubs that you can use to advertise your main site. Also, you'll be able to offer some unique content by taking advantage of the different tools provided at each site. For example, you can use My Space to post additional articles (on your blog) or bulletins for special announcements. Use your tagline space to advertise your site's URL.

Sites like Squidoo and HubPages offer even more features. You can build a network of readers by partnering with other site members who share the same interests. The ultimate goal with these sites is to build more and more areas for distributing your content, building reputation, and boosting your brand exposure. You can, in a sense, turn yourself into a sort of celebrity at each of these sites if you provide compelling content. They're ideal for sharing articles, videos, and other types of media that you'd like to see go "viral," as they get passed around and linked to by other network members. Remember to keep your primary objective in mind, though, and provide plenty of links back to your main opt-in page.

TRAFFIC TACTIC #9: VIRAL VIDEO AND PODCASTING

If you enjoy speaking about market topics, consider creating videocasts or audio podcasts. In other words, create multimedia versions of your newsletters and distribute them on sites like the following (for videos):

- YouTube

- Google Video

- MySpace TV

- AOL Video

- Revver

and on sites like these (for podcasts):

- Podcast.Net

- Apple iTunes

- PodCast Blaster

The benefits of taking this approach are many. Presenting information in audio and video allows you to convey your personality much more strongly than is possible through text. It allows you to draw people's attention to the points you really want to emphasize, because tone is conveyed so much more clearly. It is a lot harder to convey your tone to a reader through text, as all you have at your disposal are the various formatting tricks.

Also, using these types of media allows you to reach a far larger audience than you would simply by going after Web searchers. In fact, you'll find YouTube videos cross-posted to people's MySpace profiles. You'll see audios and videos ripped directly from any of these sites and posted on individual blogs all across the Web.

Media and social-networking sites feed off of each other, and this is to your advantage when it comes to getting exposure and traffic. Keep in mind that all of these sites are driven by participation among the general public. The media at these sites is shared and syndicated, often overlapping from site to site.

Using affiliate videos to generate traffic will require a little extra work setting up, but it is a cutting-edge and very effective method. The central idea of the affiliate video is to create presell content, for example, product tutorials or demonstrations, on videos that you then distribute to the various viral video sites on the Web, like YouTube and Google Video.

For example, let's say you're promoting desktop recording software that lets people compose and record their own music right on their computers. You could create a screen capture video that shows you composing a simple song. The video might include shots of you choosing instruments, cutting and pasting tracks, adding effects, and so on, to show people how easy to use the product is. Then, at the end, you'd play the track to show off your composition. At the end of the video, you could announce (or roll in credits) something like the following:

Want to create your own music on your PC? Learn how at http://www.youraffiliatesite.com.

You see, you're simply directing them to your site, where you capture their information and follow up on the offer.

This method is powerful for a number of reasons:

- **SOCIAL PROOF**

  Viewers see someone else (you) actually using the product, so they get a sneak peek at how it works and how it might work for them.

- **LIVE DEMONSTRATION OF BENEFITS**

  Some benefits are harder to put into words, and some people learn better by watching than by reading instructions. With video, both problems are solved because the benefits are demonstrated to the prospect right before his eyes.

- **HIGHER-QUALITY CONTENT**

  Multimedia presentations are fun to watch and easier for some to absorb than traditional sales letters. You're doing more than just selling to the prospect; you're giving him a real taste of ownership of the product.

For all these reasons, the affiliate video method can really generate high traffic! YouTube and Google Video are just two of dozens of such sites online that receive millions of hits and viewers per day. The sites are set up to make sharing of videos as easy as possible. Popular videos get redistributed from one site to another and even onto individual Web sites and blogs. When people want to share a video, all they have to do is copy a little snippet of code, and that video is embedded right onto their site.

TRAFFIC TACTIC #10: STEALING TRAFFIC FROM BLOGS

An easy way to "steal" targeted visitors from high-traffic sites is to post responses (or comments) on popular blogs. For a long while, most people viewed blogs as a sort of online diary, but they have become powerful marketing tools over the past few years. In fact, some bloggers, especially political bloggers, have reached celebrity status in the major media. My own blog over at http://www.EwenChia.com allows me to communicate on a far more personal level with my subscribers and customers, deliver unique content, and promote all of my other sites and affiliate products.

The point to note here, though, is that almost every market you get into these days will have at least a couple of very popular blogs providing content to the marketplace audience. What you can bank on is that the members of your market who take the time to consume this information are highly targeted and very passionate in their interest.

So, let's talk about this process of stealing traffic via blog comments. Most blog owners allow their visitors to interact with them by leaving responses to the content they've posted on their blog. For example, I can post an article to my blog sharing some new insights about affiliate marketing or announcing an upcoming product launch—and have my visitors respond with their own opinions, questions, and suggestions.

Here is a screenshot from one of my blog entries:

PS. Warning: I'll be sending you another email in the next **24-48 hours** which is rather important. There're no sales pitches there but instead, what I want to give you is a **FREE video** I just recorded today with a student.

There's a ton of **real content and information** in this video which I hope you can benefit from...including the **true 'secrets' of marketing** and what your **real keys to online success** are...

So if you don't mind receiving so many emails from me in such a short period of time, do look out for that video link :-)

Read more about the online marketing secrets series.
online marketing secrets
, online marketing, internet marketing, Marketing, marketing an online business, web site online marketing, marketing online, internet marketing online ——— **Link to comments**

This online marketing ___ is presented by Ewen Chia; 11:50 PM 9 comments ___ ks to this online marketing secrets post. ✉

Notice that just after the end of my blog entry is a short follow-up section, which includes a link to comments posted by readers in response to my blog entry. In this case, you have to click on the "Comments" link to get to them and to post your own comment. On some blogs, though, the comments will be displayed directly below the most recent entry. When you click on the "Comments" link, you'll see the replies people have posted:

Tom said...

Hello Ewen! This is great idea for little guys like my or other who is new in Online Marketing.I like your SAW system and i wait for your newbie stuff. Thank you for helping little guys.

Greetings from Croatia!

1:27 AM

Joseph said...

Hi Ewen, this project definitely is a great help. Hopefully you will add a forum in it so all the newbies can share and ask questions to seek the right info or skill needed. I look forward to hear from you!

Cheers

1:59 AM

Now, notice what you can do here. Let's say that you're in the affiliate-marketing niche like I am, and you want to steal some of my traffic. What you would do is post a thoughtful reply to my entry, then link back to your opt-in page. Your comment would need to be relevant and helpful to the overall discussion. The one thing you don't want to do is spam people's blogs with meaningless comments just to get your link out there. Instead, really pay attention to what the blog author has said, and formulate a meaningful response. Let's say I posted an article about mistakes made by newbie affiliate marketers. You might post a comment like this one:

> Hey Ewen, you made a good point about choosing high-converting products. I made the mistake of trying to promote anything that looked good in the beginning, too. In my opinion, conversion is just as important as proper targeting, if not more so. Hopefully, more marketers will start teaching this concept to newbies, as it's really too important a factor to be left out.
>
> Your name
>
> http://www.your-optin-page.com

Now, that was easy, wasn't it? You just need to speak with some authority. Your comments can be based purely on opinion, or you can also offer up some information that enhances the information given in the author's entry. You can agree with the author, or you can even disagree to stir up a little controversy. Let me show you an example. Let's say you read a blog entry by someone claiming that people can lose weight by drinking a gallon of salt water every day. You know this is ridiculous, of course, and it's your job as an information provider to help people get the facts. So, you compose a counter response with information:

> Hi Joe. I've got to respectfully disagree with you. Salt water?? If you know your science at all, you know that all

this does is dehydrate you. It's not real weight loss; it's just water weight that comes off. There are *far* better, and safer, methods people can use to lose weight quickly. I know, because I review them all the time. There are at least two methods I can think of that involve just changing what you eat for breakfast, and they work in about 7 to 10 days.

Your name

http://www.real-fat-loss.com (opt-in page)

You can bet you'd get traffic from that response! In essence, you've stolen not just traffic, but also a little bit of authority and expert status from the blog owner. You've also hinted at alternative solutions that people will want to find out about. Clicking on your link from that point becomes a natural impulse.

> *By far the easiest method of finding targeted blogs in your market is by searching through blog directories.*

By far the easiest method of finding targeted blogs in your market is by searching through blog directories. These directories are organized by categories, making it easy for you to browse through available blogs and find one that's targeted to your market. In order to find these resources, you can start with a Google search using the phrase "blog directory." You can also search using your niche market key phrases and the word "blog," for example, "golfing blog."

Here's a list of blog directories to get you started:

- http://www.blogcatalog.com/

- http://dir.blogflux.com/

- http://www.technorati.com/

- http://blogsearch.google.com/

- http://www.findblogs.com/

- http://www.blogsearchengine.com/

Finally, don't forget to follow any links you come across! Let's say you go to one niche blog and see that they have linked to similar blogs or mentioned one in a post. Make sure you follow these types of links, as they can lead to a whole universe of related blogs!

TRAFFIC TACTIC #11: STEALING EVEN MORE TRAFFIC FROM BIG-NAME SITES

As a follow-up to the blog method, I urge you to seek out additional high-traffic sites that allow visitors to post comments, write product reviews, and answer questions. Some of the major sites you'll want to visit include the following:

- Amazon.com

- Epinions.com

- Yahoo! Answers (http://answers.yahoo.com)

- AllExperts.com

- Answerbag.com

- Ask Metafilter (http://ask.metafilter.com)

Each of these sites allows visitors to interact in some way as part of a larger community. Amazon, for example, allows registered Amazon.com members to post their own reviews of books, music, and other products. Sites like Yahoo! Answers and Answerbag.com are totally user-driven. People come to these answers/advice sites looking for help on everything from how to change a tire to career advice. The range of questions people ask on these sites in limitless. What you can do is seek out the products or questions specific to your market, and get traffic by writing your own reviews and answering people's questions. For example, let's say you visit Yahoo! Answers and see that a member has asked the following question:

> Hi everyone, I'm having a huge problem with credit-card debt! I thought I would be able to pay off all of my cards (I have five and the total balance between all of them is $15,000), but my interest rates are too high—plus I've been late on some payments. This is getting out of hand, and I'm getting scared! I don't want to declare bankruptcy, though. What should I do??

Now, if you are targeting the financial-management market and have a specific offer on an e-book product that teaches people how to get out of debt, then this is a perfect question for you to answer! You might respond with something like this:

> Hi, I know just how you're feeling! Credit card debt can be a nightmare. The good news is that you are *not* trapped. I don't know your specific situation (are you managing money poorly? not earning enough at your job?), but I have some information that may help. First, you can call up each of your lenders (the ones you're making timely payments to) and negotiate better interest rates with them. Most people don't know this! It really is as simple as

making a phone call. The reason is: *they want to keep you as a customer*. Now, if that doesn't work, then you need to look into a process called "Accord and Satisfaction." This process involves negotiating with the credit-card companies for a debt settlement. This buy-out amount (determined by the lender) will usually be a percentage on the dollar of total debt. For example, if you owe $5,000, they may accept a settlement of $2,000, which means you're paying back only 40 cents out of every dollar you owe. That said, I don't recommend doing this on your own. To get the best deal, you need some kind of legal help or assistance from a debt-management company, but you have to be careful which one you go with, as some of them can get you into an even bigger mess than you're in now. I'm happy to help provide you with more information if needed, and I have a free guide available at my site: http://www.get-out-of-debt-now.com.

The goal in writing your response is similar to that in article marketing. You want to establish some credibility and expert status while fulfilling your role as an information provider. A lot of people visit these sites, and you stand to get traffic from anyone who comes across your review, comment, or answer. The traffic to your site will come from linking to your opt-in page, as in the above example. On sites like Amazon, this usually has to be done by making your URL a part of your registered username. On sites like AllExperts, you usually interact via a forum, so you'd want to use the signature file method. Lastly, sites like Yahoo! Answers usually allow you to slip your URL right into the body of your reply, and you can also link to your site from within your Yahoo! User Profile. The rules about this vary from site to site, so just make sure you explore each site thoroughly to determine their rules and restrictions on outside linking, then figure out the best way to get your URL in front of other members.

TRAFFIC TACTIC #12: CONTENT SYNDICATION AND SETTING UP YOUR OWN BLOG

Allowing people to download and manually republish your articles is still a winning, time-tested strategy. However, it is also now considered the old-fashioned way of doing things. As technology evolved, publishers found a newer, easier way of grabbing and reprinting content. After all, it's a lot of work to cut, paste, and format articles—especially on large sites. Publishers needed a way to syndicate online content more effectively—something hands-off and automated. A new standard called RSS came to the rescue. "Really simple syndication," "real-time simple syndication," or "rich site summary" is the format used for syndicating Web content. A full discussion of how RSS works is beyond the scope of this course, but I will help you to understand some of the basics.

RSS involves behind-the-scenes programming. At its simplest, all that's required is a bit of Javascript. What happens is this: when a visitor comes to a site with an RSS feed, the code behind the page is triggered to pull in content (or headline links to content) from other sites. So, for example, Site A makes all of its content available for syndication and provides the necessary code to access its content feed. Site B (and C and D, etc.) implements this code in order to retrieve Site A's content automatically.

OK, that's the techie stuff. The important thing to understand is that you can scoop up even more traffic when you submit your articles to directories that have implemented automatic RSS syndication and when you implement an RSS feed on your own Web site, allowing other sites to pull content directly from yours.

I'm going to provide you with a full list of resources to get started on this in a moment. Before I do, though, we need to squeeze in the blog factor. *Weblogs,* or blogs, are still the hottest craze online right now. Perhaps you have heard of some of the more popular blogging sites:

> http://www.blogger.com/
>
> http://www.livejournal.com/
>
> http://www.myspace.com/

You can scoop up even more traffic when you submit your articles to directories that have implemented automatic RSS syndication and when you implement an RSS feed on your own Web site, allowing other sites to pull content directly from yours.

LiveJournal and MySpace are popular among younger Web surfers. They function more like personal diaries. MySpace, however, is becoming a viral tool to contend with, especially for artists and musicians. I consider these sites of "experimental interest," meaning that if you choose to use them, tread cautiously. Test them out, but don't rely on them. My recommendation for business-oriented blogging is Blogger. Blogger is now owned and run by Google. I recommend pointing your blog to a unique domain name. In other words, choose the option that allows your blog to load up at http://www.yoursite.com rather than http://blogger.com/your-username.

There are several options available for implementing blog software on your site—some for a fee, some free under an open-source license. The most popular utilities include TypePad, B2Evolution, WordPress, and PHPNuke. These programs are server-side programs. Your Web host may already offer a few of them for free. Look in your control panel or administration area for a utility called Fantastico. This will allow you to install these scripts with a minimum of technical knowledge. You can also ask for assistance from your hosting company's tech support.

Now, to the point: **why blog?** Blogging allows you to post your own content and articles consistently and easily. If you have difficulty creating Web pages on your own, then blogging might be the solution. The typical blog interface looks a lot like a word processor. You simply type up your article right in your Web browser, click Post, and the content is automatically published to your site.

Blogs also give you an opportunity to publish content separate from your main sales site. Now, why is this important? Well, you've seen the traditional, direct-marketing offer page. All you have there is one page containing your offer copy and subscription form (plus product images if it is a sales page). Remember, too, that the function of your page is to entice visitors to make only one of two choices: respond to the offer, or leave. This is why we avoid posting article content on opt-in pages and sales letters. You don't want to give the visitor a distraction. You also don't want her to feel that she's seen everything she needs to know from your articles. If you post links to this kind of content on your opt-in or sales page, you run the risk of satisfying the visitor's curiosity before she ever gets to the Buy Now button! It's unfortunate, but this is one of the limitations of traditional, one-page, direct-marketing sites—and this is where your separate blog site comes in.

You'd like to let both potential and existing customers in on your latest product news, testimonials, outstanding results, etc. You can do all of this with a blog.

Let's say you want more room to presell to and educate your prospects. Better yet, maybe you're offering a very robust product that requires a lot of updating. Either way, you'd like to let both potential and existing customers in on your latest product news, testimonials, outstanding results, etc. You can do all of this with a blog.

Let me give you a really good illustration. There are several product owners out there who are offering keyword research software. I know of at least two who implement blogs to great effect. They use their blogs to do the following:

- Announce special offers

- Announce the latest updates to the software for existing customers

- Write in-depth articles on keyword research

- Write articles/reports on research tests they've run using the very product they're selling

This is very powerful. You see, they're demonstrating benefits in near real-time. Someone who sees the sales page and is still sitting on the fence can go over to the blog and get a better idea of what the product will really do for him. At the same time, the blog creates a sense of community. Let's say the fence-sitter reads the comments other customers have made on a given blog post. Now, this undecided prospect is very frustrated … there seems to be an insider discussion taking place. Unless he buys the product, he'll continue to be left out. Make no mistake; the desire for inclusion will compel a very large number of prospects to convert themselves into customers!

In addition to looping traffic back and forth from your blog to your sales site, you will also be able to draw in new visitors to your blog, and then funnel them to your sales site. **Blogs attract traffic** in several different ways:

- Search engines are attracted to fresh content

- Syndication and "blog and ping"

- Blog community directories

- Bloggers linking to other bloggers

We'll talk more about syndication and "blog and ping," since the other concepts are familiar to you by now. Your blog software should have a syndication module built into it, which you can start using immediately. There is also a feature called "blog and ping," which is included in some utilities. It's basically an auto-alert feature. What you do is collect a list of the sites you'd like to notify of new blog posts. You set these sites to be pinged, or alerted, basically, whenever you post new content. When you ping a site, you're inviting their syndication system to do a fresh crawl (a type of search that picks up new Web pages) for your latest content.

I've got to add one caveat here. If and when you use this function, you might want to go light on either the number of sites you ping or the number of posts you put up per day. As it goes with many automated tools, there's a point of overload—thousands of users pinging, causing strain on other sites' servers.

Here are some sites to check out for your syndication needs:

- http://www.goarticles.com

- http://www.freesticky.com

- http://www.articledashboard.com

- http://www.amazines.com

- http://www.freewebsubmission.com

And here are some good blogging resources:
- http://www.blogger.com

- http://www.wordpress.com

- http://www.masternewmedia.org/rss/top55

- http://www.rsstoblog.com

- http://netforbeginners.about.com/od/bloggingbasics

TRAFFIC TACTIC #13: VIRAL REPORTS

These reports aren't called "viral" for nothing: the name reflects the ease with which they're designed to be passed from person to person within the Internet community. What makes a report (or even a piece of software or multimedia) truly viral in terms of push and distribution? Here are the three key elements, as I see them:

- Quality content

- The right price: it's *free*

- The profit motive: distributors make money via rebranding

Let's take a look at each element in more depth. Your very first step is to create a report filled with high-quality content. Whether you write the report yourself or hire someone else to do it, your focus should be on giving people the kind of content they'd normally have to pay for. Are you

> *Whether you write the report yourself or hire someone else to do it, your focus should be on giving people the kind of content they'd normally have to pay for.*

afraid that it might be difficult to create a report like this? It's really a snap. You don't have to give away the information in the product you're trying to sell; you just have to provide market-relevant information.

Now, you can write this report yourself, or you can hire a freelancer to do it. You can also plumb the public domain to put something together. It doesn't have to be the best report ever written on the subject, but it should be useful or helpful to your prospects. Again, you're just fulfilling your role as an information provider.

> *The topic of your report should be relevant to the product or site that you're promoting*

The topic of your report should be relevant to the product or site that you're promoting. What you are doing is preselling to your niche by educating them, motivating them, and raising their interest. So, imagine that you're creating a report for one of the affiliate programs you're involved in, and the product is a $97 piece of software that searches keyword combinations for Google Adwords. A relevant viral report might cover the following areas:

- A beginner's guide to Google Adwords

- An expert's guide to Adwords containing secret tips and tricks

- How to write effective copy for Adwords to convert more traffic

- How to ethically spy on your competitor's keywords, then crush the competition!

- Keyword-mining software: choosing the best and learning how to evaluate your results

Here's another example. Let's say you're in the weight- loss niche and want to lure people onto your list using your report as an offer. You could create dozens of different reports for this market:

- "Fat Secrets: The Surprisingly High Calorie Counts Hidden in So-Called Health Foods"

- "Fat Facts: Good for You Fats, Bad for You Fats—And Why You Should Know the Difference!"

- "The Dreaded Plateau: How to Supercharge Your Metabolism and Drop Those Last 5 Pounds"

- "Hungry No More: Over 100 Delicious and Healthy Recipes That Will Leave You Feeling Satisfied"

I'm sure you're getting the idea. Any of the above titles could make for great viral reports. You deliver on the information people are really looking for, make them hungry for more of that content—that is, more of it *from you.*

Viral reports are always offered free of charge—in order for them to circulate as widely as possible. You don't want any barriers in the way of people reading the report and passing it around. People really do love freebies. In this day and age, more and more consumers are getting used to the idea of paying for information, albeit somewhat grudgingly. So, when they see something that looks good and see that it's theirs for the taking, they'll leap on it. Keeping it free also

Viral reports are always offered free of charge—in order for them to circulate as widely as possible.

builds up your image. Even though your profits are the bottom line, you've got to demonstrate that you aren't out solely for the money. You have a good product and genuinely desire to help people. Show your audience the type of content they'll receive when they do pay you somewhere down the line. Show them that you know your stuff, and you're willing to give out a free sample in return for mutual trust.

The third element I identified, of profit motivation, is the most crucial. This is the viral fuel that will boost your report off the launching pad: you need to offer an incentive to others to distribute your report. You create this incentive through rebranding. Making a report rebrandable means that you provide both a license to rebrand, as well as the means or method of doing so. Let's talk about the technical end of rebranding first, since that's where most people run into questions.

This is the viral fuel that will boost your report off the launching pad: you need to offer an incentive to others to distribute your report.

Software is necessary in order to rebrand a PDF file. The software I use and recommend is Viral PDF (http://www.viralpdf.com). This software allows you to make all or part of the affiliate links in your report rebrandable, meaning that the reader can replace your affiliate links with his own. You can retain links back to your Web site. You can even keep some of your affiliate links and allow only certain ones to be rebranded. The point is that the possibility of earning a profit by redistributing your report motivates your reader. The profit motive, more than anything else, is what's going to compel people to give your report away to others, who will also want to rebrand the report and give it away to others, and so on, and on.

It would be nice if quality were the only incentive necessary for redistribution, but that's just not the case most of the time. Even if someone loves your report, there's a natural laziness at work within us. "Maybe I'll put this up on my Web site or e-mail a copy to Mom … after the weekend." Not so when there's money involved. If people

The profit motive, more than anything else, is what's going to compel people to give your report away to others, who will also want to rebrand the report and give it away to others, and so on, and on.

believe they can turn a profit, they'll rush to get your report out to as many people as possible, right away. They see the viral power. They know plenty of other people are going to distribute the report. They want to beat them all to the punch.

Now, you might be thinking, "If everyone is rebranding it, how does anyone make any money?" Well, that's the good news. What usually happens is the distribution chain is balanced between *pure publishers* and *pure readers*. A large enough percentage of publishers will rebrand the report for you to get broad distribution. However, an equally large percentage of pure readers will download your report, read it, and decide whether to take action. It's those readers who'll make good on the incentive by clicking through the publisher's affiliate links, thus making the rebrand worthwhile for them.

You can also create viral reports in .exe format, and there are rebrand options available particular to each EXE e-book compiler. However, I generally don't recommend using the .exe format. Because of computer viruses, Trojans, and other security concerns, people are paranoid about receiving executable programs from unknown sources. Also, many readers are Macintosh users, and PDF is the preferred option for these readers.

When it comes to traffic power, viral reports have both long-term and short-term effectiveness. If you create a really good report, it won't be too long until you see your results begin to multiply. There will be a peak of viral activity when the report is at the height of popularity. After that, things will die down a little bit, but the report keeps on working. You'll still get traffic from it for months, sometimes even years down the line. The reason for this is sheer breadth of distribution. A successful viral report will be on so many people's computers and so many sites online, you won't even be able to keep track of them all! That's why the traffic just keeps on trickling, even when the initial rush starts to fade.

To create a traffic-pulling viral report, you not only need the right viral elements, you also need to distribute the report to the right people. Imagine for a moment what you would do if you really had a virus—let's say you came down with the flu and you decided to give it to as many other people as possible so you'd have some company. What would be the quickest and most effective method of spreading your flu around? The quickest way would be to give it to people who, through their jobs or other daily habits, come in contact with as many, if not more, people than you do!

And that's why the first step in unleashing your viral report involves contacting other list owners. You've researched your niche in advance, right? So, you should have a long list of potential joint venture partners and related e-zines and Web sites at your fingertips. Now is the time to begin contacting them! Shoot over an e-mail to potential partners to let them know about your report and the included rebrand/income opportunity:

Hi Dave,

This is [your name] from [your Web site]. I just finished creating a free report on [topic name] called [report title]. You may download a copy of the report here: [Web site URL].

The report is rebrandable for [affiliate program], which pays out [amount]. I've also included the option for you to rebrand with your own name and Web site URL.

If you like the report and think your subscribers would benefit from it as well, please feel free to distribute it to them.

Thanks so much for your time. Please do let me know if you have any questions.

Regards,

[your name]

Now, in addition to distributing via partner sites, there are two other outlets you need to take advantage of:

1) YOUR OWN OPT-IN LIST

Make sure you offer the report to your list first. All it takes is a quick broadcast e-mail using your autoresponder program. This is not the same thing as your usual follow-up messages. The follow-up messages you have preloaded into your autoresponder go out in predefined sequences of your choosing. Those mails are staggered because the sequence begins at the moment of sign-up and the messages go to just that individual subscriber. Broadcast e-mails go to all of the subscribers on your list, and the e-mail goes out immediately. It's just like mass e-mailing all of your friends. Whenever you need to send a quick e-mail out to your list in this way, the "broadcast" feature is the tool to use.

2) E-BOOK DISTRIBUTION SITES

E-book distribution sites (or directories) are like article directories, but the focus is on downloadable books and reports. People visit these directories for the same reason they visit article directories: they need content! Some directories focus solely on free content, while others offer a mix of both free and paid e-books. There are also sites that present strictly "for fee" e-books, and you'll want to avoid those for obvious reasons. While most directories cover the gamut of topics, some are more specialized. Nine times out of ten, the specialized directories focus on business and Internet marketing. How do you know which directory to choose? First, make sure the directory is well organized and that your e-book can be placed in the appropriate category. You'll want to avoid sites that are disorganized because you want your e-book to be found easily. Second, make sure the directory is relatively popular. Sites that come up in the top ten on a Google search will get a lot of traffic, but make sure the site is run professionally. Just because a site shows up in the top ten doesn't mean that people like what they find when they get there! Here is a list of e-book directories to get you started:

- **http://www.mindlikewater.com**
  Multiple categories. Attractive and well organized.

- **http://www.ebookpalace.com**
  Offering both e-books and articles. Very well-organized site. Even includes a list of e-book topics people are searching for on the site.

- **http://www.jogena.com**
  An excellent resource. Fewer categories. Strong focus on business, marketing, writing, and publishing.

- **http://www.free-ebooks.net**
  Well-established, highly trafficked, and popular site. One of the big guns of free e-book distribution.

TRAFFIC TACTIC #14:
NATURAL SEARCH-ENGINE OPTIMIZATION

There is an old way of thinking about search-engine optimization, and a new way. The old way of thinking is a holdover from the earlier days of the Internet—back when search-engine optimization was the main lifeline of every online business, and failing to optimize meant failing to thrive. It used to be that people spent thousands of dollars on books, seminars, insider tips, and professional services—all in the name of getting into the top ten search results of the big search engines.

However, all of this changed when the brains of the industry figured out how to set up virtual, online versions of traditional (offline) advertising channels. More and more sponsors turned to banner advertising, then affiliate programs, and then—the knockout punch: pay-per-click advertising. This was (and still is) good news for the small-business entrepreneur because it means he no longer needs to obsess over search-engine optimization. So, there's a new way of thinking today. I can best sum it up for you like this: do search-engine optimization, but don't obsess over it!

Your best bet is to put the basics I'll show you here into action, and then don't fret about it too much. You see, there is a perception (mostly accurate) that search-engine optimization is difficult and complicated. This perception bears out especially when your goal is to optimize a site for highly competitive keywords. It's almost impossible to get to the top and stay there. That's not just because of the vast amount of competition but also because search-engine algorithms are constantly changing. Well, you don't have to worry about this. You're going to learn how to do search-engine optimization the smart way:

• **KNOW YOUR KEY PHRASES**

All search-engine optimization begins with key phrases. Notice I said "phrases," not "words." Single keywords are to be avoided (too broad, too much competition). Think of all of the key phrases relevant to your site. We'll use a golfing-related site for our example. What are some appropriate phrases for a golfing site? Well, that depends on how you've zeroed down into a subniche. Maybe you've decided to sell an info product teaching beginners the rules of the game. In this case, you wouldn't want key phrases like "used golf club," because you aren't selling golf clubs. Instead, you'd have phrases like "learn to play golf," "rules of golf," "golf handicap," "golf training," "play better golf," "golf tips," and so on. Each of these key phrases, in turn, is relevant to your content. In other words, they represent the type of information that is on your site.

> *Engine optimization begins with key phrases. Notice I said "phrases," not "words."*

Now, here is where it gets interesting. You'll want to avoid using all of these key phrases on one page—with one exception—for a single opt-in page (this is true for single-page sales letters as well). You may include all such phrases in your meta tags (these are the HTML or XHTML elements—more about this later—providing structured data about your Web page) so long as you are using those phrases within your copy. Otherwise, narrow down your list to the most relevant and targeted phrases, with an eye toward weighting the frequency and density of those key phrases in your copy. You can use a free tool such as http://tool.motoricerca.info/keyword-density.phtml to calculate those values.

So, let's say that "golf tips" and "golf training" appear at a rate of 12 percent in your

The general rule to follow is this: your most important key phrases should carry a density of 12–15 percent

copy, while "rules of golf" and "play better golf" come up at 0–1 percent. In that case, you'll want to keep the former key phrases in your meta tags while tossing those latter key phrases. You'll also want to rework your copy a bit and see if you can use more of your best key phrases in order to make your optimization more robust.

The general rule to follow is this: your most important key phrases should carry a density of 12–15 percent. You should have no more than two to three key phrases that rank this high in your copy. Your other phrases, the ones that are relevant but less important (or simply not the targets of optimization for a specific page) should have densities under 12 percent. If you want to increase the odds of ranking on some of those terms, make sure their scores do not fall below 5 percent.

Now, last but not least, what if you have more than just one Web page? What if you have a large content-driven site, and you want to optimize across a range of key phrases? The same rules apply, but you have even more opportunity to improve your site's search-engine ranking. We'll stick to our golf example here. Let's say you want to fill your site with pages and pages of information for beginning golf players. The number-one way you'll do this is by posting articles—just pure, solid content.

If you want to get ranked on the key phrase "golf tip," you'll need an article optimized for that phrase. For instance, the article might be called, "Ten Golf Tips for the Absolute Novice."

OK, you've got a starting point. What next?

The next steps involve the gritty details of optimization. This is the stuff many people get frustrated with because it seems so artificial—but this is what works. First, you need your key phrase to appear once in your title tag. Here, I'm talking about the actual HTML (<title></title>) tag that causes the title of the Web page to display in the top status bar of your visitor's browser. So, your first optimization step looks like this:

<TITLE>Ten Golf Tips for the Absolute Novice</TITLE>

Second, use your key phrase in the body title of your Web page. The general theory is that after your title tag, you need your key phrase to appear once in a header tag. Header tags are commonly used for titles because they cause the text to appear larger and bolder. So, go into your HTML and find the beginning of your content. Create an <H2> header and place your article title within it like so:

<H2>Ten Golf Tips for the Absolute Novice</H2>

Third, your key phrase should appear within a bold tag at least once, early on in the page. This part is kind of tricky. Depending on how your article is written, it may not look appropriate to have your keyword in bold. You might have to tinker with your article and find a logical place to put the key phrase in bold. If your article is broken down into numbered tips, however, this works out just fine. You'd have "golf tip one," "golf tip two," etc. Regardless, here is how to perform this step:

Golf Tip

Fourth, use your key phrase multiple times within your copy. Here is where many people run into trouble. Following the "more is better" philosophy, many wind up overusing their key phrase. This produces copy that, although potentially attractive to the search engines, is awkward and unreadable to the human visitor. Here is an example of what not to do:

> We hope you find our golf tips useful. Our golf tips are the best golf tips available on the Internet among golf tips Web sites visited by people searching for golf tips.

Ugh. See what I mean? Your content needs to be real and solid and good. Try to get your key phrase density as close to 12 percent as possible, while keeping the voice of your article natural sounding. It's all about working your key phrase into the flow:

> Here at learntoplaygolf.com, we strive to offer the best tips and tricks available to the novice player. What's a birdie? What's a par nine? What's a good golf handicap? Come find out the answers to these questions, and a whole lot more, in our extensive golf-tips library.

Fifth, include key phrases in named hyperlinks. In our previous example, we could have turned the phrase "golf-tips library" into an active hyperlink, leading to a page with a table of contents of selected articles. Although search engines give more weight to key phrases in hyperlinks that point to your site from other sites, there is still value in including key phrases in your hyperlinks, making sure that the page you link to includes usages of that same key phrase. In other words, you'll get some credit for having "golf tips" hyperlinked to a page with, say, your article titled "Ten Golf Tips for the Absolute Novice." Just make sure your use of this trick is logical, relevant, and not overdone. You don't want to "stuff" your links (or your image tags, meta tags, etc.) with keywords. The search engines will penalize you for this.

Sixth, use the "ALT" tag with your images. When you place the code for an image into your HTML, the image tag has an optional parameter called "ALT." This tag, when used, displays whatever text you place in the ALT parameter to users who are browsing with images turned off. So, let's say you have an image on your golf-tips page of someone about to swing a club, and you want to place your key phrase there. You'd do it like so:

```
<img src="golfswing.jpg" width="100" height="100" border="0" ALT="Golf Tips">
```

This wraps up our tutorial on search-engine optimization. Remember, this is just a very rough guide to get you started. If you'd like to learn more about search-engine optimization and stay current on the latest search-engine algorithms affecting your Web site's ranking, check out the resources at http://www.searchenginewatch.com and http://www.seochat.com.

8C

YOUR TRAFFIC PLAN

We've just covered the many traffic-generating tactics at your disposal. In this section you will learn how to create a customized traffic plan to help drive visitors to your Web site. Why do you need such a strategy at all? First, remember that traffic is part of the big picture when it comes to targeting your market. For this reason, traffic is really the first step to conversion. It won't matter how good your offer or your sales copy is if your visitors are untargeted. Second, you need to have a daily plan of action. There are many steps you'll take each day to move your business forward, and the task of generating targeted

This is all about using your critical-thinking skills to plan ahead and make focused, deliberate choices.

traffic is no exception. Third, many of the traffic-generating techniques you'll learn about are cumulative in their effects. In other words, you won't see significant results unless you repeat and build upon these steps.

For example, let's say you want to use articles for driving traffic. If you submit only one article for publication to the article directories, you'll get (maybe) fifteen to twenty visitors within the month, and the numbers will drop off as that article ages. However, if you submit, say, ten new articles each month, then your traffic will accumulate from a few visits per month to hundreds … and pretty soon you're looking at a thousand or more visitors per year just from article marketing. Make sense? This is all about using your critical-thinking skills to plan ahead and make focused, deliberate choices.

An effective plan means all of the following:

- Looking at short-, mid-, and long-term strategies

- Seeing how all the pieces fit together and build on each other

- Factoring in your ability to leverage time and resources toward even more traffic when you start getting results

- Understanding that everything you do is cumulative and requires daily action for maximum results

You will soon learn about the top, proven traffic methods available, and I'll show you how to implement them. But right now, I want to give you a checklist to fill out in creating your plan:

☑ What are the top three *free* traffic methods I want to use first?

☑ What is the one *paid* traffic method I want to use first?

☑ How much time will it take to implement these first four methods?

☑ How much money will it take to implement the *paid* traffic method?

☑ How much time can I devote to traffic generation each day?

☑ How much money do I have in my budget for traffic?

Get out a piece of paper, write down each of these questions, and keep the checklist nearby. You'll be able to answer these questions after you've finished reading this chapter. Once you've answered each question, you'll be able to formulate a realistic plan based on how much time and money you have available to invest in getting your business off the ground. We'll walk through an illustration so you can see how this works:

☑ Top three *free* methods: articles, groups/forums, viral report

☑ Top *paid* method: pay-per-click advertising

☑ Time to implement the above methods: approximately one month if I can devote at least eight hours per week

☑ The average cost-per-click in my market is 10 cents. At roughly four hundred visitors per month, that works out to $40 per month.

☑ One hour in the mornings before going to work (five hours total); one to two hours in the evenings Tuesday–Thursday (three to six hours total); two hours on Sunday afternoons. Grand total: ten to thirteen hours per week.

☑ Current total business budget: $120. Web hosting costs: $15 per month. Autoresponder costs: $20 per month. $120–$35 = $85 available for traffic.

There are a couple of things to notice here. First, the above list is pretty good, but it also makes quite a few assumptions that may or may not be accurate. For instance, it assumes that you would already be clear on how long it takes you to write an article or how long it takes to set up a pay-per-click campaign. Depending on your past experience and skill level, you would adjust your time estimates.

When you make your list, I want you to think about what you're good at and what comes easily to you as well as what might give you difficulty. The point of creating a strategy is not simply to list what sounds good but to organize your campaign so that you begin from your strengths rather than your weaknesses.

The point of creating a strategy is not simply to list what sounds good but to organize your campaign so that you begin from your strengths rather than your weaknesses.

If you don't have enough money in your budget, for example, you'd want to focus on all the free traffic methods first. Likewise, if you've got plenty of money, you can pour that into paid advertising to get your momentum going, then take a little more time to work on articles, reports, etc.

The key is to choose at least three to four methods up front that you can implement as soon as possible, and arrange their execution relative to time and money versus return on investment. I cannot overstate the importance of this! Let's look at just one more illustration, and then I promise we'll move on.

What I'd like you to do now is compare your current ability to generate traffic against what I like to call the "commonly held wisdom" about which traffic methods are the fastest and most effective. In other words, you'll need to look at what most Internet marketers advise (refer again to the previous chapter for the common wisdom) versus what *you* can do right away. The two may not always be a match, and this affects your initial traffic strategy. Let's pretend that the following describes the circumstances of a fictional affiliate marketer:

- His monthly traffic budget is $20.

- The average cost-per-click for paid advertising in his market is 8 cents per visitor. So, at a budget of $20 per month, he is able to afford 250 visitors, so long as he doesn't get too many clicks on higher-cost keywords.

- He enjoys participating in discussion forums and educating others.

- He's a decent writer but not very confident. It takes him longer to write an article or report than he'd like.

- He feels he does a better job conveying information when he can speak to people in person or on the phone.

Now, with this scenario in mind, let's look at the commonly held beliefs about traffic generation. The methods producing the fastest results are thought to be (in decreasing order of speed):

- Pay-per-click

- Banner/text advertising

- E-zine advertising

- Forums/groups

- Articles/reports

The cheapest methods are thought to be (in decreasing order of effectiveness):

- Articles/reports

- Forums/groups

- E-zine advertising

- Pay-per-click

- Banner/text advertising

Based on the sample traffic-generating ability of our fictional affiliate marketer, we can see a couple of problems arising right off the bat:

1) He has only $20 to spend on pay-per-click advertising. Therefore, while he can get some immediate traffic, he can't get very much right away.

2) He's probably limited to using only one paid method for the time being, as e-zine and banner ads would eat up far more than $20.

3) The cheapest, most effective method available to him (articles/ reports) is also the slowest and requires him to write (a task that he's not very fast about, either).

If you were in his shoes, how would you solve this dilemma? Remember: you're always leveraging either time or money, and strengths against weaknesses.

Were I in this position, I would capitalize on the following three things:

- Natural talent for public speaking

- Affinity for participating in discussion forums

- The $20

I'd come up with an initial strategy that creates more leverage and gives me more resources to work with in the future. How? Well, keep in mind that all I really need to do is get the visitors to my site and onto my opt-in list. If I can get enough of them onto the list, then I can leverage them for more money and more traffic. All I need to do is come up with an offer that will suck them in while returning some tangible benefit back to me. So, here's what I'd do:

- Find a good, free teleconferencing service (like http://www. instantconference.com) that allows me to record the calls.

- Come up with an informative and valuable topic relevant to my niche that I want to hold a teleconference on. This could be a Q&A format with subscribers or with an expert I intend to interview.

- Include this as an offer on my opt-in page.

- Advertise the upcoming teleconference in my signature file, as I focus on participating as much as possible in my market's forums.

- Devote my $20 to scooping up additional traffic and teleconference participants.

- Make sure to mention in follow-ups that there are only 150 spots available for the call (this is the free limit with the conferencing service listed above). Participants get a free copy of the recording, while those who missed it will have to "purchase" it (see next bullet point).

- A day or two after the call, send a follow-up message to my list recapping how great the call went and what the nonparticipants missed out on. Tell them that the recording is not for sale, but they can get a copy for free as a bonus if they act on my lead affiliate offer, then forward their e-mail receipt to me.

Bingo—I should earn at least double what I spent on traffic from this, as long as I've truly created a high perceived value around the teleconference. Those who missed out will clamor to get their hands on the recording. It's exactly this type of creative thinking (and understanding of your own strengths and weaknesses) that can help you solve a traffic problem centered around "not enough money," "not enough time," or "not enough skill."

Create your plan based on careful consideration of your available time, skills, and resources.

To summarize, create your plan based on careful consideration of your available time, skills, and resources. Focus initially on what's going to give you the most leverage. Use that leverage along the way to strengthen your weak spots.

CHAPTER 9

Backend for Beginners

Any business wanting to increase bottom-line profits needs to implement a collection of backend offers and products. We discussed the definition of the backend in part one of this book, remember? The first sale you make to a customer is on what's called the *front-end*. In other words, the main product that you're advertising—the thing people have come to your "store" to buy—is your front-end offer. There are at least two other profit points near the front- end transaction: the upsell (or midlevel) and the backend.

The upsell is the equivalent of an upgrade or impulse purchase. When the customer is in the process of making payment (checking out), you offer them a related product or upgrade. For example: "For just $15 more you can also get Product X." Another version of the upsell is the *hidden* upsell, or what's more commonly known in Internet marketing circles as the *one-time offer*. Readers who have followed my work may remember I introduced this concept and called it the *hidden page* way back in 2004 in a product called Power Affiliate Marketing. Those who used it had great success.

> *Just like any smart investor, the way to take your business to the next level is by diversifying your investments.*

The backend product offer occurs after the initial sale. For example, if someone purchases a blender from you, you might follow up in a few days to offer them a book of drink recipes. The purpose of the backend is to generate repeat business. You capitalize on the interests of existing customers by offering them additional related products.

A second and equally important purpose of the backend is to gain leverage. Having a backend system boosts your profits beyond what you make in one affiliate program alone or with a single product. Just like any smart investor, the way to take your business to the next level is by diversifying your investments.

As a merchant or product creator, you can use affiliate products that are related and consistent with your main offer for the backend. As an affiliate, you can create your own products or find additional affiliate programs to fill out your backend. Either option will work, but the use of affiliate products is hands down the easiest way to fill out any backend system. We're going to look at this from a couple of angles.

STEP #1: FIND MORE AFFILIATE PROGRAMS AND AT LEAST ONE RESIDUAL PROGRAM

The first step to increasing your income through the backend is to find additional affiliate programs you can promote to your list. If you're making good money on one product, common sense dictates that your existing customers will also be interested in other, related products you might offer to them.

Residual-income affiliate programs are those that pay you on a monthly basis for the life of the customer you referred.

You can start out by offering one to two additional products each month. At least one of these should include a residual-income program. Residual-income affiliate programs are those that pay you on a monthly basis for the life of the customer you referred. These types of residual programs are usually service-based products sold as monthly memberships or subscriptions.

So, for example, if you refer someone to a site that charges a $20-per-month membership fee and pays you 50 percent of that, you'll earn $10 every month on that referral. Obviously, the key with these types of programs is to refer as many people as you can and retain them.

STEP #2: PREPARE AN E-MAIL CAMPAIGN FOR AFFILIATE PRODUCTS YOU WANT TO BACKEND

Super affiliates never promote just one product. In fact, all of the work that goes into promoting the lead product is just the beginning. As their name indicates, lead products (what you promote from your opt-in page and in your first e-mail follow-up series) are designed primarily to generate

It's not about just tossing in one product after another.

leads rather than sales. It's wonderful when you do earn some commissions from your lead product, but you are not to rely on it as a sole income generator. Super affiliates don't earn the bulk of their income from the front-end, nor do they use the front-end for high-ticket products. They save the real income generators for the backend. In other words, it is your second (and third and fourth …) offer where you begin promoting the "big money" products.

These backend offers are carefully chosen. It's not about just tossing in one product after another. You have to look not just at higher-priced products but also at products that offer you the opportunity to earn residual or passive streams of income.

Let's say that your lead product costs $49, and you earn $25 per sale. If you made fifty sales per month, you might think you were doing pretty well. This adds up to six hundred sales per year, for a total of $15,000 per year in commissions. This is definitely extra spending money, but it's not enough to free you from your day job or make you rich by any stretch of the imagination. This is why you *must* develop a profitable series of backend offers if you want the kind of massive income that super affiliates earn.

A typical super affiliate's backend structure looks something like this:

- **SECOND OFFER**

  A higher-priced product, usually about 30–40 percent more expensive than the lead product offering. For example, if the lead product costs $29.95, the follow-up product should be around $39.95 to $49.95.

- **THIRD OFFER**

  Usually a product that earns the affiliate a recurring commission. For example, some type of monthly service or membership site. This is typically a low- to midrange–priced product—something that a majority of subscribers can afford. The reason for this is obvious: it's better to earn a commission of $9.95 x 150 ($1,492.50 per month) at this point in the game than to earn $50 x 10 ($500). This doesn't mean you can't promote higher-priced residual offers in the future— just that you don't want to push them this early in the relationship.

- **Fourth offer**

  This can vary based on your interpretation of how your list is responding to the offers you've sent so far. You can surprise them with a truly valuable, low-cost offer here if necessary. Likewise, you can also test their limits by introducing your most expensive offer to date. It is not unusual to test response for a product priced double or triple above everything else you've offered so far.

NOTES AND TIPS ON PREPARING BACKEND FOLLOW-UP CAMPAIGNS

Ideally, you could take the time to have each of your campaigns written up and ready to go when you launch your site. However, 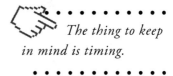 *The thing to keep in mind is timing.* you can just as easily create them after you've started the campaign for your lead product. The thing to keep in mind is timing. If your first campaign runs for seven days, and you plan to have a three-day gap between the first and second series, then you've got ten days to finish creating the second follow-up series.

It's best to get the second series created as quickly as possible. Your subscribers need to receive your e-mails consistently, or you risk losing their attention. Get your campaigns done and uploaded before your subscribers have cycled off the first series so that the transition from one to the other goes as smoothly as possible.

Also, it is beneficial to change your approach, or tone, just slightly. Your subscribers have had some time to get to know you. You can use your second campaign to deepen the relationship even further. You might, for example, point out the differences between the first and second products or use the second follow-up as an opportunity to deliver a bit more informational value. You can offer another gift or insert some unique promotional strategy, such as creating a video tutorial related to the product. Overall, the thing to remember with each campaign is that you are not only promoting a product but also building a relationship with subscribers. Be creative!

CHAPTER 10

Duplicating Your
Business Model

Duplication of your business model is what will really put your profits into overdrive! Think of it like buying up real estate. Your business is like a piece of property you acquire, fix up, and then turn around and rent for a steady stream of income. In order to build on that income, you simply acquire more property and repeat the process. Here's how:

PERFORMING COMPONENTS #1–4 IN OTHER MARKETS OR ACROSS YOUR EXISTING MARKET

In order to duplicate your success, you simply repeat the first four of the five core components:

1) Research and target a new market or find horizontal product lines you can expand into within your existing market.

2) Create an offer or solution targeted to the market.

3) Drive market traffic to your offer.

4) Build a backend for additional revenue.

Let's talk about some of the questions you should ask yourself before you duplicate your business:

- Do I want to go into a closely related market or a radically new one?

- What market can I go into that might be even more profitable?

- Do I want to sell the same type of product (e.g., e-books), or do I want to sell something else (e.g., software, videos, physical goods)?

- What were some of the obstacles I encountered in my first business that I'd like to eliminate this go around?

- What have I learned so far that will help me create my next business even faster and do it even better?

- How much of my existing profits can I reinvest into my new business?

These questions will help you make a strategic decision about when, where, how, and what to duplicate.

The fact is that you can start a second, separate business in a new market or enhance your existing affiliate business by becoming a product creator. If you choose to create a product of your own, then you add this into the backend of your existing affiliate business! This method is actually at the heart of how I started pushing my income to massive levels. So, let's take a look at duplication from the product-creator angle first.

MOVING INTO PRODUCT CREATION

You can survey your list to find out what products your subscribers might be interested in, and then either locate those as affiliate products or create them yourself. Asking your list what they want is the easiest way to deliver a solution that will be mutually profitable. In other words, your list will tell you what they want to buy. They'll tell you what solutions they need. This works out great because you'll have a lot of your list presold on the product before you even offer it.

> *Asking your list what they want is the easiest way to deliver a solution that will be mutually profitable.*

In order to survey your list, you first need to set up an account with a free online survey company like http://www.surveymonkey.com or http://www.freeonlinesurveys.com. Let's say that your niche market is weight loss. Here are some questions you could ask your list:

1) Which would you rather learn: how to eat right or how to exercise?

2) Would you rather have a book of healthy recipes or an actual meal-planning, how-to guide?

3) If you answered "how to exercise" in question #1, would you rather learn about high-impact aerobic exercise or low-impact exercise?

4) In 500 words or less, describe your most pressing weight-loss issue.

5) If a book were available that answered all of your questions, would you purchase it?

6) How much would you expect to pay for such a book?

The answers your subscribers give you to these types of questions can help you locate the right affiliate product to offer or create your own information product solution just for them. As a general rule, it is best to offer your subscribers some kind of freebie in exchange for taking the survey. When you've set it up, you'd send them an e-mail like this:

Hi First Name,

I need your help. I'm trying to come up with a brand-new weight-loss guide that will blow all others right out of the water! But I need *your* help to do it.

Would you be willing to take a quick, five-minute survey to tell me what your biggest questions are when it comes to losing weight? If so, I'll return the favor by giving you a copy of "100 Low-Fat Recipes." It's normally a $37 report, but you get it FREE just for filling out the survey at this link:

http://www.linktoyoursurvey.com

Thanks a million!

Your Name

ANALYZING SURVEY RESPONSE AND CREATING YOUR FIRST REAL INFORMATION PRODUCT

Once you've collected enough survey data and narrowed down a topic for your product, it's time to create it. Your product doesn't have to be a masterpiece; it just needs to cover your subscribers' main questions and be good enough to sell. Depending on the subject matter, you might find that your first product can be as simple as a fifteen-page report.

Now, you can create the product on your own, or you can speed the process up by hiring someone to do it for you or even buying some private label rights content. Product creation can be a very rewarding and innovative process, but I understand that many newbies have difficulty with it. Therefore, we're going to run through some surefire methods for creating products at lightning speed.

You have to have an actual product idea in mind before you can create it. This requires brainstorming and research, but one of the easiest places to start is by "stealing" other people's ideas! Let's be clear: I'm not suggesting that you rip off someone else's product or copy it word for word. Instead, think of all the products you've seen up until now that made you say to yourself, "I wish I had thought of that!" Then, see if you can come up with your own unique twist on the same theme or idea … or create a better product. Or you can simply create a "companion" product. Let's say someone has come up with a good method for training dogs, and they've even named it after themselves, for example, "The Chia Method for Well-Behaved Dogs." You could create a spin-off product like "Teach Your Dogs Tricks Super Fast Using the Chia Method." We do this all of the time in the Internet- marketing niche. One month someone will come out with a product like Google Cash and, before you know it, that idea gets followed

I recommend looking to current hot sellers for inspiration.

up with a slew of other Google Adwords, how-to products like Google Profits, Adwords Secrets, etc.

So, I recommend looking to current hot sellers for inspiration. Usually all it takes is a simple change or two on style and focus to come up with your own unique version of a hot-selling information product. Another place you can look to for ideas is in the products being advertised by pay-per-click advertisers. When you're doing market research, make sure to visit all of the sponsored listings to see what products are being sold. You can "steal" more ideas this way. You can also identify gaps in the market place.

For example, I just went and typed "candle making" into Google. Every single sponsor ad on the first-page results is selling candle-making supplies. Why not an e-book on candle making? Why not a complete home-study course with DVDs? You see, the PPC advertisers will give you an indication of how diversified the marketplace is in terms of product offerings. You'll often find gaps where a market is slanting to one type of product offering or one type of product format over another. It's the perfect place for you to sneak in.

You can also generate product ideas by reading market-specific articles. Let's cruise over to an article directory. How about http://www.findarticles. com? I'm going to enter "Italian cooking" and see what comes up:

- "Quick and Easy Italian Cooking" (a press release for a new book)

- "Bowled Over: a Rustic, Inviting Meal Based on Italian Ingenuity" The summary beneath this listing catches my attention:

Thrifty Italian cooks have long been known for their inventive ways with leftovers, and stale bread in particular has inspired a number of famous dishes.

Hmm. Could I create something using "quick and easy Italian leftovers"? What about coming up with some crazy ways to wrap leftovers into a pizza sandwich? Let's keep reading:

- Say Cheese! Diet Strategy: Boost Your Calcium Intake, Add Protein and Lose Weight by Cooking with Lower Fat Versions of This Dairy Favorite ...

I can see a lot of different products that could spin out of this idea, can you? You could create any of these:

- "All Italian Atkins Diet Recipes"

- "Strong Bones for Life: 10 Ways to Boost Your Calcium Intake for Maximum Health!"

- "Less Meat, More Protein: How to Maximize Protein Intake on a Vegetarian Diet"

- "Dairy Lover's Dream: 100 Low-Fat Dairy Dessert Recipes"

See? Four product ideas already, and some of them have helped me to target additional mini markets that might be profitable!

Likewise, you can get product ideas from news and current events. Using the news for product ideas breaks down two ways:

1) Identify markets and generate ideas based on current news.

2) Search for stories related to a market you've already identified.

After doing a quick search over at Yahoo! News, I saw the usual stories about accidents, crimes, politics, etc., then moved down to the "Most Popular Stories" and "Most E-mailed

You can get product ideas from news and current events.

Stories" categories. There was one headline that caught my attention right away: "Quitting Smoking Boosts Weight by 21 Pounds." I clicked through and read the article. It was reporting on the results of a recent study. Although it has long been known that most people gain weight after they quit smoking, the assumption was that the weight gain was around ten to fifteen pounds. The new research indicates that it's closer to twenty-one pounds—which is a lot to pack on for most people. Even if you don't look like you've gained much weight, you can usually feel it, and of course, you'll have the hassle of going up a couple of pants sizes.

When you see a news report like this, that bulb in your brain should light up! There's definitely an information product lurking here. What if you can put together an e-book that helps prevent smoking-cessation-related weight gain? The data's got to be out there somewhere. You could even interview a local expert or doctor in your town to compile the tips.

What if you've decided you want to create a video product but aren't sure how to present your information? You can snag some ideas from:

- Google Videos (http://video.google.com)

- You Tube (http://www.youtube.com)

- Revver (http://www.revver.com)

- iFilm (http://www.ifilm.com/viralvideo)

These are some of the top, free video distribution sites online today. Many of the viral videos your friends forward to you start their journey getting passed around on these sites. The really neat thing is that most of these sites have converted the videos into Flash .swf files that stream right into your browser—there's no file downloading or waiting. As for the content you'll find, it's a real mix. There are wacky and crazy videos, music videos, commercials, and even short documentaries. You can also run searches on your key phrases to see what comes up, as the videos are tagged with descriptive keywords. See if you can find some videos relevant to your market, and start taking notes. What's popular? How are people rating the videos? What feedback are they getting?

Online groups and forums are another goldmine of product ideas. Let me share a very powerful tip with you about this now: *Always go to where your market hangs out.*

always go to where your market hangs out. Whether you're researching or advertising—you've got to put yourself in front of your audience, and there's no better way to do that than find their hiding places. Groups and forums are a wealth of information because they are the places where your market comes just to talk, ask questions, commiserate, and generally connect with others of the same interests. When you go into a target forum, start by reviewing about three months' worth of threads. Take note of the following:

1) What topics come up repeatedly?

2) What types of questions do people ask?

3) Do you see any desires expressed for certain solutions? "I wish I could find …," or "Why hasn't someone come up with a way to …?"

Once you've located a good handful of forums that are active and seem to have a lot of passionate discussion flying around, go ahead and join those forums. Introduce yourself as just a regular Joe first. Don't go in with any big sales or marketing speech. Make helpful posts of your own and let people get to know you—then you can start asking questions.

Bring up the fact that you'd like to create a solution for the group members. Ask people to give you a list of their most pressing questions and problems. You can do this via a direct posting or you could have a link to a survey in your signature, something like:

> Interested in a free e-book about [niche]? Come grab your copy of [title of your lead generating e-book], valued at $30, for FREE just for taking my survey at:

> http://www.addressofyoursurvey.com

That technique is a one-two punch because you can snag some subscribers to your autoresponder, get your questions answered, and build up goodwill!

CREATING YOUR PRODUCT IN TWENTY-FOUR HOURS OR LESS

Now that we've discussed some ways to brainstorm for product ideas, let's look at how to go about creating your product. We want this to be both easy and fast. It may sound like a tall order, but it can be done. Now, there is a method to this. In order to create a *quality* product in a short amount of time, there are two goals you need to focus on:

1) Concise but powerful and value-packed information

2) Easy packaging with emphasis on high perceived value

What this means is that you'll want to get the content for your information product in very tight chunks. So the bulk of your work will involve reviewing the content, and then splitting it up quickly into all the components involved in your offer:

1) Main product content

2) Content for the backend and midlevel

3) Content for the bonuses

This may require sticking with just one product format or it may mean using multiple formats, for example, a video product as the main package with e-books to fill up the backend and bonuses.

OK, without further ado, let's move right into the product formats available to you and discuss the merits of each one relative to speed, and the tactics necessary to create them.

- **Audio interviews**

  Audio interviews can be done quickly. You can either have someone interview you or locate an expert and interview them by phone or in person if time permits. All you have to do is record the interview and put the audio file into MP3 format. This is an *instant* product.

- **Podcasting**

  Podcasting requires some technical expertise, so use this one only if you know you can set things up quickly. A podcast is basically the same thing as streaming audio but delivered via a feed, similar to the way blog updates can be delivered via RSS. The customer downloads your podcast to her MP3 player. There's extra perceived value here, and there's also a way to buy yourself a little extra time. Let's say you need a couple more days to fill out your product and create some extra products to go along with it. What you'd do in this case is package your product as a subscription. In other words, you set up a Web site and have people pay to be on your podcasting feed. You can start getting advance sales on this before your first podcast even goes out. Better yet, instead of one-time payments, you'll develop a recurring income with this that's super easy to maintain. Just keep creating new audio products via the interview method!

- **Video tutorials**

  Video tutorials can be put together a couple of different ways. Let's say that your tutorial involves showing people how to do market research online or how to use a program like Photoshop. You can capture your computer screen as you walk through the process, step by step. All you need is screen capture software. The software that almost everyone uses for this is called Camtasia Studio, and you can find it here: http://www.camtasiastudio.com. The other way to create tutorials is use your own Web cam or handheld video camera. This method is fast if you're experienced with this sort of thing or have a video-savvy friend who can help you out.

  The only caveat I would attach is this: if you're concerned about production quality and you don't think you can put together a good product quickly, then you'll need to choose another format for your product. This really becomes a concern only when you're creating products that can't be demonstrated on your own desktop. For example, if you wanted to create a tutorial showing people how to do yoga, you'd have a lot more work involved in creating the video.

- **Software**

  Maybe you'd like to create a software product. You can have this done quickly by a freelance coder over at places like:

http://www.elance.com/

http://www.rentacoder.com/

http://www.scriptlance.com/

Now, with that said, you aren't going to come up with the next Windows XP on a rapid-development timeline. In order to get a piece of software created quickly, it needs to be a relatively simple program. In fact, it would be best if your software was some kind of script program in PHP or Javascript. These are the kinds of things a good coder can whip out in an afternoon.

- **RESALE RIGHTS AND PRIVATE- LABEL RIGHTS**
  First, let's talk about the difference between resale rights and private-label rights. Resale rights grant you the right to resell a product. However, they do not allow you to present that product as your own. In other words, the original producer of that product retains authorship. Private-label rights allow you to sell a product as if *you* wrote it yourself. You get the raw product, and you slap your name on it.

  Rights products are by far the fastest information products to get going from a sales perspective because all the work has been done for you. Even better, you'll typically find that multiple products have been created for a given niche, and this will give you plenty of material for filling up the backend and bonuses. In order to obtain these products, you'll have to spend some money. There are offers out there where you get to download a whole package of premade products, and there membership sites that provide a constantly updating storehouse of new rights products. I'd recommend going the membership route simply because you'll have access to multiple niche topics.

- **SHORT REPORTS AND WHITE PAPERS**

  Your information product doesn't have to be a nine-hundred-page novel! People have made hundreds of thousands of dollars on short reports … sometimes no longer than twelve pages! Your report can be your main product, or it can even be a lead generator. Let's say you whip out a twelve-page report and sell it for $12. That won't be a ton of profit at first, but you'll have built a database of existing customers to market to when you come out with an even bigger, better product.

  OK, now you're probably wondering, "What's a white paper? And how does that differ from a report?" Well, for our purposes here, it really doesn't differ that much. Using the term *white paper* can add perceived value to the product. However, if you look at some of the traditional definitions of white paper, you also get product focus and packaging ideas. Here's the definition I found online that I think fits best: "an authoritative report issued by an organization" (dictionary.com). This could prove really useful if you're targeting "new entry" consumers of a market—for example, new parents, first-time car buyers, freshmen college students, recent graduates of professional schools, new real estate investors, etc. Now, I hate to put it this way, but it's kind of an opportunity for you to get off easy. It's so simple to put together the basics when your goal is to educate someone completely new to a given subject. You don't have to go into the finer points at all, just the ABCs!

- **JOINT-VENTURE PRODUCT CREATION**

  You can create products with your joint- venture partners. When you're doing market research, you'll find sites that you can team up with. A good example of when and how to use this is if you've got specialized knowledge but aren't good at the technical aspects of creating e-books, videos, etc. So, find a joint-venture partner who is good at it—someone who's already done it. Team up and share your specialized knowledge with them, while they turn that knowledge into the finished product. Then, you can both promote the product together and share the profits! It's super quick, too, to use a joint-venture partner for creating products out of interviews and teleseminars. Set up a coregistration event and have your JV partner interview you, then you interview your JV partner. Record the event and wrap it up into an audio product or e-book transcript. The possibilities are endless.

- **THEMED COLLECTION**

  Let's say you've gathered up tons of content for your market. You've got so much, in fact, you could create dozens of products from it. Consider packaging it all as a themed collection. You can sell a themed collection as a one-off, or you can drip it out slowly. For example, maybe you've come across a thousand low-fat chocolate dessert recipes. This would be way too much for one product. So, you can create volumes:

  "100 Low-Fat Chocolate Desserts Volume 1"

  "100 Low-Fat Chocolate Desserts Volume 2"

… and so on. That would give you ten products! You could release one every other month or so. Other types of themed collections could be ranked in difficulty (basic, intermediate, advanced, etc.), time-based (retro, current, future, etc.), age-targeted (kids, teens, adults, etc.), progressive (level 1, level 2, level 3, etc.), or class-differentiated (students versus teachers, amateurs versus professionals, budget versus luxury, etc.).

- **E-CLASSES, TELESEMINARS, WEBINARS, ETC.**

  Sometimes the information you want to provide to your market is complex. Sometimes you need to be able to deliver information interactively or near real time. You can do this by setting up e-classes, telesiminars, and Webinars—any type of format where the customer has to come to you and interact in some way. This often involves structured course material as well as homework and question-and-answer sessions. If you want a really good example of this, check out http://www.richdreams.com or head over to http://www.scienceofgettingrich.net. Sign up for their newsletters. These two sites focus on wealth creation and prosperity coaching. It's a complex subject, and many of their customers and subscribers have questions on the material, even after reading it through several times.

  These merchants have solved that problem (and created tons of extra product/profit centers) by offering e-courses and teleseminars. The Rich Dreams folks, in particular, are very savvy at this, as they've broken down the material into several levels—and they turn almost every teleseminar into a new e-book or CD product! Part of what they've done is used the "themed collection" model. The basic introduction product of Rich Dreams is the e-book *I'm Rich Beyond My Wildest Dreams.* After customers digest this, they have the opportunity to expand their learning through two different e-courses: Quantum Selling and Quantum Marketing. And Rich Dreams is charging a premium for those classes. Roughly $1,500 for a seat in a six-week course. If you prefer to interact with your customers this way, it is a tactic you should seriously consider. You'll have much more control over when, where, and how you deliver content, and you'll be able to charge a lot more for it, too.

- **MEMBERSHIP SITE (CREATE AS YOU GO ALONG)**
Membership sites get you recurring income and a way to deliver product from one streamlined location. A script such as Lock Area Lite (http://www.locked-area.com/lite) will let you get a protected membership site set up quickly. You can roll out your first information product right way, then create more products and add them to the membership site as you go along. This is a time-tested packaging model. Customers love the sense of abundance and value they get from accessing quality products each month for one low fee.

- **PAID BLOG MEMBERSHIP (COMBINE BLOG + HIPCAST.COM)**
This is similar to the podcasting idea we discussed earlier, but you can use a really cool tool to expand the format of your offerings. The tool is called Hipcast (http://www.hipcast.com) and it lets you record and publish audio, video, and more, all online, and then post all of it to your blog. There aren't any out-of-the-box

solutions for paid blogs right now, but what you can do is use your blog platform to lock content away behind a registered member's area. (Most blog platforms have user-registration modules.) Then charge for registration, and send the username and password after payment is received. You might also be able to put your blog behind a membership script like Locked Area Lite, but I haven't tested this.

- **Raising perceived value**

  Perceived value is something wealthy marketers know all about. It is one of our little tricks that leaves the average person scratching his head and saying, "How did you get people to pay you $97 for a book?" You see, the person who doesn't understand perceived value is looking in the wrong direction! The product offer is never "just a book" or "just a piece of software." The value is in the information. The value is in the perception of high return on investment. The customer doesn't care how that information is presented; they just want access to that information right away because they see it as highly valuable. The only way format really has any influence is through toying with people's preconceived notions about offline costs. For example, when you add audio and video to a package, the perceived value jumps even more because the average person still has the idea that CDs and videos can be priced upward of $30 or more. That said, let's take a look at some packaging tricks that will help you up the value of your product in your potential customer's eyes.

  The **module system** is often used in home-study courses. Modules themselves are just ways of putting information into tightly focused categories for the purpose of structured learning. While similar to regular book chapters, modules are really beefier, more along the lines of college textbook chapters or the components of a complex computer program. Let me give you an example of a module system for a fictional product. We'll use a weight-loss program as our model.

The 10-Day Crash Diet

Module 1: Preparing Your Mind and Body

Part A: The Psychological Game

-How to visualize your 10-day goal

-Thought stopping and conquering negative messages

-Seeing food as your friend, not the enemy

-Get psyched about exercise

Part B: The Body Tune-Up

-Cleansing your system of toxins and why this is important

-The 48-hour cleansing recipe

-Time for more water

-Getting onto a deep sleep schedule

… and so on. Just imagine if you had a rather large information product. You could end up with ten to twenty modules or more!

Now, what does a customer say to himself when he sees a full listing of the modules on your sales letter? He says, "Wow! Look at all of that! I'm getting serious bang for my buck if I buy this, and it looks like it is organized well enough for me to get the most out of it."

The module system gives your customer a sense that your product is professional, high quality, and in depth. Every single item listed in your module outline is like a benefit. Not only that, every item is a curiosity booster. People will wonder, for example, "What's in the forty-eight-hour cleansing recipe?" "Can I really get excited about exercise?" And this is what you want. This literally skyrockets the perceived value of your product … and all you're really doing is using a good outline!

As noted earlier, **mixing your media** (for instance, adding audio and video to text) also helps to raise perceived value. People have a general idea about what things are supposed to cost offline, but they don't know just how cheaply you're producing your online content. If you were to go to a bookstore and buy a book, a CD, and a video, how much would it cost you? Let's say the paperback costs $19.95, the CD is $15.99, and the video is $30. The cash register rings you up $64.95 before sales tax.

Now, imagine you go online and you find "The Ultimate Real Estate Investing Package." It contains one main e-book, three bonus e-books, four video tutorials, and two audio interviews. It would be ridiculously easy to charge $64.95 for this—and completely realistic to charge up to $197 or more! Why? All of these products, if purchased offline, would likely cost you about $120–150. Now, add in some of your other "value" tactics into your sales letter, and you can tack on an extra $50 or more to the price.

- **GRAPHICS**

  Graphics go a long way toward increasing perceived value and inspiring more confidence in your customer. People love product images and screenshots. Graphics not only make your sales letter more professional looking, they give people a visual taste of your product. This is important. Remember that your customer has no way of touching your product before she downloads it. People do use their physical senses of touch, taste, sight, and sound when evaluating a purchase. You don't want to be the purveyor of the "invisible mystery product, which may or may not be any good, hiding behind a $97 price tag." So, whenever you can, use screenshots (especially for software products), e-book covers, box covers, "before" and "after" photos, photos on testimonials, and any other "use" or "results" graphics, for example, photos of dishes created from the recipes.

- **BONUSES**

  Bonuses, as you probably know, are *de rigueur* these days in the information-product industry. There's hardly a product out there that doesn't come with a bonus or two or ten. The perceived value equation here rests on the idea of over delivering. It is about giving the customer more for his money. It may not cost you anything to create the bonuses, but your customer sees it as getting a two-for-one special. You can also think of it as a lot like buying a new car or computer. Whenever people buy such items with hefty price tags, there's a bit of anxiety going on. Potential buyer's remorse. Worries about whether they've gotten everything they need to use this big, expensive item they just spent a month's salary on to get. That's why merchants offer free accessories with such purchases. It's kind of like follow-up therapy. You buy a computer and you expect to get some free software and a mouse pad out of the deal. You buy a fancy mountain bike, and the bike shop throws in a free helmet, gloves, and a security lock. Make sense?

Adding relevant and valuable bonuses will always raise perceived value—and you need to explicitly lay out that value to the customers, as well. What I mean by this is you need to tell them what this bonus would normally cost if they were buying it separately. Like so:

Bonus 1: How to Instantly Boost Your IQ ($67 value!)

Bonus 2: Tips, Tricks, and Tactics to Beat the SATs ($97 value!)

Bonus 3: How to Never Overdraft Your Bank Account Again (… priceless!)

Remember, too, to make sure that your bonuses are relevant and complementary. Each bonus should fit in with the theme of the main product.

- **CREATE THE BACKEND FIRST AND BREAK IT UP**
  Backend products are follow-up products that you can offer to existing customers. The backend is where additional sales and

profits can be made. But you don't have to limit yourself to the backend. You'll also want to break your products up for midlevel and one-time offers. One-time offers, for example, provide a way to raise the price tag without extra work on the sales letter. You get your customer convinced of the value of your front-end product. When he goes to order, you present him with the option to tack on this other product for an extra fee. He's already in the process of buying, so there's a good chance he'll go ahead with this. People often reason this way: "Well, if I'm already spending $50, what's an extra $20?" So, when you are putting your information product together, gather up enough content so that you can break it up into pieces. Break it up for each of your objectives. Pull out the content that will create your main product, set it aside for a moment, and start compiling the remaining content into super fast backend offers, bonuses, and lead generators. This way, you have all of your leads and sales tools in place, even if you don't have the main product finished yet.

LAUNCHING YOUR PRODUCT AND CLONING YOURSELF

This step of the blueprint will have you setting the stage for viral traffic and promotion. The key to this piece of the puzzle is in setting up your own affiliate program. Using affiliate programs as traffic boosters is not a new idea. What's new, under my system, is the special focus put on turning your customers into affiliates. You're going to integrate affiliate sign-up into your sales funnel. As you read the forthcoming steps, it will be clear how this takes place and why it makes such a difference. The first thing you must do is repeat the setup steps used in creating your offer. In order to launch your first product, you will need the following:

- A new domain name just for that product

- A sales page for the product

- Another opt-in page you can use to capture leads for follow-ups on that product

- A separate opt-in list within your autoresponder account for that product

- Payment processing

For payment processing, I recommend most newbies start out with Clickbank. It is easy to sign up. You are charged just a one-time fee of about $50 to get your sales page approved. Also, Clickbank has a ready-made affiliate program that is automatically associated with your product once your account is set up. This is vital, because you want to make it as easy as possible to turn your customers into affiliates!

The reason it's so easy is because Clickbank allows affiliate marketers to set up global accounts. In other words, when someone creates an affiliate account with Clickbank, they have the ability to promote any product in the Clickbank marketplace, not just your product. This is because each merchant is assigned a special Clickbank hoplink that looks like this:

http://AFFILIATEID.MERCHANTID.hop.clickbank.net/

Let's say that you're selling a dog-training product, and you decide to use this theme in your merchant ID name—"train-dogs." The hoplink that

Clickbank will assign your account will look like this:

http://AFFILIATEID.train-dogs.hop.clickbank.net/

This URL is set to redirect to your sales page while tracking the visitor on behalf of the affiliate who replaces "AFFILIATEID" with her own Affiliate ID. So, for example, an affiliate with the ID of "janedoe" would promote your product with her affiliate link like this:

janedoe.train-dogs.hop.clickbank.net/

Make sense?

Now, let's continue with how and why you want to set things up this way. One of the things you want to include and emphasize in your sales letter is the business opportunity customers will have in promoting your product as an affiliate. You want to make this opportunity appear to be a part of the product itself. This may seem a little strange at first if you're selling a non-Internet-marketing product—but it really isn't too much of a stretch. Remember: you're selling more than just one product. You've got midlevel and backend opportunities integrated into your sales funnel. This gives not just you, but also your affiliates, an opportunity to earn income on three different levels.

Anyone who is interested in your product is also likely to be interested in making a profit from it. The only thing is that many of your customers will be new to the idea of affiliate marketing. In essence, what you're really doing is introducing these customers to the concept of affiliate marketing itself. You're also going to give them the necessary tools to make promoting your product easy, step by step.

CREATING INCENTIVE BY PAYING COMMISSIONS ON ALL LEVELS

When setting up your program, you'll want to pay your affiliates on all levels: front-end, midlevel (if any), and backend. This will give them plenty of incentive to promote your product. Remember, for every level an affiliate makes a sale, you've made a sale, too. So, there's no need to be greedy. If you feel you want to bump up your own profits a little more, you can always add your own affiliate products on the backend, keeping those commissions for yourself. Setting up this step of the system should be pretty straightforward, though you may have to do some creative hacking in some cases.

For example, with Clickbank you technically can't sell multiple products from the same account—that is, unless you implement one of the commercial scripts designed to get around Clicbank's one-product rule. For a more in-depth discussion on that issue, see http://www.clickbankguide.com/multipleaccounts.htm. Alternatively, you could have multiple accounts for each product. This shouldn't affect the crediting of your affiliates, because their Affiliate IDs will already be on the customer's computer from the initial referral. The main reason I point out this Clickbank issue to you is the cost involved in opening multiple accounts.

MAKING SURE YOUR SALES FUNNEL IS SET UP CORRECTLY

This will save you the most time. Don't launch until your product funnel is set up correctly. The funnel looks like this:

- Front-end product (your main product)

- Midlevel products (your one-time offers)

- Backend products (your related offers, affiliate products, etc.)

Now, why set all of this up first? Glad you asked. It's all about timing and organization. Let's say you intend to have a one-time offer on the midlevel. However, you're in a hurry and you decide to launch without putting it into place, telling yourself, "Well, I'll do it later." Does "later" ever come? How much profit have you lost while you put it off? Might you mess up your main sales letter in the process of going in and futzing with your shopping cart and payment processor once you finally get around to adding in your one-time offer? These are the kinds of things you need to get out of the way from the start. If you save it all for later, you risk not only interrupting your current sales funnel but also having your new offers fall flat.

Don't launch until your product funnel is set up correctly.

Everything needs to be there when the customer purchases, when he's in buying mode and paying attention, when he's excited about his new purchase. This is the time when he is most likely to take you up on anything else you offer him. If you wait until long after the fact, however, you can expect the response to be lukewarm. So, get your sales funnel set up before you launch. Work out all the kinks and bugs, and then you'll be ready to set sail.

CREATING A STRONG SALES LETTER

You need a strong sales letter. If you aren't good at writing sales letters, hire someone to do it for you. You can find some decent copywriters on freelance sites such as http://www.elance.com and http://www.rentacoder.

com. You can also copy elements from sales letters you've read that made you want to buy. Study them and try to pinpoint how the author used pacing, tone, style, and formatting to draw your attention where she desired. Make sure your sales letter has all the components of solid copywriting in place:

1) A killer headline

2) Focus on benefits over features

3) Good graphics

4) Focus on the customer (the word "you" appears more than the word "I")

5) Bonuses with estimated value listed

6) Powerful closing offer and guarantee

For a quick crash course on writing good copy, check out these "20 Tips to Writing a Strong Sales Letter" (http://www.cheap-copy.com/sales-letter. html). Once you've completed your letter, make sure you run it through spell-check. Invite friends, relatives, JV partners, etc. to review, edit, and critique the letter. They'll spot things that you've missed and give you their feedback on how strong your message really is.

LAUNCHING YOUR PRODUCT AND TURNING EVERY CUSTOMER INTO AN AFFILIATE

This is where your autoresponder is going to come in handy again. What you're going to do is build your customer list after the sale and use that list to recruit affiliates from your customer base. Remember that you'll be promoting your affiliate program as an inbuilt part of your product. Therefore, it is only logical to get your customers registered for this right away.

You'll do this by presenting the customer with an affiliate registration form just after he completes the sale and reaches your thank-you page. This form is really just the subscription box for your autoresponder. Keep in mind, you've got two different lists you need to set up in your autoresponder—the leads list, where you collect opt-ins from visitors to your sales page, and the list dedicated to your existing customers. This second list is the list you'll point to on the affiliate registration page. Here is a screenshot showing how this is done:

As you can see, this list will serve a number of purposes. Once customers are registered, they're sent the link to download the front-end product, just in case they miss the main download page the first time for whatever reason. They'll also receive any future product upgrades or offers via this list. Now, this list will also be your link to affiliate recruitment. You can follow up with your customers about your affiliate programs right away. Here's a sample e-mail you might send:

Dear First Name,

Thanks again for your purchase of "Dog-Training Secrets of the Masters!" Just in case you missed it, here is the link to download your product:

http://www.downloadlink.com/

First name, how would you like to earn some extra $$ by selling "Dog-Training Secrets of the Masters!" yourself? Well, you can! In fact, just minutes from now you could be on your way to making back the cost of the book plus a whole lot more. All you need to do is sign up as my affiliate, and you can begin promoting right away. In order to join my affiliate program, you first need to sign up as a Clickbank affiliate through this link: http://www.clickbank.com/accountSignup.htm

Once you've created your account and chosen your Affiliate ID, all you need to do is insert your ID into this link: http://AFFILIATEID.train-dogs.hop.clickbank.net/ where AFFILIATEID = the ID that you chose at sign-up. That's it! Use that link to promote "Dog-Training Secrets of the Masters!", and you'll earn commissions on THREE different levels …

To Your Success,

Your Name

It is important you explain to them all the levels of your sales funnel. Your affiliates will have the opportunity to earn commissions on the front-end, midlevel (if any), and backend. Although you'll need to set up Clickbank accounts to handle payment processing for each level, you will not have to set up separate affiliate links for those levels. The reason is that the visitor will already be cookied with that affiliate's ID from your main sales page. As long as that visitor doesn't clear his cookies, your affiliate will get credit for midlevel and backend sales, even if those products are being sold from a different Web address with a different Clickbank hoplink.

FOLLOWING UP WITH AFFILIATES AND ENCOURAGING THEM

You should continue to follow up with your customer list about the affiliate program. In order to maximize participation, you need to send more than one or two e-mails about the program. Your goal should be, first, to continue to encourage your customers to take part in the affiliate program (if they haven't done so already). Second, you'll want your existing affiliates to know about any changes or additions to your affiliate program. Increasing participation can be as simple as sending an enthusiastic "Good job!" to your affiliates. For example, let's say your sales have been through the roof due to your affiliates' efforts. You could send them an e-mail like this:

Dear First Name,

Sales have been crazy this month at "Dog-Training Secrets," and I owe it all to my affiliates! You guys are doing a great job! Some of you will be getting really big checks soon. :-) In fact, I know at least one of my affiliates made over $10,000 in commissions this month!

Since things are going so well, I want to give you even more incentive to promote "Dog-Training Secrets."

For THIS MONTH ONLY, commissions are going up on ALL LEVELS. That's right, instead of the usual commission structure you're used to, I'm giving you a fat raise by boosting your commissions to:

- 75 percent on the front-end

- 85 percent on the mid level

- 90 percent on the backend

You're getting a 30 percent boost in commissions on each level! It's just my way of saying thank you for being one of my valued affiliates.

Also, if you haven't yet signed up as an affiliate, this should give you extra incentive to take action. ;-) You can sign up here:

http://www.clickbank.com/accountSignup.htm

Doing things this way not only encourages your existing affiliates, it also motivates more of your customers to take part in your affiliate program. Lastly, remember to follow up with your affiliates about any new tools or resources you've put together for them. You should periodically send out a reminder link to your affiliate resources page.

MOTIVATING AFFILIATES INTO INSTANT ACTION

If you want to see your profits skyrocket, you need to really motivate your affiliates to take action. You see, a lot of people are intrigued by the idea of affiliate marketing, but they don't truly understand how to get started.

They sign up for various programs and then play around at them, never really getting serious or earning any money. As an affiliate program owner, you want to prevent this as much as possible. The way to do this is by making it as easy as possible for every affiliate, especially newbie affiliates, to take action right away. There are two things you can do to ensure that every affiliate, from the beginner to the pro, is gung-ho about promoting your product:

- Offer attractive commissions

- Give them the tools for success

First, your commission structure should be generous. High commissions are one of the main things that motivate affiliates to promote a product. If you want them to put in their own time and money into advertising your product, you need to make it worthwhile for them. I recommend offering at least 50 percent commissions on all levels, even more on the front-end. For example, you might offer 75 percent on the front-end and 50 percent on the midlevel and backend.

Next, you need to give them the right tools. To do this, you need to create an affiliate toolkit, and make that toolkit available from a special affiliate resources page on your site.

What is an affiliate toolkit? Essentially, it is a collection of helpful promotional material your affiliates can use to promote your product. Here are some of the things you can include in an affiliate toolkit:

- A list of keywords your affiliates can use to promote your product in the pay-per-click engines, like Google Adwords

- A full set of follow-up e-mails your affiliates can send to their own lists

- Solo ads your affiliates can run in e-zines

- Classified ads your affiliates can place at classifieds sites

- Rebrandable e-books or reports your affiliates can give away to their lists

- Product images, banner advertisements, or other graphics for your product

- Some text-link ads (e.g., for Google Adwords)

Basically, what you want to give them is the same kind of promotional material you use to promote your site. This is especially important for helping newbie affiliates, who may not know where to start and need some hand-holding. You need to make things 1-2-3 easy for them. Giving them a cache of prewritten material does just that.

In order to deliver this toolkit, all you need to do is upload it to your site and create a Web page where affiliates can access the material. Just set up a new directory on your site, like so:

http://www.yoursite.com/affiliates/

and direct your affiliates to that page. Make sure you repeat all the important information about the program there (e.g., commission structure, format of their Clickbank hoplink, etc.). You can also direct them to other resources that might help them, such as link cloakers, Web hosting, autoresponders, etc.

FINE-TUNING AND CREATING YOUR OWN SYSTEM

After reviewing your existing model, you may come up with a whole list of things you'd like to change. What would you like to do faster? Is there a way to cut costs? Did you find one form of advertising more effective than another? These are the issues that come into play when you're fine-tuning this whole process into your own system. You look for what works, as well as any areas of weakness that need to be addressed. For example, let's say that writing follow-up e-mails is a real problem for you, but you're really great at writing reports, and you find that those pull sales in even better. You could decide to focus on using reports as one of your primary tools in the future—or you could choose to work on your follow-up copywriting skills.

It's all about determining what the most effective process is for you.

Likewise, maybe you've discovered that you really enjoy creating products. You could choose to focus on that, and switch your affiliate marketing into a tool for your backend system. It's all about determining what the most effective process is for you.

AUTOMATION—PUTTING YOUR BUSINESS(ES) ON COMPLETE AUTOPILOT

Automation is a required step in duplicating your business model into new markets. As you've seen throughout this book, you can set things to run mostly hands-free once you've created your sales funnel and tied it to your autoresponder. Everything from product delivery to affiliate sign-up can be automated.

To review, here are the key things to do:

- Use your autoresponder to automate lead capture, follow-up, product delivery, and affiliate sign-up.

- Use Clickbank to handle payment processing and manage your affiliate program.

- Use your affiliate links to drive customers through both front- and backend offers on affiliate products.

- As a product owner, turn your customers into an army of affiliates in order to generate massive amounts of traffic, hands-free.

That's it! Once you've linked all the pieces of your sales funnel together, you just need to send traffic to your offer. Your autoresponder will deliver your content, handle page redirects, and deliver product-download links.

MANAGING YOUR BUSINESS

Daily business management really comes down to three core areas:

1) Money

2) People

3) Tools and time

Time is likely your most valuable asset, so let's address that first. Creating a daily management plan will really help you out. You need to have a set list of marketing tasks you can refer to each day. Write down everything you need to get done. It's important that you write it down—get it out of your head and onto paper. This clears your mind and frees up your focus.

Creating a daily management plan will really help you out.

Connect each task with an intended purpose or anticipated result. Try to describe briefly the intended successful outcome of that task. Here's a sample plan:

9:00 AM—Focus on building free traffic:

  a. Submit press release

  b. Submit article

  c. Finish working out details of JV with so and so

11:00 AM—Get ready for PPC campaign

  a. Sort through my key phrases and pull out most targeted

  b. Write first set of advertisements

  c. Log in to Adwords and start keying in the information

If you find yourself getting bogged down with a lot of what-ifs and vague feelings about tasks, then make sure you get them out of your head by writing them down. Then ask yourself, "Is the task actionable right now? Yes or no?" If the answer is no, then toss it and move on. Put these tips into place, and I think you'll find that your work day is very well structured and your promotional efforts will yield fruit much more quickly.

The second crucial element to managing your business is consistency and commitment.

The second crucial element to managing your business is consistency and commitment. It's obvious, but do you really know why? Let me tell you what I've seen happen in the past. An aspiring newbie comes up with a great idea and creates a killer information product. However, he hasn't sat down for any goal planning, nor has he laid out a definite strategy. The product launches, but something isn't finished. So the product gets pulled back while he works on "this other piece I forgot about." The product never really gets off the ground, and motivation is lost. You see, you can't just toss up your sales page, send out an ad or two, and expect the money to start rolling in. Promotion requires consistent effort. You've got to build on your efforts every single day. This means doing the following:

1) Watching over your PPC campaigns and tweaking them on a consistent basis. Change up your ads. Add or subtract key phrases, bid prices, etc.

2) Continually write articles and submit them to article directories.

3) Consistently seek out new e-zines, Web sites, blogs, etc., that offer targeted advertising.

4) Create new content and newsletters monthly for your current subscribers. You've got to keep your leads interested.

5) Never let more than a week go by where your hands are off your business. If all you do is just one promotional tactic per day, you're still in the ballpark. Even this amount of effort will reap results for you.

So stay committed and focused. You've already come this far and worked this hard on your product; it would be a waste to do things any other way.

The third secret of management is to save both time and money by leveraging your traffic. Traffic, whether free or paid, is gold. It's the steam that runs the engine of your business. Leveraging your traffic means getting a feedback loop going so that any given visitor to one part of your sales funnel can be channeled toward yet another part of

Save both time and money by leveraging your traffic.

your funnel. This could mean channeling them to an opt-in form, another sales page, a backend offer, or even one of your other product sites. The point is that once you've grabbed that visitor, you do everything possible *not* to let her go. There are two primary ways of doing this:

1) Send all your traffic to your lead-capture page first.

2) Make sure that both your lead-capture page and your sales page have "exit" pop-ups.

If he tries to leave, however, you need a way to grab his attention one more time. An exit pop-up will allow you to do this.

Your visitor is either going to subscribe, buy, or leave. If he buys or subscribes, you've nabbed him! If he tries to leave, however, you need a way to grab his attention one more time. An exit pop-up will allow you to do this. Let's say he sees your lead-capture page but decides he doesn't want to subscribe. This is bad, because now he could walk away for good and never see your sales page. What do you do? Have your sales page come up in an exit pop-up when he clicks away. The same principle applies to your sales page. Your visitor decides she's not interested for some reason and tries to leave. You hit her with a pop-up that's got a special offer or maybe a time-sensitive one-time offer. Now you've captured her attention one more time and you've got a second chance to leverage profits out of her.

Remember: all of your traffic represents an expenditure of either time or money. It's sweat and equity that you've put in. Really, you've put in far more effort than your visitor. So you've got to use leverage in order to even the score. Otherwise you end up having to double your efforts, when—if you'd thought to use a pop-up or some other traffic funnel—you could have redoubled your existing results.

Being a good money manager means watching both what you're earning and what you're spending. You need to know how much profit you've earned for the day as well as what you spent to generate that income. Another thing you should consider is setting up a bank account dedicated to your business. Especially at tax time, you're going to want to know the details of your business-related expenditures and income. It is much harder to do this if you're mixing business transactions into your personal account!

People are the reason you're in business.

People are the reason you're in business. It's very important that you stay on top of customer-service issues. Check your e-mail each day to find out whether someone has written to you with a question, problem, refund request, etc. People are impressed by speed. The faster you're able to respond to a customer, the more they're going to trust you. Other people can also be very valuable in the overall growth of your business. It is important that you learn how to network with other marketers and business owners, as this will present you with many opportunities to share resources and ideas.

Focus on seeking joint ventures, super affiliates, and market leaders. When you research your market, you'll find some sites stand out as leaders in the industry. These sites and their owners make excellent joint-venture partners, and they are also super affiliates. You see, due to their position in the industry, they have the resources you need: traffic, subscribers, and contacts to other potential super affiliates and JV partners. Contact them and work out a deal. Offer them a higher commission percentage. Offer them free product or access to your list in exchange for their help. This is going to multiply your efforts and your reach all across the board, because you'll have even more traffic flooding in to your site and more eyeballs checking out your affiliate program.

Turn your competitors into your joint-venture partners. Some of those same market leaders will be your competitors. Don't be afraid to approach them, though! You can easily turn a competitor into a partner with the right incentives. It's all in how you present the deal to them. Find out what you have in common. Target the areas where you can both mutually benefit each other, rather than compete with each other.

Turn your competitors into your joint-venture partners.

As for **managing your tools**, it is important to make sure your Web site, autoresponder, and advertising accounts are running as intended. Although this won't happen every day, there will be times when something breaks. For instance, your PPC ads might stop running due to technical problems (on the service end) or due to problems with your account. Other times, your Web site might go down unexpectedly, or your autoresponder host could have a server crash. While these situations can be a headache, every marketer will face them at some point. That's why you need to stay on top of things, and catch any problems before they get out of hand. Also, it is a very good idea to back up your work. Make sure you have copies on your hard drive of all of your materials so you can easily reupload them if anything happens.

DOING SOMETHING EVERY DAY!

Your business won't build itself overnight. You must do something every day. Take focused action. Part of a solid business plan is having a daily action plan within your long-term strategy. It doesn't have to mean a lot of work—it just has to be something that moves you a step closer to your goals. You might pick any or a combination of these:

- Write and submit one new article for traffic

- Post to a forum

- Write a new report to send to your list as a surprise gift

- Tweak your copy

- Research more market key phrases

- Read up on the latest market-related news

- Learn a new skill

Whatever you do, make sure you keep your momentum going. Success is a matter of degree; each step you take, no matter how small, will pay off for you in the long run.

REINVESTING YOUR PROFITS

Your profits give you the power of leverage. Leverage is a measure of how much you can do with what you have. It is about your resources. So, when your first business becomes profitable, you're going to be in an even better place than you were when you first began. You'll have more money available, and more money means more options.

Reinvest your profits in a way that either improves upon your existing business or facilitates the process of starting a new one (duplication). You can get yourself more education, more tools, more time—whatever you need. For example, you might invest in the following:

- Expanding your PPC campaigns

- Buying more advertising space on market Web sites

- Creating offline advertising material

- Creating a new product

- Grabbing a new piece of software, an e-book, a subscription—anything that will help your business

- Buying new leads

- Hiring a professional to redesign your Web site, if needed

- Having a pro copywriter tweak your sales material

- Buying up some resale rights or private-label products you can use as lead generators, list bonuses, or even backend offers

- Investing in any tools needed to start a new business

Any of the above (or more!) could be just what your business needs in order to move to the next level. Reinvesting your profits today can mean an even bigger return on income in the future.

CREATING YOUR OWN STREAMS OF PASSIVE INCOME

You can earn residual or passive income through your own products and services. In fact, I would highly recommend creating a recurring income business as soon as you reasonably can, because recurring income gives you leverage and it's another way of putting things on autopilot, depending on the nature of the product or service.

For example, let's say that you decided to create a set of professional Web-site templates to sell as your first product. You decide to sell them for $39.95 as a one-time download. Web templates are certainly an in-demand product, but why stop there? After all, it's a good bet that many of your customers will also be looking for a place to host their Web sites. You could make even more money per customer if you offered Web hosting as part of the total package. For instance, you could include a hosting account with each order of Web templates. Give your customer the first month of hosting for free, and then let them know they will be charged $15 per month for hosting after that. This is really easy to do if you purchase what is known as a "reseller" account with a good Web-hosting company. Many of these companies will allow you to rebrand the look and feel of the payment and hosting interface so that it looks like you're running your very own hosting company.

This is just an example to get you thinking about some possibilities. The point is for you to create a business where you get to charge the customer on a regular basis for an ongoing service. I wouldn't recommend technical services (like Web hosting) to most newbies, though. Instead, I would recommend creating some form of information-based membership site. Here are some of the products and services offered under this model:

- Newsletters, e-zines, magazines, newspapers, journals, etc.

- How-to content sites

- Resale rights sites

- Database services (lists of wholesalers, public-records searches, research databases, etc.)

- Multimedia content and services (dating sites, clipart or royalty-free images, music downloads, ringtones, screensavers, movie rentals, etc.)

- Product of the month: products delivered monthly by subscription. Typically includes things like chocolate, coffee, general groceries, seeds, small clothing items, etc.

These are the minimum requirements for a subscription/membership business model:

- Your own Web site

- A payment processor with the ability to receive recurring payments

- The ability to limit access to content/scripts to generate usernames/passwords and guard access to members' areas

- Access to enough content and/or products to maintain membership benefits

THE POWER OF MEMBERSHIP SITES: A CASE STUDY

Late in 2007, I launched a new membership site at http://www.SuperAffiliates.com. It is by far one of the most successful membership sites in the world, and it attracted over 3,500 members within four days. Here is a screenshot from the sales page:

Now, what exactly am I selling month after month with the Super Affiliates Inner Circle Membership? Quite simply, I am providing my members with turnkey niche affiliate businesses based on well-researched markets for which there are high-paying affiliate products and programs. Of course, I also include a boatload of training material to help them get started. Members have access to the training blueprint right away and access to each month's business kit as soon as it is available. So, my members learn not just how to be successful affiliate marketers, they also receive ready-made marketing packages to help them get started. The first affiliate kit was designed to help members promote multilevel-marketing affiliate programs, but the site is not focused strictly on business-opportunity programs. Members will also have the opportunity to promote affiliate products in niches such as guitar playing, golf, dog training, and so on. Each monthly kit includes the following tools to help members with their affiliate marketing efforts:

- A twenty-plus-page report they can give away to their opt-in lists
  as a means of preselling the affiliate products they want to promote

- A list of the top fifty keywords for the market

- A set of ten keyword-rich articles they can submit to article directories for traffic generation

- A set of ten prewritten Google Adwords advertisements based on select key phrases from the top fifty list they can plug into their Adwords accounts right away

- A set of five signature files they can use in their e-mails and when posting in market forums

- A set of five preselling e-mails they can plug in for their autoresponder series

In essence, I'm selling information or content to people who rely on information to sell products. The reason this is so attractive is that creating all of that content takes a lot of time and effort. Most new affiliates are eager to get started making money and loathe the idea of having to create that much content first on their own. There's a huge learning curve to master before they even see their first sale. If they have these content-based tools already in place, though, they can get into a market quickly. This allows them to learn by example while also getting positive results much more quickly.

You might be wondering how much time it takes me to create these kits. The answer is: not very long! I'm fanatical about keeping all of my businesses as automated as possible. I research the markets each month, create the requirements for each kit, and then outsource the actual writing and editing to freelancers.

I definitely recommend that you consider outsourcing before you start a membership site, or come up with products that are easier to put together.

Whatever you do, just make sure you can deliver your product on time to your members and that you're providing real value in exchange for their ongoing payments!

It really depends on what you are good at and like to do. If it is easy for you to create videos or do teleconferences, for example, then you could create a membership site based on those types of products. Likewise, you could also change the billing schedule.

If you wanted to deliver extremely high-quality products that require more development time, then you could create a membership site based on a quarterly billing cycle or something similar. Whatever you do, just make sure you can deliver your product on time to your members and that you're providing real value in exchange for their ongoing payments!

SUMMARY
AND CONCLUSION

Running your own successful Internet business requires focus, commitment, and consistent action. Also, as you have learned in this blueprint, it requires having a solid plan. You need a market, an offer, targeted traffic, and a profitable backend system. You must also learn to test your offers and track your results. Improvements to your bottom line will be made only insomuch as you are willing to learn what works and what doesn't. Even small changes in your copy, your offer, or your sources of traffic can have significant impact on your profits.

There are also **two basic lifetime principles of money-making** (online or offline), which you must fix firmly in your head before you start—because they will serve you for life, make you incredibly rich, and set you free financially:

1) **You'll make the most money when you provide a product or service that people truly *want* and are willing to pay for.**

It's not entirely true when they say "find a need and fill it"—
because it's not exactly what people need, it's what they *want*
and attach their emotions to. You do not have to find a need,
as very often needs are already identified by your competitors.
You just have to provide the want faster and better. So find
out what people want and what they're willing to pay for—the
answers are *everywhere,* online and offline.

2) You must learn the two most profitable and necessary skills of
all time in business: copywriting and marketing.

These two skills will surely make you wealthy beyond your dreams when
you combine them with a hungry market and in-demand products or
services that you can offer. When you learn how to move money with the
written word alone, and then learn *all* about promoting and marketing your
business, you'll always be able to depend on yourself for financial survival
in a good or bad economy. Combine these principles with the information
you've learned in my blueprint, and you are virtually guaranteed to build
your own thriving Internet business! I look forward to hearing from you
when you make your first million online, and I wish you all the best in
business and in life. To your success!

Bonus Chapters

CHAPTER 11

Blogging

I have made reference to blogs throughout my blueprint. Blogs are powerful tools for both traffic generation and for building the list relationship. If you are new to blogging, it is probably best that you go with a solution that is as easy to set up and use as possible. I recommend Blogger for this, and I am going to walk you through a step-by-step tutorial on how to get started using it in your own business.

Blogger is a free blogging service run by Google. It is ideal for newbies because the interface is very straightforward. Creating your first post is about as easy as typing up a regular text document.

STEP #1: SIGNING UP FOR AN ACCOUNT

First, go to the Blogger homepage at http://www.blogger.com. There you will find a graphic in the center of the page showing you the three easy steps to creating your blog. Click on the orange arrow that says "Create Your Blog Now":

On the next page, you will be asked to create a Google account. Now, if you have already created a Google account by signing up for Adwords, you can skip the next steps by logging in with your preexisting Google account. Otherwise, you will need to go ahead and set up a Google account by following the instructions on the screen. Then click Continue to move on to the next page.

Now, you should see a screen asking you to name your blog. What you want to do here is give your blog a title as well as select a username that will appear as part of the Web address for your blog. For example, you might name your blog "Jane Doe's Dating Tips." This is the title people will see when they visit your blog. Now, let's say that the username "janesdatingtips" is available. This will create your blog address at: http://janesdatingtips. blogspot/com, which is the URL you'll use to send visitors to your blog.

Click Continue again, and you will be taken to a page where you can choose the template for your blog:

Your template is going to set the overall look and feel of your blog. It determines the color scheme, layout, and text styles for things like links and headings. You have a number of templates to choose from, so choose the one you think looks best and fits with the image you want to convey. You can't go wrong choosing a clean and simple template. Simply click on the image of the template you want, then click Continue. *Voila!* Your blog has been created! Now you can move on to step two.

STEP #2: CREATE YOUR VERY FIRST BLOG POST

After clicking Continue, you'll be taken into the main administration area for your account, and you'll see the blog entry tool waiting for your first post. Take a look at the screenshot below. You'll notice that the functionality is much like that of a regular word processor. This is where you will type or cut and paste the text for your first blog entry:

Notice that you can preview your entry to see what it will look like on your blog. You can also save your post as a draft if you need to stop working on your entry and come back to it at a later time.

In order to officially publish your blog entry to your blog, you'll click the Publish button. If everything went OK, you should receive a message telling you that your post was published successfully. To see the finished results, click on View Blog. Here are the results we got for the sample post I created in the previous step:

And there we have it! A real, live blog created in just a few simple steps. If you've already got something written for your blog prior to setting it up, then this whole process shouldn't take you more than five or ten minutes to complete.

ADVANCED BLOG SETUP

If you already have some experience with blogging, you might want to consider using an advanced blogging platform such as WordPress or Movable Type, and use scripts for customizing the look and feel and monetization features of your blog. Here are some resources to get you started:

BLOGGER TEMPLATES/THEMES

http://www.layoutstudios.com/themes

http://blogger-themes.blogspot.com

http://freetemplates.blogspot.com

WORDPRESS TEMPLATES/THEMES

http://www.alexking.org/software/wordpress/theme_browser.php

http://www.wordpress-themes.net

Movable Type Templates/Themes

http://www.blogskins.com

http://www.sixapart.com/movabletype/styles/index

http://www.blogfashions.com

http://www.stopdesign.com/templates/photos

CHAPTER 12

A Beginner's Guide to Writing Great Ad Copy

The ability to write effective ad copy is one of the most important skills you can develop. Notice that I said it is a skill you can *develop*. You don't have to be a natural born writer to create great advertising copy, although having some talent does help. However, all good copywriters follow a formula, and you are going to learn about that formula here. It works regardless of whether you're a natural writer or feel totally intimidated by the idea of creating your own ad copy. You'll be thrilled once you master it, because you'll find it applies to a variety of situations:

- In your opt-in page and sales-page copy

- In your pay-per-click advertisements

- In your classified ads

- In your e-mail follow-ups and newsletters

Basically, any time you need to communicate with others and get your message across effectively, you'll be able to count on the formula.

STEP #1: ASKING THE RIGHT QUESTIONS

Are you intimately familiar with your market? Do you know your product and your offer inside out? If you don't, then you should—because this is 90 percent of what you need to know in order to write effective advertisements.

Know your market. Know your product. Know your offer.

Know your market. Know your product. Know your offer.

More importantly, you need to know what the prospects in your market really want to buy, not just what you want to offer. If you've done effective market research, then you should be able to address this by answering the following questions:

1) What is the problem?

2) Is there a solution?

3) What is the solution?

4) How does the product solve the problem?

5) Why is this product the best solution to the problem?

6) How will the customers' lives be improved once they consume the product?

7) What is the next step they should take?

The answers to these questions help generate the foundation of your advertisement. Write out as many answers to these questions as you can, and phrase them in as many ways as you can.

STEP #2: START THINKING AIDA-PLUS

Have you heard of *AIDA* before? It is an acronym for attention, interest, desire, action. Each of these elements creates great copy. AIDA also represents the logical flow of how the process of persuasion works in advertising:

1) Grab the prospect's *attention*—with an interest-raising headline.

2) Maintain the prospect's *interest*—with additional copy designed to support (and flow from) the claims made in the headline.

3) Create *desire*—for more information, for ownership, etc.

4) Make a call to *action*—compel the prospect to follow through on the offer by clicking on a link, signing up for a newsletter, purchasing a product, etc.

That's AIDA. Now, here is where the "plus" comes in: it is one thing to grab a prospect's attention and get him to read your ad—but there are some other important tasks you need to address in the copy as well:

- Build credibility

- Highlight the product benefits

- Address objections

- Be persuasive

Of course, it is quite difficult to achieve all of the above in a short ad (such as a pay-per-click ad), and it is not always necessary to do so. Instead, you'll use the AIDA formula first to write your shorter advertisements, then use AIDA-plus to flesh out the long copy items (like follow-up e-mails, sales letters, and so on). Now that you know the basics, let's look at how to jumpstart the process.

STEP #3: BUILD A PLATFORM

Every good advertisement needs a platform to spring from and to set the tone for the rest of the copy. Can you guess what your platform is? It is your headline. Why are headlines so important, and why do marketers spend so much time writing them, rewriting them, testing them, and tweaking them? It's very simple: your headline is the premise of the entire ad.

Your headline is the premise of the entire ad.

The headline focuses and defines your angle, so to speak. It sets up your tone and approach. This will be easier to understand with an example, so let's pretend for a moment that we're writing a headline advertising a weight-loss e-book. Imagine that this e-book shows people how to turn their everyday activities into powerful, calorie-burning exercises. Take a look at the following two headlines, and see if you can spot the approach used in each:

1) "Finally Revealed: The Key to Rapid Weight Loss Without Harsh Dieting or Exercise!"

2) "Amazing Fat-Burning System: Lose Up to 10 Pounds Per Month, Guaranteed! Gentle, Painless Exercise Method Uses the Natural Fat-Burning Ability of Your Muscles …"

The first thing I'd like you to notice here is that either of the above headlines could be used to advertise the same e-book. If you pick out the promised benefits from each headline, you have: "no dieting," "no strenuous exercise," and "rapid results."

You need to be able to support the claims of your headline, and those claims must spring from a logical premise.

But notice that the first headline appeals to (and I hate to say it) the lazy portion of your market, while the second headline emphasizes a gentle and natural method. The first headline implies some sort of secret is at play, and the second headline acknowledges the fact that there is some form of work involved in the solution.

Either headline would grab attention, but the second is more credible—it tells more and the claims made are not as outrageous. All you would have to do in your ad copy following such a headline is support the premise that the exercise method in question works gently and naturally.

Remember: all copy flows from the headline. You need to be able to support the claims of your headline, and those claims must spring from a logical premise. The thing you don't want to do is create an ad with a flashy, hyped-up headline that has nothing to do with the rest of the ad copy. So, always begin with a solid platform; doing so will make the rest of the writing process much easier.

STEP #4: OUTLINE YOUR COPY STRUCTURE

There is one step I skipped above that you'll want to take into account before you outline the structure of your copy. That step is choosing the tone of your copy. The tone is basically the "voice" that you write in, and this can change your entire approach. For example, your tone could be any of the following:

- Professional, businesslike, serious

- Personal

- Lighthearted

It is important that you maintain consistency of tone throughout your copy—in both the headline and the body. If you begin with a businesslike headline, for example, don't suddenly switch gears in the rest of your copy and try to do comedy.

It's like writing a short story. Good copy is like a story in the sense that you begin with an introduction, build to a climax, and then come to a resolution. In advertising, your headline and subheadline make up the introduction. Your objective is to grab the readers' attention and pull them in, just like pulling them into a good story.

That part is easy enough—but how do you build tension in advertising copy? You build tension by accruing benefits. Take your prospect through a journey in her own mind where benefits keep adding up—so much so that she's ready to make a buying decision based on emotional reasoning, rather than logical reasoning. Remember this: emotion motivates people more powerfully than logic. People will buy based on emotion, then justify their purchase (via logical reasoning) after the fact. Therefore, you need not concern yourself with convincing your prospect that A=B, or that Product A is worth the equivalent price B. Rather, your job is to lead him to the conclusion that Product A is worth ten to one hundred times more than price B in terms of perceived value and benefits. Then … you hit him with your offer!

Your offer is not the resolution of tension in this storyline, however. Your prospect resolves the tension for himself when he buys the product. Your offer should compel your prospect to take action and resolve the fever-pitch of desire you've built up in his mind. In a way, it is almost like cowriting a story with your potential customers. If your copy does its job correctly, they'll choose the "Buy Now" ending.

This is all somewhat abstract, so let's review the actual elements involved in the process:

- Headline—to grab attention and initial interest

- Subheadline (optional)—maintain interest and lead prospect into main body of sales letter

- Body—summarize your sale in this general order:

  A. Introduce or discuss the problem.

  B. Raise the promise of a solution ("What if I told you I have a product that solves your problem?").

  C. Describe the solution, focusing on benefits. Back this up with examples, data, and/or testimonials.

  D. Make the offer.

- Sales or Affiliate Link

- PS (optional)—Encourage prospect to take action once more; remind her of any bonuses or time-limited aspects to the offer, a money-back guarantee, etc.

- Signature (byline or contact info)

That's it—that's the basic structure of nearly every direct-marketing sales letter you'll see online today. It is also representative of the basic structure of most opt-in or lead-capture-page offers when you shorten the copy and introduce a lead-capture form in place of a sales link.

STEP #5: MIND YOUR LANGUAGE

What you say and how you say it counts for just as much as the structure (or formula) you use in your advertising. Your words must be powerful, even provocative—and at the same time they must also convey the crux of your offer without too much hype. Easier said than done? Let's look at some simple guidelines you can follow:

- Talk directly to your reader

Try to write as if you are talking to one person—think of a friend sitting across from you at the table. This will help you avoid the trap of sounding too formal or stuffy and also help you keep the focus where it needs to be: on your potential customer. This means using lots of "you" language rather than "I" language. Now, this does not mean that you have to avoid talking about yourself entirely. In fact, if you are using a personal, storytelling approach in your copy, it will be necessary to use some "I" language in order to help the reader connect with you. The difference is in how you frame the discussion.

Imagine for a moment that you are sitting across from a friend and talking to him about a sport you both enjoy. Let's pretend for a moment that the both of you are avid golfers and often share tips and tricks with each other. If you wanted to keep your friend engaged and excited, and avoid sounding boastful, how would you tell him about a new method you discovered to improve your golf swing?

Would you say, "Hey, Fred, I just played a perfect game the other day! I'm so amazed by this new golf swing technique I found. It makes me feel like Tiger Woods …"? Well, you could approach your friend that way. He might ask you to share the information if he isn't too put off by your bragging. However, this approach simply won't work when it comes to writing copy for a general audience.

So, imagine instead that you have the following conversation with your friend:

You: "Hey, have you ever wanted to improve your golf swing?"

Him: "Yes, definitely!"

You: "Me, too. There are so many books on the subject, though, I haven't been sure where to start."

Him: "Tell me about it! I wish there was an easier way."

You: "Well, that's why I wanted to talk to you. It turns out there *is* an easier way. It's an unusual method, though … nothing like either of us has ever tried. Would you be interested in learning about it?"

Him: "Absolutely!"

Now, in order to turn this imagined conversation into good copy, you have to remove your friend's responses. You must assume the existence of what I like to call the "silent affirmation" when writing to a general audience as if it were an audience of one. Why? Because you can't see or hear the people sitting at their computer screens. You have no body language or audible responses to help guide you. So, you must write as if you know what they're thinking. This means being a good study of human behavior. It means understanding, at minimum, the beliefs and biases held by an average member of your market. In other words, you must try to anticipate how an average prospect will respond to your claims.

Following our example conversation above, you could come up with the following piece of copy that would work well as an introduction to a sales letter, opt-in offer, or even follow-up message:

Dear Fellow Golfer,

> Have you ever wanted to improve your swing? Yes? Keep reading then, because you are going to love this. There's a new method available that turns even the most amateur golfers into club-swinging pros virtually overnight. I stumbled across this top-secret, highly unorthodox technique after years of poring through all the traditional books of advice. It is like nothing I've ever seen before, and I'm willing to bet it's like nothing you've ever seen before, either!

Notice the difference? The focus is almost entirely on the reader. Further, when I mention anything about me, it is framed in a way that helps the reader relate to me as someone who has struggled with the same problem and who is here to share the solution—the way a friend would share it.

The silent affirmation (or silent conversation) going on behind the scenes is assumed:

- I assume that the reader wants to improve his golf swing.

- I assume that he is wondering what type of information I can provide (top-secret, unorthodox).

- I assume he wants to know how I came across it (after years of reading through traditional advice).

- I assume his initial skepticism and the need for me to boost my credibility by admitting I wasn't always the expert ("It is like nothing I've ever seen before")—yet I still know more than he does ("I'm willing to bet it's like nothing you've ever seen before, either").

If I were writing this copy as part of a lead-capture page, I'd follow the introduction with a list of benefits, phrasing them so as not to give away the secret. After that, I'd hit him with my subscription offer and lead-capture form. Let's run through an example. This time I'll create a headline and also pull out a subheadline directly from the copy.

HEADLINE:

Get a Hole-In-One Every Time!?

SUBHEADLINE:

New Method Turns Even the Most Amateur of Golfers into Club-Swinging Pros Virtually Overnight!

BODY:

Dear Fellow Golfer,

Have you ever wanted to improve your swing? Yes? Keep reading then, because you are going to love this. There's a new method available that has golfers everywhere raving with excitement! I stumbled across this top-secret, highly unorthodox technique after years of poring through all the traditional books of advice. It is like nothing I've ever seen before, and I'm willing to bet it's like nothing you've ever seen before, either!

Imagine a technique that does all this:

- Lets you hit the ball farther, without having to hit it harder

- Guarantees perfect follow-through on every swing

- Gives you razor-sharp aim and automatically corrects for mistakes

- Is so powerful you could literally hit a hole-in-one any time you choose

Sounds too good to be true? Well, it *is* true ... but there's a catch. This information is so powerful and creates such an unfair advantage for those who possess it, that it will only be made available to a select few for a limited time.

OPT-IN FORM OFFER:

> Don't get left behind! Find out how you can get a hole-in-one every time when you subscribe by filling out your name and e-mail address in the form below. I'll rush you my FREE report, "Forbidden Golf Secrets," right away.

STEP #6: LOOK OUT FOR CLICHES

A cliché or two won't destroy your copy, but you should avoid them as much as possible. In fact, you may want to do a very close reading of your copy for hidden clichés, as some turns of phrase are so common they can slip right past you. Take these, for example:

"Been there, done that."

"Cry all the way to the bank"

"To coin a phrase"

"Plumb the depths"

If you need more examples, you can find hundreds online at http://www.westegg.com/cliche/.

What's the problem with clichés, you ask? Mainly, it's that they are so overused, your readers' minds will tune out and skip right over them. You want to maintain your prospect's attention at all times rather than give him the opportunity to ignore your message.

STEP #7: PUTTING IT ALL TOGETHER

We've gone over all of the basic guidelines to good copywriting. Thus far, we've focused almost exclusively on the elements that go into long-copy formats. Now it's time to look at how to use these techniques in short-copy situations. Short copy refers to things like pay-per-click ads, classifieds, and any situation where you don't have the space to talk at length about benefits. All you have are a few sentences at most to grab attention and encourage the reader to click on your link. What should you do?

First, go through the same process as you would when writing long copy. Flesh out all of the benefits of your product, generate as many potential headlines as you can, decide how to position your offer, and choose your tone.

Then pull out the most compelling headlines and benefits. Pare these headlines and benefits down into short sentences. Can you find a way to convey the information in fewer words?

The result: you should have a pretty good-sized list of potential headlines and subheadlines (or extremely short body-copy elements). If you are writing a pay-per-click ad for Google Adwords, for example, you may need to shorten things even more than you think. The character limits on Adwords advertisements are twenty-five characters max for the headline and seventy characters max (thirty-five characters per line) for your two subheadlines. As you can see, this limited space requires that you craft as concise and powerful an ad as possible. Further, your ad must include the type of information that will attract qualified prospects while filtering out unqualified prospects (e.g., mentioning the product price in the ad). Below is an example of a standard Google Adwords advertisement:

Web Marketing

New Web customers to your

Web site in 15 minutes for $10

http://www.GoClick.com

Notice how the focus of the ad (Web marketing) and the primary benefit are compressed into one sentence, with a price qualifier on the end? If you're having trouble seeing it, it breaks down like this:

- Primary product/service—"New customers to your Web site" (the focus is Web-site traffic)

- Benefit—Get these results fast (in 15 minutes)

- Benefit/Qualifier—$10 price listed to attract marketers looking for affordable traffic, turns away freebie seekers.

It's important to note that there's nothing wrong with getting clicks from freebie seekers in certain cases. If your sales funnel is designed to convert, you'll be able to turn a good portion of them into buyers.

Here's a tactic many marketers employ with good results: if you can offer a free trial or some other type of gift, make mention of that in your advertisement. Next, set up a dedicated landing page on your site for just that one offer. Your URL would be something like this:

http://www.yoururl.com/freetrial

You'd then use that as the display URL in your ad, and this will attract more click-throughs.

Now that you know how to use these techniques, it's time to put them into action. This will require focus and an eye on working consistently. You need to develop a precise advertising action plan. Let's imagine that you want to set up a weekly strategy. It might look something like this:

- Sunday: Create at least five quality, keyword-rich articles.

- Monday: Create PPC advertisements for at least twenty of your top key phrases.

- Tuesday: Create at least five classified advertisements.

- Wednesday: Create at least two alternative versions of your landing page for testing purposes.

- Thursday: Add additional content (or do some tweaking) to your autoresponder series.

- Friday: Create five more quality, keyword-rich articles, and then upload all ten of the articles you've written to the article directories.

- Saturday: Set up PPC campaign and place classified ads.

Remember that some advertising techniques, such as pay-per-click advertising, start working to drive traffic to your offers almost immediately. Other tactics, like article marketing, take a little bit longer because you have to wait for your articles to be approved and put into circulation. Do your best to stick to whatever plan you create, and you'll see positive results in due time.

TROUBLESHOOTING

MISTAKE #1: NOT USING THE PROPER TOOLS

THIS HAS A LOT TO DO with professionalism. One common thing a lot of newbies do is play for a while at marketing. They don't want to invest in any business tools until they think they've got a sure thing. The problem is that you'll never know the real profit potential of your market until you're taking your business seriously and really giving it all it's worth. In order to do this, you need to project a professional image and invest in the marketing tools that make your life easier. Here I am talking about things like a proper domain name, real Web hosting, and an autoresponder. If you're trying to get by with, for example, a free Web host, you're leaving a lot of sales on the table. The reason is that the perception of credibility is a big factor when it comes to what influences your customer's buying decisions. It's also a matter of targeting. Think about this example: let's say you're searching for a dog-training e-book. Which URL would you rather visit:

http://www.freehosting.com/user/allboutdogs

or

http://www.ultimate-dog-training.com/

You'd go to the second one, right? Just looking at the URL you'd intuitively believe you're going to find something close to what you're looking for there. Having a generic but market-specific domain name is the key. You need your own URL hosting on a real, dedicated Web host. Those free hosting sites you might be tempted to use aren't all they claim to be. Often, they'll place their own advertisements on your home page. Plus, you're often limited in terms of how much control you have over editing your Web pages, uploading images, and inserting code for things like autoresponders.

You'll never know the real profit potential of your market until you're taking your business seriously and really giving it all it's worth.

Speaking of autoresponders, this is another tool you've got to invest in. You've got to have a way to capture the contact information of the people visiting your site. Otherwise, you're just wasting traffic. Most sales are not made on the first visit to a Web site. People come to you in search of information first. In order to give them that information, you've got to capture their name and e-mail address so you can follow up with them. Autoresponders make this process a snap.

Now, those are the two big ones—but there are other tools you need to employ whenever you can. Let me refer you back to chapter 5 for the goods. So, if you do nothing else, get yourself up to speed with professional tools. This means at minimum getting your own domain name, Web host, and autoresponder account. Here are some that I recommend:

- http://www.hostgator.com

For domain registration and hosting

- http://www.monsterresponse.com

For an autoresponder service

Don't be afraid to spend some money on your business! Honestly, you can grab all the essential tools you need for around $40–50 per month. The difference this makes in your results will be worth it and will more than pay you back.

MISTAKE #2: FAILURE TO TARGET

THE RIGHT MARKET

This is probably the most common newbie mistake. Unfortunately, it's also the one thing that can kill your results even if you're doing everything else right! Improper market targeting is usually a case of choosing a market that is too broad. If you're currently making this mistake, don't feel bad. Even experienced marketers fall prey to this mistake. It's easy to get lost in all the options.

The one thing that can kill your results even if you're doing everything else right!

What happens when you're in too broad of a market, and how can you tell? Well, your conversion rates will be low. You'll be driving a lot of traffic that you think is targeted, but you find that the sales just aren't where they should be. You keep pumping more and more traffic, you keep changing your offer, and still … no one is buying.

There are two things you have to look at here:

1. Your product

2. The keywords you use to describe your market

There needs to be a close match between the two. It's not just about targeting a market but about targeting the product to the market. Let's look at some examples of proper and improper targeting:

- **When your market is too broad**

  Let's say you decide to go into the dating and relationships niche. You've got plenty of affiliate products to choose from—everything from matchmaking Web sites to e-books about how to attract the opposite sex or mend a broken heart. Now, one of the biggest mistakes you could make is to take key phrases like "dating advice" or "dating tips" as the basis for driving traffic to your offers. While those key phrases are relevant, they likely aren't targeted enough for your products. Why? Think for a moment about the number and types of people who might be searching for "dating advice." The market is huge! You've got people of all ages and situations searching for this information. There is no "one size fits all" solution. Yet there you sit trying to promote a very general e-book about dating, when you've got not just hundreds but thousands of competitors—competitors with much more in the way of resources and brand exposure. Your market is too broad and too risky because it's one where people have an unlimited number of options. They could literally go anywhere to get advice; and, unless you've got something really special, you're left to rely on sheer numbers and luck to make sales.

- **Proper targeting**

  OK, let's counter the situation from scenario number one. We're still interested in dating and relationships, but we want to find a much smaller segment of that market to target. If you're in business as an affiliate, this is the point where you need to research as many products as you can in order to find ones that fit a relatively narrow audience. The goal is to specialize in one subject. A good example of this would be deciding to target men who want to learn how to attract women. There are some unique products out there devoted solely to this subject. One that comes to mind is David DeAngelo's Double Your Dating program (http://www.doubleyourdating.com).

Notice you've narrowed your market here by exclusion. You aren't targeting women. You aren't even targeting every man out there looking for dating advice. You're just after the guys who need some extra help in the romance department. Now, this changes everything. It changes the types of sites you advertise on and the types of keywords you use in your pay-per-click campaigns. You're not going after "dating advice" anymore. Instead, you're after those guys who enter key phrases like "attract women," "why nice guys finish last," "date a model," and so on. Both your product and your market match up perfectly.

Even your follow-ups will be easier. Instead of trying to be all things to all people, you can focus on the one subject your audience is most interested in. This makes it a cinch to give them exactly what they want, and your sales will go through the roof.

The key is to start brainstorming through your own interests. What you're looking for is what I call an *affinity market*. An affinity market is simply a market based around a subject for which you have

An affinity market is simply a market based around a subject for which you have an affinity or liking.

an affinity or liking. This can be a lifelong hobby or even some area of expertise from your education or work life. Reread chapter 6 for more information and examples.

You'll see why this is important a bit later when we talk about the newbie mistake of not building a good list relationship. The main thing to understand now, though, is that having an affinity market makes everything you do ten times easier. It is very difficult for a newbie to go into a market of which she has limited to no knowledge. To begin with, you'll be hampered by lack of familiarity with market language or lingo. Imagine, for example, trying to go into the real estate niche when you don't know about things like adjusted exercise price, living expense insurance, negative amortization, and so on. If you don't understand what your market means when they search for this information, then you really don't know what they're looking for or whether it's the type of information they'll pay a price to get their hands on.

After affinity marketing, some of the other tricks I reveal center on narrowing down your market to a laser-targeted submarket, or niche. One of the ways you can do this is just by going to places like Amazon.com and checking into popular titles. You can see clusters of information this way. For example, let's say you're interested in birds as pets. You might find that information on how to teach parrots to talk is currently more popular than general care and feeding titles. You can also start pulling out keywords and phrases from these titles, and use those to do further keyword research on the market and find out how popular it is (based on the number of searches in the search engines for those keywords).

The final key is to get a profitability estimate on your market. This isn't as simple as determining popularity or demand. You've also got to look at the profit margin on the products you want to sell, weighed against things like advertising costs and competition.

If you're having trouble with the market you're in currently, I suggest that you revisit your research. You might be in the wrong market. However, it might also be that you've targeted the wrong product to that market or just need to switch over to a different segment of that market. If you think market targeting might be what's holding you back, then don't hesitate to make the necessary changes. It is far better to take a step back now than to keep plugging away with the same unsatisfactory results for another month or more.

MISTAKE #3: DRIVING THE WRONG KIND OF TRAFFIC

One problem most newbies face is a lack of knowledge about how to drive targeted traffic to their Web sites. Too often, newbies fall prey to traffic scams and fads that suck away valuable time and money but don't produce results. Usually, these bogus traffic systems promise to deliver things like "one million visitors for $99." Avoid these types of schemes at all costs! Not only is that traffic untargeted, it's usually not even real people going to your Web site! They just use computer programs to generate a bunch of fake hits to your site to make you think you're getting what you paid for! If you're new to online business and wondering what you need to do to generate real traffic, then you need to focus on learning about the following methods:

- Pay-per-click advertising

- Article marketing

- Social networking

- Market-specific blogs, forums, and groups

Reread chapter 8B on traffic tactics. These are the methods that really work to drive qualified visitors to your Web site. These are the methods that allow you to laser-target your market and drive quality traffic without squandering your budget. Further, when using these methods, you'll also be learning even more about how your market thinks, what their hot buttons are, and how best to communicate with them. Let me give you some examples of what I mean.

First, let's look at keyword-based (pay-per-click) marketing. One thing you'll find is that certain keywords will convert for you better than others. Sometimes, the keywords that convert are going to surprise you. You'll have at least one keyword you think is super targeted, yet it fails to bring in qualified visitors. Meanwhile, you'll probably have some keywords you tossed in on a lark, and it turns out they convert like crazy. The real lesson will come in finding out why this happens. Often, certain keywords describe your market generally, but they don't reflect the segment of your market that your product is targeted toward. And sometimes, well, it can be a mystery. But you can take the keywords that do convert and start looking for variations and synonyms that you might have missed—then focus more of your budget on those terms while dropping the losers.

Now, let's look at yet another example: driving traffic from market-specific forums or groups. In order to do this, you have to join these groups and become an active member of the community. This provides an opportunity to do even more market research. You'll be in the thick of things and learning a lot about your market's needs just by reading the threads and discussions people post to these groups. There's really a domino effect in play. The better you understand your market, the better you become at driving qualified traffic. Likewise, the more traffic sources you learn to exploit, the more you'll know about your market.

By digging out all the places where your market hides online, you get the big picture about how they operate. Where do they go? What do they talk about? What sites and products are already popular with them? Do they make a lot of word-of-mouth recommendations? How trusting are they of online businesses, and what do you need to do to gain that trust?

So, you see, there's more to traffic than just paying for clicks. There's a definite strategy involved, and you need multiple traffic-generating strategies in your arsenal—and those strategies need to allow you to target your market dead-on.

MISTAKE #4: NOT HAVING A PROVEN SALES SYSTEM

How will you make sales online? Do you know? Do you have a step-by-step plan for driving traffic to your site and then converting that traffic into paying customers? You've got to have a system in place. What action do you want your visitors to take when they reach your site? How are you going to introduce them to the product?

There's one method I teach that works like gangbusters for affiliates. It's called an *affiliate review page*. Instead of using a traditional squeeze page, you create a page that displays a full-length product review with an opt-in form below it. Visitors read your review, and if they like the information you've given them, they opt in to your list, where you follow up with them using more mini reviews and no-hype information.

The power of this system rests on the fact that you're positioning yourself more as a helpful expert than as a salesman. You presell the product by putting more information and more power back into the hands of your subscribers. You do the job of educating the potential customer, and let the merchant's sales page do the job of selling and hyping things up. You get a lot more sales this way, and you also get less in the way of refund requests.

It's a simple system to set up, and it takes a lot of the guesswork out of your marketing. Eliminating the trial-and-error approach will make your life a lot easier. Newbies far too often get into a pattern of switching around their sales funnel before it's had time to work. Maybe you started off with a squeeze page, didn't like the results, and so you took it down and replaced it with articles or direct links to products. What happens is your site becomes unfocused, and visitors don't really know what action to take.

It's only when you have full control over directing that visitor to where you want him or her to go that the real sales results start coming in.

That's why using a proven system, like the affiliate review opt-in page, can make all the difference. It gives your site one focus and basically forces your visitor to make a decision: opt in or leave. And it's only when you have full control over directing that visitor to where you want him or her to go that the real sales results start coming in.

MISTAKE #5: INEFFECTIVE (OR NO) FOLLOW-UP

Following up with an opt-in list is a process that also benefits from having a plan or system in place. In other words, you need to be strategic in your follow-ups. Some of the common follow-up mistakes include these:

- Using the solo affiliate e-mails written for you by a product owner without editing them or changing them up

- Too much emphasis on hype and hard sales pitches

- Failing to educate or presell prospects

You could sum all of these mistakes up into just one: failing to develop your own voice. It's really crucial that you cultivate your own style and tone. Remember, your subscribers are going to see plenty of hype on the merchant's sales letter. What they really need from you is solid information.

What's so special about the product you're promoting to them? Will it address their concerns? How does it fit in their big picture? Answering these questions for your prospects should be deliberately paced over a span of days, or even weeks. You've got to resist that urge of trying to hard sell them in the first couple of e-mails.

One of the concepts I teach is that of continuing your affiliate product reviews on a smaller scale in your follow-ups. So, for example, let's say that the review on your affiliate opt-in page covers the main pros and cons of a product. However, there are still a lot of subtle details you've left out, and this is exactly the type of information you start feeding to your prospects in your follow-ups.

Now, in order to do this, you really need to own the product. You've got to be able to pull out information from the product itself as well as talk about your experience from a customer's perspective. Let's pretend that you're promoting a weight-loss e-book. You'd want to be able to send out something like this:

Hi First Name,

I don't know where you are in your current weight-loss program. Maybe you're just getting started. Or you may have already lost a lot of weight, and you're just trying to shed those last 20 pounds.

There's one thing I know for sure, though: at some point you're going to hit a plateau. You know, it's that point where you get stuck at a certain weight and just can't seem to drop those last few pounds no matter what you do. This is exactly where I was when I got my copy of [insert product name here]. I didn't expect to see that topic covered in depth in the book, but it was! And I was very impressed by what I learned. While I can't explain it quite as well as [author's name] does, it works something like this …

Basically, your body does *not* like to lose weight! Big surprise, huh? It's the very things you do to start the initial weight loss that will eventually cause you to plateau. This is because your body strives to maintain balance between energy intake and output.

One big mistake people make is to cut their calories *too much* to try and trick their body into losing more. But the body sees this as a sort of attack, and so it ends up hanging on to all your extra fat in an act of self-preservation. The more calories you cut, the more your body doesn't want to let go of the fat it has stored up.

[Product name] has a truly mind-blowing trick for getting around this, but it's too involved to go into here. What I *can* recommend to you for now is to go calculate how many calories it takes to maintain your current weight, and then cut those calories to *only slightly below* that number through either diet or exercise. Don't cut more than about 100–200 or it won't work.

http://www.youraffiliatelink.com

Cheers,

Your Name

Now, do you notice how different that type of message is from a traditional affiliate sales pitch? You're giving people information they can use right now without buying any product. A lot of newbies are afraid to do this because they think people will just take that info and run with it. But nothing could be further from the truth. By giving people a taste, you're actually proving the value of the product to them and giving them an even bigger reason to buy. You're making the product relevant to their lives in a way they can touch, see, feel, and test. This approach completely trumps stock solo ads and hyped-up sales pitches. Just put this to the test in your own business. The results will speak for themselves.

This approach completely trumps stock solo ads and hyped-up sales pitches. Just put this to the test in your own business. The results will speak for themselves.

MISTAKE #6: MISSING THE LIST RELATIONSHIP

This is really related to mistake #5. Part of the follow-up process involves going beyond mere promotion. There's nothing that deadens the responsiveness of a list faster than hitting them with the same information, in the same format, over and over again. You've got to build a real relationship, and you've got to keep your subscribers on their toes. In other words, you want to increase their perception of you as a trusted source of high-quality information, and throw in an element of surprise so that they always want to open and read your e-mails.

One of the methods for this that I recommend is that of using *insertion messages*. Insertion messages are just e-mails that you send to your list apart from your preprogrammed, product-focused autoresponder sequences. Let's say you've got a five-part follow-up series for a product. Somewhere in between the messages in that sequence, you want to send out a surprise mailing.

The purpose of the mailing is to jolt your subscribers back into full attention by surprising them with a gift. This gift can be anything from a free report to a longer, information-packed article (or a link to a blog post). The key here is you give them a gift in the form of super valuable content or information. Something they normally would expect to pay for. It's all based on the principle that you do have to give in order to receive. You see, people are much more likely to do business with you when they see that you're truly focused on helping them and not just trying to get them to cough up their money.

I really can't stress this enough: find a market you can relate to, build a list, and build a solid relationship with that list!

That said, you really should be in a market where you feel you can help people. If you're just in it for the money and don't really care what product you're selling or who you're selling it to … well, it shows. People can sense this a mile away. The people who join your list do so because they are the experts when it comes to their own interests and concerns. If you don't share those interests with them, they'll be able to tell. Your lack of interest and experience will show in everything you do. When you don't care, you can't connect, and you really can't write anything more than a shallow follow-up. Your subscribers will know that you don't know what the heck you're talking about. I really can't stress this enough: find a market you can relate to, build a list, and build a solid relationship with that list!

MISTAKE #7: FAILURE TO MONETIZE THROUGH ADDITIONAL CHANNELS

I hate using clichés, but I can't think of a better way to say this: when it comes to making real money online, there's no such

The big profits come from having multiple revenue streams.

thing as a one-trick pony. The gurus and the super affiliates you hear about? They aren't raking in that money off of just one product or one sales model. The big profits come from having multiple revenue streams. Now, money-making opportunities are everywhere, and all you have to do is use your imagination. Almost anything can be monetized. You can squeeze way more revenue out of your existing traffic than you realize.

There are two different channels of monetization I tend to focus on:

1. Multiproduct affiliate marketing

2. Content monetization via blogging

In the first case, what I recommend is that you roll all of your affiliate products from one market into one site. What I mean by this is that you collect a themed group of products for a target market, and you promote them from one central location rather than setting up different Web sites with different squeeze pages. This model works when you are presenting the products from an "affiliate product review" approach. You basically create product reviews for all of the products you want to promote, and roll out each of those in your autoresponder. So, when someone signs up to your list because of your lead review about Product X, your follow-ups don't stop at Product X. Instead, you put a little break between sequences, then start following up on a totally new product to that same list.

What's great about this is that you can create follow-up promotions for as many products as you want. You could load your autoresponder up with enough follow-ups to last you a year—which means you'll have all of your promotions on complete auto-pilot. The other reason to do this is so that you can present of a variety of product options to your subscribers. Maybe some of your subscribers decided they weren't interested in the first product you offered them. That's OK. You'll have plenty more offers to present to them, and you don't have to lure them onto a second list to do it. You'll also be able to experiment with different types and prices of products. Why stick to promoting one e-book, for example, when you can present additional offers for things like videos, home-study courses, and membership sites? And don't forget to throw in some recurring revenue streams while you're at it. You should definitely be promoting at least one product that pays you a recurring commission!

Creating a blog is actually an extension of building the relationship with your list.

Now, let's talk about blog monetization. Creating a blog is actually an extension of building the relationship with your list. You need a place where you can post in-depth content—things like articles and videos that just don't fit into an e-mail format. So, when you send your subscribers over to your blog, you've got a whole new piece of real estate where you can insert additional profit opportunities for yourself. For example, you can place Google Adsense onto your blog. You can put up product banners that are linked over to the merchant's sales page with your affiliate link. You can even sell some advertising space on your blog if you've got enough readers.

The point is that your list is a ready-made source of traffic you can send directly to your blog. You may have someone sitting on your list who has never bought a thing from you, but he may click on one of your Google Adsense advertisements. Ding! That's a few more cents added to your bottom line. See what I mean? It's a cumulative effect. You've worked hard to build your list, so you don't want to just leave it sitting there. You've got to find ways of continually recycling your traffic and placing more profit opportunities in its path.

RESOURCES

ADVERTISING PLATFORMS AND NETWORKS

http://www.aaddzz.com

> A performance-based pay-per-click network with automatic site targeting.

http://www.adace.com

> Gives you a choice between centrally served or site-hosted advertising.

http://www.adcenter.microsoft.com

> This program is Microsoft's attempt to muscle away some market share from Yahoo! and Google.

http://www.AdSmart.net

> Boasts a large inventory of sites that attract highly targeted audiences.

http://www.Ad-venture.com

> A large range of options, and you can target by site, group of interest category, or targeted demographics across all sites in the network.

http://www.adwords.google.com

> An advertising platform offering both cost-per-click and cost-per-impression pricing for advertisements served on Google.com and partner sites.

http://www.burstmedia.com

> Providing ads for special-interest and niche-focused Web sites.

http://www.doubleclick.com

> Serves some of the most heavily trafficked sites on the Web. A good option to test once you've got some experience under your belt.

http://www.enhance.com

> Offers advertising through a network of hundreds of distribution partners, including Excite, EarthLink, and MSN.

http://www.GoClick.com

> A leading pay-per-click search engine, receiving over 1.5 million unique visitors a month.

http://www.searchmarketing.yahoo.com

> A Yahoo! search marketing program.

http://www.valueclick.com

Guarantees to buy 100 percent of advertising space on host sites. Performance-based pricing for advertisers.

http://www.Webconnect.net

Ad- placement service. Delivers highly targeted advertising coverage in a variety of market areas.

ARTICLE MARKETING

http://www.ArticleBase.com

Your free online articles directory.

http://www.ArticleDashboard.com

Submit articles to the Article Dashboard directory, search and find free Web-site and e-zine content, and open an author submission management account.

http://www.articlesubmitterpro.com

A tool to submit your article to multiple directories at once.

http://www.EzineArticles.com

Allows expert authors in hundreds of niche fields to get massive levels of exposure in exchange for the submission of their quality articles.

http://www.ezine-dir.com

Lists thousands of the best e-mail newsletters available on the Internet today. Search, browse, or add your e-zine for free!

http://www.ezinelisting.com

A source for all the best e-zines (online magazines, newsletters).

http://www.FindArticles.com

Contains articles from the back issues of over nine hundred magazines, journals, trade publications, and newspapers.

http://www.GoArticles.com

Free content search engine and article directory.

http://www.IdeaMarketers.com

Unites writers, Webmasters, and publishers.

http://www.Magazines.com

Offering a wide selection to choose from.

http://www.masternewmedia.com

Daily online magazine targeted at individuals, small businesses, communicators, and media professionals.

http://www.oclc.org/fristsearch/periodical/index_title.asp

The search database for serial periodicals that have chosen to obtain ISSN numbers through the Library of Congress.

http://www.onlineforsuccess.com/ezine-marketing-directory.htm

Free browsing and searching. Provides data on list size, frequency of mailing, and cost.

http://www.SearchWarp.com

Writer's community for relationship advice and do-it-yourself (DIY) information.

http://www.SubmitYourArticle.com

Submit your articles to thousands of publishers using this article submission service.

BLOGGING

http://www.alexking.org/software/wordpress/theme_browser.php
Free WordPress templates.

http://blogger-themes.blogpost.com

Free blogger templates for Blogger-powered sites by Ezline Design.

http://www.blogcatalog.com

Directory of top blogs from around the world. Blogs are listed by category.

http://www.blogfashions.com

A good place to find Movable Type templates, skins, and themes.

http://www.blogger.com

Free, automated Weblog publishing tool that sends updates to a site via FTP.

http://www.blogsearch.google.com
Search any of the dozens of other blog search sites.

http://www.blogsearchengine.com
A search engine and directory listing of Weblogs and tools.

http://www.blogskins.com

    Find hundreds of templates for your Moveable Type blog.

http://www.dir.blogflux.com

    Based on tagging with related Weblogs.

http://www.findblogs.com

    A blog directory.

http://www.freetemplates.blogspot.com

    Free blogger templates for Blogger.

http://www.layoutstudios.com/themes

    Free blogger templates, themes, skins, etc.

http://www.livejournal.com

    Free service for all your journaling and blogging needs.

http://www.myspace.com

    Meet people from your area in the country and keep
in touch.

http://www.netforbeginners.about.com/od/bloggingbasics

    The ultimate free resource for learning to blog.

http://www.rsstoblog.com

    Automate your blog posts. Post RSS feeds to your blog.

http://www.sixapart.com/moveabletype/styles/index

    One of the best places to find Movable Type templates, skins,
and themes.

http://www.stopdesign.com/templates/photos

> Creative design for your blog.

http://www.technocrati.com

> Real-time search for user-generated media (including Weblogs) by tag or keyword. Also provides popularity indexes.

http://www.WordPress.com

> A popular blog platform for Internet marketers.

http://www.wordpress-themes.net

> The official site for WordPress and for WordPress templates.

CLASSIFIED ADS

http://www.adlandpro.com

> Free classifieds, advertising, and promotion.

http://www.adpost.com

> Free classifieds for over a thousand cities and five hundred regions worldwide.

http://www.classifiedads.com

> Free classified ads for cars, jobs, real estate, and everything else. Find what you are looking for or create your own ad for free!

http://www.classifieds.yahoo.com

> Post free classified ads or search for classified ads in jobs, apartments, housing, tickets, for sale, personals, and pets.

http://www.craigslist.com

> Provides local classifieds and forums for jobs, housing, for sale, personals, services, local community, and events.

http://www.domesticsale.com

> The most effective trash-free classifieds. Online local, nationwide, and worldwide auto, real estate, vacation rentals, jobs, and general ads.

http://www.usfreeads.com

> Free classifieds. Huge traffic, active buyers, and tens of thousands of fresh daily visitors ensure your items sell fast.

COPYWRITING

http://www.cheap-copy.com/sales-letter.html

> Get your crash course on writing good copy.

http://www.westegg.com/cliché

> A great place to find hundreds and hundreds of clichés.

DIRECTORIES

http://www.AffiliatePrograms.com

> A comprehensive affiliate marketing guide that includes a complete directory of affiliate programs, industry news, forums, and helpful resources.

http://www.AssociatePrograms.com

> A comprehensive, searchable directory of affiliate programs, tips, helpful affiliate forum, resources, and award-winning newsletter.

http://www.blogcatalog.com

> Directory of top blogs from around the world. Blogs are listed by category.

http://www.blogsearch.google.com

> Search any of the dozens of other blog-search sites.

http://www.blogsearchengine.com

> A search engine and directory listing of Weblogs and tools.

http://www.dir.blogflux.com

> Based on tagging with related Weblogs.

http://www.findblogs.com

> A blog directory.

http://www.ebookplace.com

> Offering both e-books and articles.

http://www.ezineadvertising.com

> A comprehensive search engine and directory for e-zine advertisers.

http://www.ezine-dir.com

> Lists thousands of the best e-mail newsletters available on the Internet today. Search, browse, or add your e-zine for free!

http://www.ezinelisting.com

> A source for all the best e-zines (online magazines, newsletters).

http://www.free-ebooks.net

> A well-established, highly trafficked, and popular site.

http://www.jogena.com

> An e-book and e-zine directory with excellent resources.
> Strong focus on business, marketing, writing, and publishing.

http://www.mindlikewater.com

> An e-book directory with multiple categories. Attractive and
> well organized.

DOMAIN REGISTRATION AND HOSTING

http://www.hostgator.com

> A place for domain registration, Web hosting, and Web page
> building resources.

E-ZINE ADVERTISING

http://www.ezineadvertising.com

> A comprehensive search engine and directory for e-zine advertisers.

FREELANCERS

http://www.Elance.com

> An online workplace where businesses find and hire people
> on demand to get work done quickly and cost effectively.

http://www.FreelanceWarriors.com

A place where buyers of programming and Web-design services and sellers who provide programming and Web-design services meet.

http://www.rentacoder.com

An international marketplace where people who need custom software developed can find coders in a safe and business-friendly environment.

http://www.scriptlance.com

Outsource your projects to freelance programmers and designers at cheap prices.

GENERAL INFORMATION

http://www.answers.yahoo.com

A new way to find and share information.

http://www.ask.metafilter.com

Got a problem and need an answer? Log on to this community Weblog, post your questions, then await advice from the "hive mind."

INTERNET MARKETING

http://www.AffiliateFirst.com

Lists affiliate program offerings from the U.S., UK, and worldwide merchants.

http://www.AffiliateGuide.com/residual.html

>Your guide to residual-income affiliate programs, associate programs, and referrals and profit sharing.

http://www.AffiliatePrograms.com

>A comprehensive affiliate marketing guide that includes a complete directory of affiliate programs, industry news, forums, and helpful resources.

http://www.AssociatePrograms.com

>A comprehensive, searchable directory of affiliate programs, tips, a helpful affiliate forum, resources, and an award-winning newsletter.

http://www.AutopilotInternetIncome.com

>Autopilot Internet Income Pte Ltd is headed by world-famous Internet marketing expert Ewen Chia to provide proven advice and information on Internet Marketing.

http://www.AutopilotProfits.com

>An online course to teach you how to set up your own automated income strands on the Internet.

http://www.ClickBank.com

>The Web's premier affiliate product marketplace. It costs nothing to sign up, and you'll have immediate access to affiliate products that offer 50 percent to 75 percent commissions.

http://www.eEntrepreneur.com

A one-stop Internet self-help Web site that will help any entrepreneur achieve success in his online business.

http://www.EwenChia.com

Ewen Chia's main Web site where you can get insider tips, resources, and more to help you make real money online.

http://www.LifetimeCommissions.com

A directory of lucrative affiliate programs that pay lifetime commissions or residual commissions for life.

http://www.NewbieCashMachine.com

The official Internet cash system for newbies.

http://www.OneNetWork.DigitalRiver.com

Your new home for better product selection, better features, and the best payouts available.

http://www.SecretAffiliateWeapon.com

Proven, simple step-by-step system to start making money online.

http://www.SuperAffiliates.com

Shows you exactly how to make a fortune from other people's products.

MARKET RESEARCH

http://www.7search.com

A search engine that provides Web-site information, including e-mail addresses, location, age, and site popularity.

http://www.50.Lycos.com

> Top-fifty keyword searches in Lycos that include lists of
> people, places, and things.

http://www.Amazon.com

> Online shopping from Earth's biggest selection of books,
> magazines, music, DVDs, videos, electronics, computers, etc.

http://www.eBay.com

> Buy and sell electronics, cars, clothing, apparel, collectibles,
> sporting goods, digital cameras, and everything else.

http://www.Google.com

> Major Internet search engine that enables users to search the
> Web, Usenet, images, and more.

http://www.MSN.com

> A search engine by Microsoft.

http://Pulse.eBay.com

> Delivers a snapshot of the eBay marketplace.

http://www.technocrati.com

> Real-time search for user-generated media (including Weblogs)
> by tag or keyword. Also provides popularity indexes.

http://www.Trendwatching.com

> The world's most visited source for consumer trends
> and insights.

http://www.Yahoo.com

> A search engine to quickly find what you're looking for.

http://www.YahooShopping.com

Find great products online, compare, shop, and save.

PAY-PER-CLICK ADVERTISING

http://www.aaddzz.com

A performance-based pay-per-click network with automatic site targeting.

http://www.miva.com/US/content/advertiser/pay_per_click.asp

An excellent program that not enough people are taking advantage of.

http://www.GoClick.com

A leading pay-per-click search engine, receiving over 1.5 million unique visitors a month.

PODCASTING

http://www.Podcast.Net

A source for thousands of podcasts covering a wide variety of topics and interests.

PUBLIC ARCHIVES

http://www.Archive.org

A digital library of Internet sites and other cultural artifacts in digital form.

http://www.gutenberg.org

>A library of 17,000 free e-books whose copyrights have expired.

RIGHTS ISSUES

http://CreativeCommons.org

>Provides a flexible range of protections and freedoms for authors, artists, and educators.

http://www.ResaleRightsSecrets.com

>Easily transform cheap resale rights products into money-pumping machines anytime you desire.

http://www.viralpdf.com

>Brings full rebranding functionality to all your PDF e-books.

SEARCH ENGINE OPTIMIZATION

http://www.Adwords.Google.com/select/KeywordToolExternal

>Use the Keyword Tool to get new keyword ideas.

http://www.Featuring.com/wtt

>Free keyword suggestion tool from Wordtracker to help your Web site rank higher in the search engines.

http://www.searchenginewatch.com

>The authoritative guide to search-engine marketing and search-engine optimization.

http://www.seochat.com

Learn search-engine optimization and latest search-engine algorithms.

SOCIAL NETWORKING

http://www.facebook.com

A social utility that connects people with friends and others who work, study, and live around them.

http://www.friendster.com

A leading global social network emphasizing genuine friendships and the discovery of new people through friends.

http://www.hubpages.com

An online space to share your advice, reviews, useful tips, opinions, and insights with hundreds of other authors.

http://www.myspace.com

An international site that offers e-mail, a forum, communities, videos, and Weblog space.

http://www.squidoo.com

Fast, free, and easy way to build a page on a topic you're passionate about.

http://www.tagged.com

Allows users to send messages, leave comments, browse photos, watch videos, play games, give tags, and chat.

TELECONFERENCING

http://www.instantconference.com
> Free teleconferencing service.

TOOLS

http://tool.motorerica.info/keyword-density.phtml
> Free tools to calculate the keyword density of your sales page.

http://www.Adwords.Google.com/select/KeywordToolExternal
> Use the Keyword Tool to get new keyword ideas.

http://www.animationonline.com
> Offers free animated banners, Flash animation software, and Flash components. Try the components online.

http://www.articlesubmitterpro.com
> A tool to submit your article to multiple directories at once.

http://www.AutoResponsePlus.com
> Sequential autoresponder software for Web sites.

http://www.Aweber.com
> An autoresponder option that gets raves within the online-marketer community.

http://www.camtasiastudio.com
> Camtasia Studio screen recorder and presentation software

http://www.EwenChia.com/clone

>An excellent link-cloaking software product that allows you to conceal your affiliate URL, link to an order page, link to a specific product page, and more.

http://www.Featuring.com/wtt

>Free keyword suggestion tool from Wordtracker to help your Web site rank higher in the search engines.

http://www.freeonlinesurveys.com

>Create an online satisfaction survey, customer survey, employee survey, etc. Free, easy-to-use survey builder.

http://www.hipcast.com

>The ultimate multimedia tool for bloggers. Create audio and video blogs, podcasts.

http://www.locked-area.com/lite

>A password protection and member's area management system.

http://www.MiniEbook.com

>Promoting an affiliate program by creating free e-books fast for super-affiliate income.

http://www.MonsterResponse.com

>Ewen Chia's professional autoresponder service.

http://www.MyFreeWebsiteBuilder.com

>A simple, free tool for creating beautiful Web sites, even if you're not a technical person.

http://www.surveymonkey.com

> Offers a Web-based interface for creating and publishing custom Web surveys, and then viewing the results graphically in real time.

VIDEO SHARING NETWORKS

http://www.ifilm.com/viralvideo

> A video-sharing network.

http://www.Revver.com

> The first viral video-sharing network with original Webisodes, animation, comedy, vlogger, gaming videos, and more.

http://www.video.google.com

> Search and browse all kinds of videos, hosted on sites all over the Web.

http://vids.myspace.com

> Upload and share videos, find and watch funny clips.

http://www.YouTube.com

> Hosts user-generated videos. Includes network and professional content.

GLOSSARY

Adsense An ad-serving program run by Google that allows Web-site owners to gain revenue by displaying ads on their Web sites. Google provides text, image, and video advertisements that appear on participating Web sites. These ads appear based on the keywords and content present on the Web site. Webmasters are paid when an Internet user clicks on an ad on their Web page. Depending on the ad, the revenue may be a few cents up to a dollar per click.

Adwords Google's advertising product and main source of revenue. Adwords offers pay-per-click advertising for text and banner ads. When advertisers use Adwords to promote their product or service, their ads appear on any related Web site that is using Adsense. Advertisers pick keywords that relate to their ad, and then bid on these keywords. They pay each time someone clicks on their ad. The advertisement will take the clicker to the merchant's Web site. Keywords cost more when they are more popular. Depending on the keyword, a click may cost anywhere from 10 cents to several dollars.

Affiliate

Affiliate marketing is one of the most popular forms of business on the Web and an effective way to promote businesses and products. As an affiliate, you first find a company or product you would like to promote. You join the affiliate program of the company and receive the tools for sending customers to the company's Web site. This most often includes a special URL link that will let the company know that the customer has come from you. You will get credit when people visit the company's Web site. Details can vary, but in most cases you receive a percentage of the revenue from sales that customers make from following your link.

Applet

A small program or application that is usually written in Javascript and runs on a Web browser. Applets power some of the fancier features of Internet pages, such as animation. They download quickly and are used both online and offline.

Autoresponder
An autoresponder is an automatic e-mail response program. It will send preentered e-mail messages instantly to people who request information from a Web site, newsletter, or online merchant.

Banner ad
An online ad on a Web page that links to another Web site or landing page. Banner ads are one of the first methods of advertising on the Web. They have different costs depending on how much traffic and page views the Web site gets and can cost up to $150,000 per month. Banner ads are so named because they are placed at the top or bottom of a Web page. However, they can also be placed on the sides of the Web site content.

Blog
Short for *Web log*, a Web site where entries are made similar to a journal or diary. The entries are presented in reverse chronological order, with the newest entry on top. Although blogs were originally used as personal journals, they have evolved into a multipurpose tool. There are blogs on every topic imaginable, from food to politics to celebrity gossip. Generally, blogs combine text entries with images, links to other blogs, and other related media. A blog entry can also include comments from readers, categories (commonly called tags) that label the blog entry by subject, and trackback links, which are links to other sites that refer to the blog entry.

Blogger   A blogger is anyone that uses a blog to post information on topics that are of interest to them. Some of the most popular blogging software platforms are Blogger, Livejournal, Typepad, Wordpress, and Xanga. These sites will host your blog, generally for free, and provide you with the tools to create blog posts without having to know a lot about software.

Branding   In marketing, and especially Internet marketing, branding is important to establishing the company identity. Branding is the result of an accumulation of experiences that consumers have with a particular company or product. A brand creates associations and expectations among the products made by a company. The brand is a symbol for all of the information that is connected to a company, a product, or a service. Branding can include a logo, font selection, color schemes, and symbols that work together to create an impression of the values, ideas, and personality of the company. Branding has significant importance in Internet marketing, where the competition is huge. Having a noteworthy and unique branding strategy can help companies stand out in the vast online marketplace. Individuals can also develop a form of personal branding, which can help establish credibility with their online customers and target a specific niche of people.

Chat room One of the most popular ways to make connections with real people over the Internet. A chat room is basically an interactive message board that allows live, online conversation for two or more users.

Copywriting The process of writing words to promote a business, person, opinion, or idea. Copywriting can include plain text messages and a variety of other online media. The main purpose of copywriting is to persuade the reader to act somehow, whether that is buying a product, signing up for an e-course, or clicking on a link. Copywriting can also refer to the search-engine optimization methods that are used to achieve higher rankings in search engines. This type of copywriting is often referred to as content writing. Copywriting for Web-site placement involves the strategic repetition of keywords and phrases within articles.

Domain name This is the address or URL of a particular Web site. For example, http://www.Google.com is the domain name for the Google search engine. The domain name is the text name that covers up the numeric IP address of a computer that is hooked up to the Internet. Domain names make the World Wide Web more user-friendly. Instead of having to remember a string of numbers, we can remember the name of the Web site. Registering a domain name for an online venture can cost as little as $8. Web site domain names are registered to prevent people from using the same name for their Web site. There are several different companies that allow you to register a Web site, and many of these companies offer hosting packages as well.

Double opt-in
A technique used in opt-in or permission-based marketing. It ensures that a potential customer actually wants to receive the marketing materials and is a way to prevent unwanted spam. In the double opt-in process, a potential customer requests information from a Web site and is asked to confirm that he wants the information to come to his e-mail address. The potential customer then receives a confirmation e-mail in his inbox. This e-mail requires him to click on a verification link to receive further information. Once the potential customer receives verification, he will receive future messages from the mailing list, e-course, or autoresponder series.

Download
The act of transferring a file or files from one computer to another using the Internet.

E-book
This is a book that can be downloaded and read on a computer. Most e-books are saved in Adobe

Acrobat and require Adobe Acrobat Reader (a free program) to be accessed.

E-business	An e-business is defined as any business that is drawing a majority of its income from selling its products or services in an online format. E-business can also be used to refer to any business practices that are handled electronically (such as supply chain management, order tracking and processing, and payroll).
E-mail	E-mail, or electronic mail, is mail that is electronically sent to your computer. It is delivered instantly. To use e-mail, you need a computer, an online connection, an e-mail account, and an e-mail program. The e-mail account can be obtained through your ISP or from one of several free e-mail services online, including G-mail (www.gmail.com) provided by Google; Yahoo! Mail (www.yahoomail.com) provided by Yahoo!; Hotmail (www.hotmail.com) a service of MSN; Fastmail (www.fastmail.fm); AIM (www.aim.com), an AOL e-mail service; and Inbox (www.inbox.com).
Forum	An Internet forum is a place on the World Wide Web for holding discussions. Normally, forum members will either discuss one specific topic or have a common thread among all of the members.

For example, there are discussion groups for work-at-home mothers where they discuss not only business-related topics, but also parenting, budgeting, and time management. Unlike e-mail, messages posted to the forum are viewable by all forum members. Some of the other common terms for forums are discussion forums, bulletin boards, message boards, discussion boards, and discussion groups.

FTP
File transfer protocol—the standard method for downloading and uploading files on the Internet. Understanding FTP is necessary if you want to create your own Web site.

Handle
Login name or username.

Hosting
The business of providing the equipment and services that are required to display Web sites. Hosting also involves maintaining files and providing fast Internet connections. If you run a Web site or do business on the Web, you need to find a reliable host. Hosting packages are available for very reasonable rates. Do research based on customer service and quality of technical service before choosing a hosting company based only on price.

HTML
Hypertext markup language (HTML) is a language that was designed for the creation of

Web pages. While many people directly use HTML to create Web pages, there are many intermediary programs that allow you to create Web sites without using HTML. However, it is helpful to understand how HTML works. There are three main types of markups that are used: structural, presentational, and hypertext. Structural markups allow you to set up headings, paragraphs, and lists for your Web page. Presentational markups can create bold, italic, and underlined text and also change the size of the text. Hypertext markups create a link from one page to another. Keep in mind that when information is in HTML, it is sandwiched between two tags. For example, if you wanted to make the word "cat" bold, you would write: cat. Some other useful html tags include <title>Title</title>, <h>heading</h>, <p>paragraph</p>, <i>italicize </I>, <u>underline</u>, and emphasize.

Internet   The Internet is also referred to as just the Net and is a worldwide system of interconnected computer networks. The computers are connected through copper wires, fiber-optic cables, or wireless connections. The Internet consists of millions of smaller networks that have been established by businesses, academic institutions, and government networks. All together these networks carry information and services (like e-mail, online chats, and Web pages). It is a common misconception that the Internet and the World Wide Web are interchangeable terms. Actually the Internet refers to the physical or wireless connection between computers. The World Wide Web refers to the connected documents that exist on the Internet.

Internet marketer An individual or company whose primary income comes from marketing products or services on the Web.

IRT In real time. For example, chat rooms allow individuals to converse IRT.

ISP Internet service provider—a company that provides users with access to the Internet. Before you can connect to the Internet, you must first establish an account with an ISP.

JV Joint venture—although "joint venture" is not exclusively an Internet term, the concept is an important part of any Internet marketing program. At its most basic level, a joint venture is a business move that is made by two or more entities to the mutual advantage of each. In the Internet world, this process can take one of many forms. Person A can offer Person B's product on

Person A's mailing list. This is done when Person B has a great product but few means of distribution. Person A will normally receive a percentage of the profit from sales made on the mailing list. Alternatively, Person A and Person B collaborate to create a brand-new product or service. Both parties will promote the product on their mailing lists. This normally happens with information products and can include three or more collaborators. A third type of JV is when Person A interviews Person B for an article, short report, or audio program. Person B will get promotion for her current product, and Person A gets exclusive information that he can use to sell Person B's product as an affiliate. Joint ventures are a driving force in the Internet marketing world, and savvy marketers find ways to make JV deals part of their long-term success strategies.

Keyword A term that you type into a search engine to begin an online search. Keywords are also used in HTML to help search engines identify and index a Web site. Keyword research is the search for keywords related to your Web site, in order to analyze which ones yield the highest return on investment for pay-per-click and other types of advertising. Wordtracker (http://www.Featuring.com/wtt) and other keyword research tools help advertisers pick appropriate keywords for their campaigns.

Message board   See "Forum."

Meta tags   See also "Tags." Meta tags are part of the HTML
                      code that makes up what you see on a Web site.
                      When Webmasters create Web pages, meta tags
                      are used to provide structured information about
                      a Web page. These tags are placed in between
                      the <head> and </head> sections of an HTML
                      document. However, the meta tags are not visible
                      to the person looking at the Web site through an
                      Internet browser. Meta tags are part of the hidden
                      code of the Web page that is recognizable to the
                      Web browser only. Meta tags are used by search
                      engines (like Google or Yahoo!) to generate and
                      display a list of search results based on what a
                      user enters into the search engine. Tags do the
                      same thing, but meta tags refer to the overall
                      keywords for the entire Web site, while tags refer
                      to the specific Web page. Meta tags have been
                      used as a key component of a technique called
                      search-engine optimization. Since Web sites are
                      listed based on their meta tags, it is commercially
                      advantageous to pick the right meta tags to drive
                      traffic to a Web site.

MSN   Microsoft network. MSN (www.msn.com) offers
                      a wide variety of programs and features to Internet
                      users. Most MSN services are free of charge.

Newbie	Newcomer; any person who is new to the online world or a specific forum or chat room.
Niche	A focused and targetable portion of the market. A business that focuses on a niche market is attending to the need for a product or service that is not being addressed by the mainstream market. The niche market narrowly defines a group of potential customers. Niche marketing is the process of finding and serving one or more small yet profitable markets. Niche marketers design custom-made products or services for the markets that meet specific needs.
Online, offline	The state of being connected to the internet through an ISP, OSP, or network. "Offline" is the state of being disconnected from the Internet. As an adjective, "online" describes a variety of activities that users can do on the Internet. For example, it is used in the phrases "online shopping," "online gaming," "online search," "online store," etc.
Opt-in	A form of marketing also called "permission-based" marketing—a popular sales approach that is used online to make sure that the customers being contacted are actually interested in the products being sold. A prospective customer will give his consent to receive marketing information

(normally through e-mail). Opt-in marketing aims to tailor the messages and communication between the marketer and customer to the customer's needs. This is often done using the principles of niche marketing.

OSP Online service provider. An organization that provides an information service over the Internet. Examples are search engines, online backup services, and application service providers.

Page impressions Also known as page requests or page views. Page impressions refer to the number of times that a Web page is requested from a server. This is the preferred method for counting traffic.

Pay-per-click Also called "cost-per-click"—an online advertising payment model in which payment is based on the number of clicks that are generated. As an advertiser, you bid for certain keywords related to the content of your site (the information or products that you offer). When a user searches with these keywords in a search engine, they are shown your listing, as well as others that are bidding on the same keywords. If the user clicks on your listing, you pay the amount that you have bid. The highest-bidding advertisers will appear first in the search results, and the subsequent listings are ranked by the amount of their bid.

Bids for keywords can be anything from a few cents to a few dollars per click.

PDF A file format for documents that are viewed and created by Adobe Acrobat Reader, Adobe Capture, Adobe Distiller, Adobe Exchange, and Adobe Acrobat Amber plug-in. PDF technology has created a standard format for transferring documents on the Internet. One of the benefits of using PDFs is that they are easily accessible, even by the newest of Internet users. E-books are commonly delivered in PDF format, which makes them instantly downloadable.

Plug-in A small software program that can extend the capabilities of your Internet browser. It can give your browser the ability to play audio files or movie files. Some of the most common plug-ins are Shockwave, Flash, Acrobat, Real Player, and Quicktime. Once you download a plug-in, the small program will be on your computer to be used by other Web sites.

Podcast The term is a combination of "iPod" and "broadcasting," although it is not necessary to own an iPod to listen to podcasts. This term can be used in several different ways, but podcasting normally refers to the publishing of audio or video files to the Internet. The files are referred to as "podcasts" or "shows" and are similar to talk-radio programs or public-access television shows. People who create podcasts are called podcasters.

PPC   See "Pay-per-click."

Reprint rights   Permission to print a work that has been previously published. In the online world, buying e-books with reprint rights is one way to profit from information products.

RSS   Really simple syndication, real-time simple syndication, or rich site summary—the format used for syndicating Web content. RSS is a technology that allows Web sites to distribute new content to Internet users without the user having to revisit the Web site. RSS feeds are the syndicated information sent through RSS technology from Web sites to Internet users. Users can subscribe to feeds from a variety of Web sites, and then new information from those Web sites is sent directly to them through an RSS reader.

Search engine   A Web site that acts like a card catalog for the Internet. Search engines use spider programs to index and locate desired information. The search-engine program will find information on the Internet based on the keywords that are entered by the user.

SEO Search engine optimization—the process of using targeted keywords in the content, tags, and meta tags of a Web site in order to gain traffic through search engines. SEO techniques also include testing the search engine results to make sure that the site is well placed in the keyword results. The better the SEO, the higher your Web page will appear in the search-engine results for that keyword.

Signature file Sometimes referred to as a "sig file," a signature is a short statement at the end of an e-mail message. It can be used to identify the sender and provide additional information. Sig files can also include a small picture file, a link to a Web site, or a personal quote.

Site, Web site A place on the Internet or the World Wide Web. The term *site* refers to the body of information as a whole for a domain name. A Web site is a collection of Web pages. The pages can contain text, graphics, audio, or video content. *Site* can also refer to an FTP site or archive site. These types of sites are directories that store files for downloading and uploading.

Spam Also unsolicited commercial e-mail or junk mail—messages that are sent to people without their consent. Spam is characterized by its large volume. A spam filter or spam-blocker program is used to detect any unsolicited or unwanted e-mail in your mail program's inbox. This prevents spam messages from getting into your inbox. A spam blocker will filter through messages based on a certain criteria.

Spider   See "Crawler."

Spyware   A type of software contracted from using the Internet. Spyware gathers information about the Web sites that you visit in order to build a profile of your preferences for the purpose of marketing. Spyware is often included in free downloads that you get from Web sites. The license agreement for these free programs may mention the use of spyware, but very few people actually read the details of these agreements. As a result, spyware often gets onto a computer without the user's knowledge. There are many programs available that will find and remove spyware programs from your computer. Some of the more popular are Ad-Aware and Spybot.

Social networking   The process of meeting and networking with people through the use of specific Internet technology. The largest social-networking site on the Internet today is MySpace. Social-networking sites offer several things to their members, including the opportunity to meet members that share similar interests.

Software

A set of instructions that tells a computer how to execute functions and tasks. Software code is written in a programming language that makes computer systems and hardware work. Some programs contain millions of lines of code. The two basic software categories are system software (which makes the computer run properly) and application software (which includes programs).

Source code

The format in which a computer program or Web site is written. Online, the source code for a Web page is normally in HTML but can also be written in another computer language. To find the source code of a Web page, select View from the top of the Internet Browser. In the View menu, there should be an option that says View Source or something similar. The source code will appear in a pop-up window.

Subdomain name

A domain name that is part of a larger domain. If you've ever seen a Web address that doesn't start with the letters *www*, then you've encountered a subdomain. Some examples of subdomains are http://news.google.com or http://mail.yahoo.com.

Tag

A tag is a keyword or descriptive term that is associated with a piece of information, sound clip, or video on the World Wide Web. Tags have become one of the most prevalent forms of classifying information on the Internet. Tags are used in two specific ways. The first use of tags is hidden to the viewer but visible to Internet search engines. When a Webmaster creates a Web page, tags are added to indicate what type of content is on that page. This allows the search engines to give you results based on keywords that you enter. Tags also provide users with a quick and easy way to navigate the information on the Web site. Many sites now have tag lists so users can click directly on the tag words that interest them the most.

Target market

This refers to the market segment to which a particular product is marketed. Members of a target market have similar interests that may be based on age, gender, lifestyle, or socioeconomic grouping. By using target marketing, an Internet marketer can develop a product that speaks to a certain group of people.

Tech support

A service that you call when you have questions regarding your computer hardware or software. The tech support personnel will guide you through fixing your problem over the phone.

Thread

A topic thread is a string of consecutive message posts to newsgroups, mailing lists, or forums. Threads can be organized in ascending or descending order based on the date posted. Open threads are blog posts that allow readers to comment and discuss topics relevant to the blog.

Tracking

Online businesses use tracking to tell whether or not their advertising, copywriting, and Web-site design are converting to sales. Using advertising link-tracker software is one of the quickest methods to track where customers are coming from. The software measures the number of clicks that are received on individual advertisements and then the sales or subscriptions garnered from those clicks.

Traffic

Internet traffic is the term used to refer to user activity on a Web site. Each time someone visits a Web page, an entry is automatically registered on the Web page server's log file. The log file records the number of times that a piece of information has been requested from the server. This request is commonly referred to as a *hit*.

Trojan

A Trojan horse computer virus gets its name from the infamous legend of the same name. Just like the Trojans were fooled into letting opposing forces in their gates, a Trojan horse virus is sneaky.

This type of virus disguises itself as a helpful program. Once the program is downloaded and opened (run) on the user's computer, the virus is released. Commonly the virus will erase the hard drive or destroy parts of the computer. Sometimes a Trojan will hide on the computer undetected and slowly start transforming files and documents. This way the user does not know how or where he or she downloaded the virus.

URL Uniform resource locater or universal resource locater—the Web address that you'd type into the address bar of your Web browser to take you directly to the Web site you are looking for. The term is either pronounced with each letter said ("Yoo Are Ell") or as an acronym ("Ural").

Username/UserID The name used to log into a user's account. See also "Handle."

Viral Originally coined to describe viral marketing, this adjective has expanded to refer to any practice that moves a product from person to person. The ease of passing information on to others with e-mail addresses has made it possible for information, videos, and graphics to spread like wildfire through the Internet community. There are viral videos, viral jokes, viral hoaxes, etc.

Virus   A program that multiplies itself on computer systems and incorporates itself into shared programs. Some viruses are harmless pranks, but others can destroy computer files or disable a computer entirely. A key characteristic of viruses is that they spread quickly, from user to user, commonly through e-mail attachments. Most, if not all, Internet service providers offer some kind of protection from viruses within the structure of the Internet connection. If you use the Internet frequently, you might also want to invest in an additional virus-scanning program, such as McAffee VirusScan or Norton Anti-Virus.

WAHM   Work-at-home mom—a mother who chooses to raise her children and run a home-based business instead of working outside the home and placing the children in daycare. A variation is WAHD (work-at-home dad).

Web 2.0   The second generation of services that are available on the World Wide Web. Web 2.0 applications include blogs, podcasts, pay-per-click marketing, wikis, tagging, and RSS syndication.

Web designer   The person who is responsible for how the site looks and feels. The Web designer handles the entire aesthetic and navigational creation of a Web site. A Web designer is also responsible for ensuring that the graphics are clear, the links are working, and the navigation on the site is intuitive. Although Web designer is usually responsible for the creative aspects of a Web site rather than the programming, a knowledge of Web programming is necessary.

Web marketer   See "Internet marketer."

Webmaster   A person involved with creating and/or managing a Web site. A Webmaster is the person who maintains the content and functioning of a Web site. This may include receiving all of the feedback from Web-site users, maintaining graphics, supplying content updates, and handling all programming matters. A Webmaster may or may not have designed the initial layout of the Web site. Some larger Web sites have one Webmaster to handle the content of the site and another to handle the more technical aspects.

World Wide Web   The connected documents that exist on the Internet. See also "Internet."

XML   A programming language similar to HTML, used to develop Web pages. The main difference between XML (sometimes called XTML) and other programming languages is the ability to add customized tags to the Web page design.

XML provides a platform for developing Web sites that encompass the principles of Web 2.0. It is a lot more abstract and complex than previous programming languages, and it's not quite certain whether XML will replace HTML entirely.

ZIP file   A compressed file used on Windows. ZIP is the standard technology for data compression. On the Internet, larger graphics and programs are normally compressed as ZIP files before they are made available for download. This allows downloading to go much faster. After downloading a ZIP file, you need to use a decompression software (such as WinZIP, a free program) to unzip it and access the data. The technology is very useful when sending photos through e-mail.

YOUR *FREE* BONUS WORTH US$397.00:

Instant Download!

THANK YOU FOR YOUR INVESTMENT in *"How I Made My First Million on the Internet...And How You Can Too!"*. As a special gift for readers only (for a very limited time), here's your...

"THE EASIEST WAY TO MAKE A MILLION ON THE INTERNET!" (AUDIO MP3 RECORDING + TRANSCRIPT TRAINING PROGRAM)

CONGRATULATIONS! With your investment in this book, you also qualify for a **FREE BONUS worth US$397.00** for a limited time only...

This bonus is a **complete audio training program** called *"The Easiest Way To Make A Million On The Internet!"*, and in your package, you will instantly get:

353

- A full 86-minute MP3 recording of the audio training

- Entire word-for-word transcript of the audio training

- PLUS a mystery "money-making bonus" too!

Here's a small sample of what you'll discover in this training program:

- An ultra SIMPLE step-by-step system to start your Internet business in the next 30 minutes

- How to make your first sale on the Internet in just 24 hours from now...

- How to generate unlimited PASSIVE income every single day... on complete autopilot!

- The secret blueprint to creating a MILLION-dollar business online from day one...

And much more!

Visit The Website Below
To Download your FREE BONUS now
- before it's gone forever!

WWW.INTERNETMILLIONAIRES.COM/BONUS

Printed in the United States
138916LV00003BA/2/P